DISTURBANCES OF THE MIND

Sergei Korsakoff, Alois Alzheimer, James Parkinson, Hans Asperger ... all eminent scientists whose names have become synonymous with a disease, a syndrome or an autistic disorder. Although the names of these psychiatrists and neurologists are familiar, we often know little about the individuals themselves and the circumstances surrounding their discoveries. What exactly did they discover, and who were their patients? Douwe Draaisma expertly reconstructs the lives of these and eight other 'names' from the science of mind and brain. *Disturbances of the Mind* provides a fascinating, illuminating, and at times touching insight into the history of brain research. Thanks to Draaisma's unerring eye and elegant, engaging style, the case histories of Asperger, Bonnet, Capgras, Clérambault, Korsakoff and Gilles de la Tourette syndromes; Alzheimer's and Parkinson's diseases; the areas of Broca and Brodmann; Jackson's epilepsy; and the Gage matrix are all brought to life and transformed into unforgettable tales.

DOUWE DRAAISMA is Professor in the History of Psychology at the University of Groningen in the Netherlands. He is the author of *Metaphors of Memory* (Cambridge, 2000) and *Why Life Speeds Up as You Get Older* (Cambridge, 2004).

Disturbances of the Mind

Douwe Draaisma

Translated by

Barbara Fasting

CAMBRIDGE
UNIVERSITY PRESS

CAMBRIDGE UNIVERSITY PRESS

Cambridge, New York, Melbourne, Madrid, Cape Town, Singapore, São Paulo, Delhi

Cambridge University Press
The Edinburgh Building, Cambridge CB2 8RU, UK

Published in the United States of America by Cambridge University Press, New York

www.cambridge.org
Information on this title: www.cambridge.org/9780521509664

Originally published in Dutch as *Ontregelde Geesten* by Historische Uitgeverij, 2006 and
© Douwe Draaisma 2006
First published in English by Cambridge University Press 2009 as *Disturbances of the Mind*
English translation © Cambridge University Press and Barbara Fasting 2009

This translation was supported by a grant from the Foundation for the Production and
Translation of Dutch Literature.

Printed in the United Kingdom at the University Press, Cambridge

A catalogue record for this book is available from the British Library

ISBN 978-0-521-50966-4 Hardback

Contents

Introduction: Not the Draaisma syndrome

Sometimes memories don't take on meaning until years later. As a college student, I used to work weekends in an old people's home. One of my responsibilities was the bread cart: towards the end of the afternoon I did the rounds of the rooms, together with a geriatric assistant, delivering the day's cold meal. If someone was visually handicapped or had trouble walking, we also laid the table. One afternoon, as we were rummaging in the cupboard of one of the residents for china and cutlery, the lady suddenly announced that there was a little man outside in the garden. A little man? We followed her gaze. There was nothing unusual in the garden. But she insisted: 'There's a little man there.' I looked to see if there was anything she could have mistaken for a man. I saw a lamp-post among the bushes, about a metre high, with a cap that looked vaguely like a hat. 'Do you mean that lamp over there?' 'Of course not! I can see it's a lamp!' We assured her that neither of us saw anyone outside. As the assistant pushed the woman's chair closer to the table, she rolled her eyes and tapped her forehead with one finger. At the time, that seemed to me a satisfactory explanation. We called out a cheery 'Enjoy your meal!' and continued on our way.

It was some twenty years later that I read about quite a rare syndrome that affects mainly older people with failing eyesight. They begin seeing things – usually images of people, often miniaturized. They appear just as twilight falls and it starts to go quiet. The phenomenon, which is quite harmless, is called Bonnet syndrome. It is named after Charles Bonnet, a Swiss naturalist and philosopher, who in 1760 was the first to describe these images. Bonnet hadn't seen them himself; he had been told about them by his grandfather, who began seeing images of people when he was almost 90, after several failed cataract operations.

I had met someone with Bonnet syndrome and hadn't noticed anything unusual. I realized then how easy it is *not* to discover something. And even if I had, it would have been a 'rediscovery'.

Why is it that Bonnet 'saw' it and I didn't? One obvious difference, though not the only one, is that he took his grandfather seriously. That in itself was no mean accomplishment, for the old man insisted that he saw not only people, but also fountains, carriages some 30 feet high, a rotating wheel floating through the air. Instead of concluding that his grandfather was failing mentally, Bonnet accepted the authenticity of the images and considered possible explanations. He went on to describe in one of his books a neurological disorder that can cause visual sensations without affecting one's judgement. In the following chapter, we will see how in 1936 that disorder became Bonnet syndrome, and how subsequent generations of psychiatrists and neurologists have attempted to explain those images.

But what if there had never been a Bonnet, and I had taken the woman with her 'little man in the garden' just as seriously as Bonnet took his grandfather? Would there now be a 'Draaisma syndrome'? The answer is an unequivocal 'no'. If I've learned one thing from this study of twelve name-givers active in the field of brain science, it is that what happens *after* a discovery is more important than the discovery itself.

To focus on just one element in those further developments: the discovery must be registered. In this respect, each era has its own conventions. Where Bonnet described his observations in a book, today's neurologists and psychiatrists communicate via specialist journals, and there are specific criteria for the research and the presentation of findings. Today, a simple description of a single case carries very little weight. An aspiring name-giver must collect a considerable number of similar cases (100 is better than 50) and provide the particulars of each one, such as age, sex, vision, medication and educational level. He must also come up with an explanation for the phenomenon, preferably one borne out by experiments that make it clear which factors influence the occurrence of such images. Then the beginnings of a consensus must be arrived at within the scientific community as to whether the phenomenon in question is indeed one which cannot be classified within any existing psychiatric or neurological syndrome. After that, an authoritative colleague (or a committee) must propose that the name of the author be attached to the disorder. And only when the scientific community actually begins to refer to that name can we say that a new 'discoverer' has been added to the annals of brain science. Clearly, all this lies far beyond the possibilities of a college student with a part-time job. In fact, even Bonnet wouldn't have stood a chance today. 'Your grandfather, you say? And what exactly did he see?'

Linguistically speaking, 'Bonnet syndrome' is an eponym: a proper noun turned common noun. The 'donor' invariably drops his or her first name, while in the case of the best-known eponyms – Alzheimer, Parkinson, Korsakoff and Asperger – even the designation 'disease' or 'syndrome' has become superfluous. And not only do their first names disappear, but after a while the rest also fades away, including recollections of their lives and the circumstances surrounding their discoveries. For twelve of these eponymists I have tried to serve as a 'resurrectionist' – not in the grim sense attached to the term in the days of James Parkinson, but as a historian striving to bring to life their thoughts and ambitions, their struggles and hopes, in short, turning names into people again. It was a privilege to give the eponymists the attention they deserve, by making each one the subject of a chapter.

Why eponyms? And why these eponyms? There are valid reasons for choosing them, but valid reasons are not always the original motive. What initially drove me was curiosity, pure and simple. *Who were these people?* What was the drive behind their discoveries? Later, as I began to explore those lives long past, other questions presented themselves. Who saw to it that their names were immortalized? Is the condition we call the Tourette syndrome the same disorder that Gilles de la Tourette described all those years ago? What was Parkinson's disease before Parkinson? What form did Alzheimer's disease take before the neuro-pathologist Alzheimer revealed to his colleagues what he had found in the brain of Auguste D? Why was the disorder described in 1944 by the Viennese paediatrician Asperger not discovered earlier, since everything indicates that there have always been individuals with the behavioural abnormalities which are today grouped together as 'Asperger'? How is it possible that Asperger himself was not discovered until 1981, a year after his death, and his original article went almost unnoticed?

The valid reasons referred to above have to do with the key position of eponyms within the scientific enterprise. They are among the pro-cesses which regulate scientific prestige and recognition. According to the sociologist of science, Robert Merton, it is through eponyms that 'scientists leave behind their indelible signature in history; their names enter into all the scientific languages in the world'.[1] High on the firmament we find eponyms like Newtonian physics, Euclidian geometry and the Copernican system. The echelon which follows consists of a long series of 'fathers' of sciences, disciplines or special-izations: Bernoulli, 'father of mathematical physics'; Wundt, 'father of experimental psychology'; Hughlings Jackson, 'father of British neurol-ogy'. Many of these 'fathers' (Merton predates the first 'mothers') live on in such 'ordinary' eponyms as the theorem of Bernoulli and Jackson's epilepsy. Literally everything that exists, in whatever form, can be named after its discoverer: propositions, plants, laws, hypotheses, distributions, instruments, tests, narrows, comets, craters on distant planets, scales, effects, classifications, proofs and visual illusions. Even mistakes or conjectures can be crowned with an eponym: it appears that the 'conjecture of Poincaré' has recently been demonstrated (even though the mathematician in question has vanished without a trace). A less desirable form of immortality is the eponym that designates something which upon further consideration does not exist, like the 'canals of Schiaparelli', which the Milanese astronomer Giovanni Schiaparelli observed on Mars in 1877. Outside the scientific world, immortality is decidedly short-lived: the name of James Watt does not spring to mind every time we change a light bulb, nor do we think of John Loudon McAdam whenever we turn onto a highway.

Down through the ages, physicians have honoured one another with literally thousands of eponyms. There are eponyms for parts of the body, operations, symptoms, reflexes, diseases, syndromes, instruments, tests and reactions.[2] An extensive list can be found at www.whonamedit.com. At the moment of writing, the site contains 3,225 entries. It is in English, so that it may be slightly skewed in favour of Anglo-Saxon medical science, but its sheer size enables us to draw a number of interesting conclusions. Physicians active during the last quarter of the nineteenth century or the first quarter of the twentieth century had the best chances of being so honoured. After that, medical research became increasingly a matter of teamwork, and individuals were less likely to be immortalized in an eponym. Today, eponyms continue to be bestowed (relatively more often in clinical genetics), but there is a clear preference for descriptive designations

[2] A selection of over fifty neurological eponyms appear in P. J. Koehler, G. W. Bruyn and J. M. S. Pearce (eds.), *Neurological Eponyms* (Oxford, 2000). For my chapters on Broca, Korsakoff and Jackson, I drew upon the relevant contributions in that collection. Other useful sources were D. Arenz, *Eponyme und Syndrome in der Psychiatrie* (Cologne, 2001), and P. Beighton and G. Beighton, *The Person Behind the Syndrome* (Berlin, 1997).

or abbreviations, as in AIDS, ADHD or ALS (previously known as 'Charcot's disease').

Of the eponyms which appear on www.whonamedit.com, the highest number come from the United States (819), followed by Germany (636), France (428), the United Kingdom (340) and Austria (155). The Netherlands (46) just misses the top ten, coming after Sweden (52) and Denmark (48). Where the date of attribution is concerned, there are considerable differences between the various nationalities. Of the Americans, some 39 per cent were born after 1900, whereas only one of the 25 Czech eponymists was born in the twentieth century, a reflection of the fact that the Czech Republic's heyday as a centre of medical research lies in the past. Austria's high ranking is likewise due mainly to its illustrious past: fewer than 13 per cent of its eponymists were born in the twentieth century. Germany, France and the United Kingdom have traditionally been among the medical superpowers, and that holds true even today; they also have a high proportion of relatively young eponymists.

The 340 UK eponyms span over four centuries of medical history. The seventeenth century is represented by such luminaries as Willis and Sydenham. Thomas Willis, an Oxford anatomist, first described the circle of arteries at the base of the brain, and was also the name-giver of Willis' disease, an obsolete term for diabetes mellitus. Thomas Sydenham, 'the father of English medicine', identified a disease of the nervous system which causes involuntary movements of trunk, arms and legs that resemble a kind of jerky dance: Sydenham's chorea. Some nineteenth-century eponyms that were once well-known have disappeared or been rechristened. William Smellie, a Scottish obstetrician, was known for the Smellie manoeuvre, a manipulation during breech delivery in which the after-coming head is delivered while the child rests on the physician's forearm. This procedure now goes by various names, each country favouring its local inventor. Most eponyms, in the United Kingdom as elsewhere, have their origin in the nineteenth century. That was the era of James Parkinson and John

Hughlings Jackson, whose eponymic contributions will be dealt with in separate chapters. But there are many more. Sir Charles Bell found his name attached to a nerve, a paralysis and a type of spasm. His main claim to fame is probably the Bell-Magendie law, stating that the anterior spinal nerve roots contain motor fibres and the posterior roots sensory fibres. Pathologist Thomas Hodgkin lives on in the name of a particular type of cancer which attacks lymphatic tissue.

As befits a British list, it features more than a few eccentricities. The 'albatross reaction', described in 1967, refers to patients who after a gastrectomy start pursuing their surgeon, like the albatross that followed the ship in Coleridge's 'The Rime of the Ancient Mariner'. A more recent work of literature inspired the identification of the 'Alice in Wonderland syndrome', first described in 1955 by a psychiatrist called John Todd. This syndrome involves distortions of time, space and body shape which are sometimes experienced as a consequence of migraine headaches. Lewis Carroll himself is known to have suffered from migraines.

There are almost a dozen women among the British eponymists, such as Yvonne Barr, whose name is associated with the Epstein-Barr virus. They include many paediatricians and geneticists. Of the 3,225 entries on persons listed at www.whonamedit.com, only 117 are women eponymists. A number of factors seem to have conspired against them, since by the time the study of medicine was opened to women and they began to make their contribution, the great wave of naming was already over.

The vast majority of medical eponyms are intended to honour priority: the designer of a new operation, the inventor of an instrument, the first person to describe a part of the body, the discoverer of a disease. When that priority is challenged, bitter conflicts can result, giving rise to issues that are of greater interest than priority alone. What exactly is a 'discovery'? Which factors determine whether something is a 'discovery' in the eyes of the scientific community? Can we call someone a 'discoverer' when he himself had no clear understanding of what it was he discovered, as seems to have over-come the man who first identified the area of Broca? Questions such as these are at the heart of the scientific enterprise. Eponyms are at once accolade and arena. They are the site of manoeuvre and manipula-tion, where power and authority are at issue, where conflicts over what constitutes a scientific proof are settled, and where decisions are taken on matters of classification and categorization. As the historian of neurology, Anne Harrington, once remarked, 'the modern-day scientist, interested above all in how the human mind and brain "really" work, should also give some thought to the question of how science "really" works'.[3] Eponyms mark the spot where these two questions intersect.

But why *these* eponyms in particular? For the most part, I was guided by my own curiosity, although the end result is not entirely arbitrary. There was a striving to make the selections representative, in a historical, geographical and disciplinary sense. Gilles de la Tourette, Capgras and Clérambault are all representative of French psychiatry, with its focus on patient demonstrations. Capgras described a syn-drome whereby the patient is under the misapprehension that his loved ones (wife, children and friends) have been secretly replaced by *doppelgängers*. In Clérambault's syndrome, the patient (usually a woman) is convinced that someone is in love with her. These three – Gilles de la Tourette, Clérambault and Capgras – all carried out their investigations within the psychiatric institutions to which they were attached. Capgras and Clérambault published their results in the form of clinical lessons, a method of communication which was then held in high esteem in France. Alzheimer and Brodmann (who drew up a map of the human brain) were both a product of the German tradition of neuropathological research. Their studies were carried out in a laboratory, and their most important instrument was the microscope. Alzheimer was an institutional physician who did his rounds with

[3] A. Harrington, *Medicine, Mind, and the Double Brain* (Princeton NJ, 1987), p. 286.

great dedication, but believed that his greatest service to his patients was rendered after their brains became available for microscopic examination.

Representativity with respect to disciplines is a far more difficult matter. Throughout history, many diseases, syndromes, disorders and conditions have regularly changed position with respect to what we now call 'neurology' and 'psychiatry', which up until the late nineteenth century were regarded as a single field of science. James Parkinson, a GP in one of the poorest neighbourhoods of London, had no inkling as to the cause of the 'shaking palsy' which he described in 1817, although he suspected that something had gone awry in the brains of his patients. But Charcot, the Paris neurologist who in 1876 named the disease after Parkinson, believed that it might well be related to psychological factors, such as a violent shock or severe emotional stress. As a result, Parkinson's disease underwent a shift in the direction of psychiatry. Today, the degeneration of a small area of the brain that produces the neurotransmitter dopamine is seen as the cause of Parkinson's, which brings the disease back into the field of neurology. These changes in perspective are the rule rather than the exception. The syndrome of Gilles de la Tourette has never ceased hopping back and forth between neurology and psychiatry. While the syndrome of Capgras had long ago been defined in psychoanalytical terms, in the last twenty years it has shifted in the direction of neurology. In the case of the Asperger syndrome, a disturbance which is part of the autism spectrum, the role played by neurological factors is still unclear.

As noted above, the decision to study eponyms almost automatically placed the centre of gravity of the selection in the nineteenth century and the consequences of this fact are reflected in the portraits in *Disturbances of the Mind*. Despite the differences, what the eponymists have in common is the fact that they all made use of case studies. Together, they are representative of a scientific style which disappeared half a century ago. In case histories, the elements of care and treatment, observation and research are still closely intertwined. Parkinson writes with compassion about a patient who had his servant run ten metres ahead, so that the man could catch him when his slow shuffle turned into a headlong dash. That same compassion resonates in Alzheimer's description of the state of desolate confusion in which Auguste found herself, and in Korsakoff's account of the total lack of imprinting skills among his patients. In Hans Asperger's 1944 case histories of his 'difficult children', the experience of the patient echoes throughout each account. If in these twelve portraits I have succeeded in transforming names into people of flesh and blood, then it is because their case histories are about people of flesh and blood.

ONE

Towards dusk the images appear: Bonnet syndrome

In the spring of 1759, in Geneva, the retired magistrate Charles Lullin called in his secretary for a long session of dictation.[1] He was advanced in years (close to 90) and his eyes were beginning to fail. In October 1753, he dictated, he had undergone a cataract operation on his left eye; until September 1756, he had been able to see with the help of a convex lens, but now the light had gone completely. The right eye had also been operated on for cataracts and there was some light left, although not enough to enable him to read or to write. Since then he had had a servant read the newspaper to him. Lullin was convinced that the curious experiences which he was about to record were related to his eye problems.

In February 1758, strange objects had begun to float into his field of vision. It started with something that resembled a blue handkerchief, with a small yellow circle in each corner, about the size of a fives ball. The handkerchief followed the movement of his eyes: whether he was

---

[1] It was not until a century and a half later that the piece appeared in print, under the title *Visions de Monsieur l'Ancien Syndic Lullin, Seigneur de Confignon*: Th. Flournoy, 'Le cas de Charles Bonnet. Hallucinations visuelles chez un vieillard opéré de la cataracte', *Archives de Psychologie*, 1 (1902), 1–23. The quotations are taken from this publication.

looking at a wall, his bed or a tapestry, the handkerchief blocked out all the ordinary objects in his room. Lullin was perfectly lucid and at no time did he believe that there really was a blue handkerchief floating around. Nor was it difficult to make the image disappear: all he had to do was move his eyes to the right, and he again saw the familiar objects in his room. The handkerchief was not the only object he saw. One day in August, two granddaughters came by. Lullin was sitting in his armchair opposite the mantelpiece, and his visitors were to his right. From the left, two young men appeared. They were wearing magnificent cloaks, red and grey, and their hats were trimmed with silver. 'What handsome gentlemen you've brought with you! Why didn't you tell me they were coming?'[2] But the young ladies swore that they saw no one. Like the handkerchief, the images of the two men dissolved within a few moments. In the next few weeks they were followed by many more imaginary visitors, all of them women. They were beautifully coifed and several of them had a small box on their head. One day, when his servant came into the room after running an errand, he was followed by two gigantic ladies, both of them so tall that their heads almost touched the ceiling.

> 'Who are those ladies you've brought with you?'
> 'Excuse me, sir, there is no one here.'
> 'Have you gone blind, man? They're so tall and portly that you could hardly miss them.'[3]

The ladies had walked away without uttering a word. Somewhat later, Lullin was standing at the window when he saw a carriage approaching. It came to a halt at his neighbour's house and, as he watched in amazement, the carriage grew bigger and bigger until it was level with the eaves of the house some 30 feet off the ground, with everything perfectly in proportion. On another occasion, four girls aged around twelve walked into the room, one of them holding a

---

[2] Lullin, *Visions*, p. 8.   [3] *Ibid.* pp. 8–9.

child of about three by the hand. They were all richly attired, decked out with colourful ribbons, pearl necklaces and pear-shaped diamond earrings. They seemed to be chatting together. Then one of them turned in his direction and gave him a most charming smile, revealing perfect white teeth. Then they disappeared again.

Lullin was amazed by the variety of images he saw: one time it was a swarm of specks that suddenly turned into a flight of pigeons, another time a group of dancing butterflies. There was a rotating wheel floating in the air, the kind you saw in dockside cranes. On a stroll through the town, he stopped to admire an enormous scaffolding, and when he arrived home he saw the same scaffolding standing in the living room, but then in miniature, not even one foot high. What first appeared to be a small cloud turned into a window, which he recognized as the attic window of a house further down the street. He also saw landscapes framed like paintings, a city in the distance, a woodland scene, a forest, a fountain with its spray dispersed by the wind. Once, he decided to carry out an experiment involving the size of the images. About a hundred paces from the house there was a small square with a fountain. He noticed that if he saw the blue handkerchief next to the fountain, it was the size of a large table-cloth. But if he saw it against the background of the table where he took his meals, it was no larger than a thumbnail. The size of other images also tended to vary according to how far away they were.

In closing, Lullin dictated a number of other things he had noticed. He never saw the images when he was in bed, either awake or asleep. They glided by in total silence, even the images of people engaged in conversation. After the two gentlemen who had accompanied his granddaughters, no more men appeared in the room. On the street, by contrast, he saw no women. All the individuals appeared on the left and also passed behind him to the left before disappearing. But he established that this had nothing to do with his left eye: the images also appeared when he closed one eye at a time, and even when he covered both eyes with a handkerchief.

Figure 1.1: Charles Bonnet (1720–1793). Engraving after a painting by J. Huel (1777)

But above all, Lullin was struck by the individuals themselves. One morning as he was quietly smoking his pipe at the window, he saw on his left a man leaning casually against the window frame. Except for the fact that he was a head taller, the man looked exactly like him: he was also smoking a pipe, and he was wearing the same cap and the same dressing gown. The man was there again the next morning, and he gradually became a familiar apparition. The images of people began on 10 August and lasted until September. That was the last he saw of them. Only his pipe-smoking alter ego continued to appear well into October. The images were somewhat fainter, doubtless because the mornings tended to be hazy at that time of year.

'A most remarkable case'

These experiences are recorded in a large exercise book containing eighteen pages. No fewer than five signatures attest to the authenticity of the document: the first is that of Lullin himself, little more than a scribble; followed by those of the secretary, a reader, the family doctor and Lullin's grandson, Charles Bonnet. The latter was to play a key role in the story of a phenomenon which, much later, would come to be known as Bonnet syndrome. Lullin wrote that he had recorded his experiences in such detail at the insistence of Bonnet, 'this great naturalist and physicist'.[4] Charles Bonnet did indeed have an established scientific reputation.[5] That reputation was based above all on his work as an entomologist: at the age of 20 he had recorded his observations on the ant-lion or doodlebug, and this gained him an appointment as a corresponding member of the Académie des Sciences. At the time his grandfather was seeing his strange apparitions, Bonnet was working on a book devoted to various psychological topics. It appeared in 1760 under the title *Essai analytique sur les facultés de l'âme*.[6] In the chapter on the sense of sight, Bonnet gave a brief account of the experiences of 'a greybeard'.[7] He described it as a 'most remarkable case, which one would be inclined to reject as far-fetched, were it not for the fact that it was based on a totally reliable source'.[8] Bonnet was intentionally brief, as he intended to comment on the case in greater detail at some later date. However, he never got around to doing so. In the second edition, published in 1769, he explained in a note that the greybeard in question was his maternal grandfather. He had died in 1761, lucid to the end and blessed with an excellent memory. Bonnet added that the exercise book was now in his possession, referring to it as 'a most curious piece of psychology'.[9] After Bonnet's death in 1793, it ended up among the papers of an eye doctor in Geneva, where it surfaced by chance around 1900. Lullin's exercise book did not appear in print until 1902, when the

---

[4] *Ibid.* p. 16.

[5] G. Bonnet, *Charles Bonnet (1720–1793)* (Paris, 1929). See also L. Anderson, *Charles Bonnet and the Order of the Known* (Dordrecht, 1982).

[6] Ch. Bonnet, *Essai analytique sur les facultés de l'âme* (Copenhagen, 1760; 2nd edn, Neuchâtel, 1769). Also as Part 6 in *Œuvres d'histoire naturelle et de philosophie de Charles Bonnet* (Neuchâtel, 1779–1783). Quotations from the *Essai* are taken from the latter publication.

[7] Bonnet, *Essai*, p. 317.　　[8] *Ibid.* pp. 315–16.　　[9] *Ibid.* p. 317.

psychologist and philosopher Flournoy made it the focus of the opening article in his new journal *Archives de psychologie*. Until then, Lullin's experiences were known to the scientific community only through Bonnet's brief account.

The body of literature devoted to Bonnet syndrome is relatively small. Even if we cast our net wide, across various sciences, language areas and historical periods, the number of articles does not exceed a hundred.[10] Between 1760 and today, philosophers, neurologists, psychiatrists, ophthalmologists and psychologists have written about the phenomenon, but it has remained on the margins of scientific interest. Well into the 1960s, case histories regularly appeared which were unrelated to the existing literature: it seems that there were multiple discoverers of Bonnet syndrome. According to a 1989 review article, some forty-six cases had been described thus far.[11] What is striking about these case histories is the enormous variation in the type of images, ranging from faces or individuals to animals, vehicles, buildings and landscapes. And among the individuals, there is likewise considerable diversity. They are strangers or acquaintances, children, adults or old people; some only stroll by, while others are engaged in some activity or other, like the hammering blacksmith and the farmer behind his plough. They may be wearing a doctor's white coat, a dressing gown or some old-fashioned costume; many are quite ordinary, while others display some unusual detail, such as a flower growing out of their head; sometimes they are of normal height, at other times they are miniaturized or elongated until they reach gigantic proportions. And some people see a copy of themselves ('autoscopy'). Everything that the old Lullin saw has also been seen by others, in endless variations.

[10] A. Fernandez, G. Lichtshein and W. V. R. Vieweg, 'The Charles Bonnet Syndrome: a review', *Journal of Nervous and Mental Disease*, 185 (1997), 195–200.

[11] K. Podoll, M. Osterheider and J. Noth, 'Das Charles Bonnet Syndrom', *Fortschritte der Neurologische Psychiatrie*, 57 (1989), 43–60.

It is perhaps tempting to skip the intervening two centuries or so, and present only the findings of the research into Bonnet syndrome carried out over the last twenty or thirty years. But then we would be depriving ourselves of the pleasure of the journey. It was not until 1936 that a condition resembling Bonnet syndrome was named and defined, and even that statement is slightly coloured. While several attempts have been made to establish the existence of a syndrome of Bonnet, there is still no agreement on the inclusion and exclusion criteria. Over the last two centuries, the experiences which Lullin dictated to his servant in 1759 have figured in various conceptions of the human mind. They have served as a projection screen for psychoanalysts and perception psychologists, eye doctors and geriatricians. Behind this neat term – 'Bonnet syndrome' – lies a world of manoeuvring, confusion and conflict, as well as curiosity and astonishment. So, first the journey and then the destination.

Charles Bonnet was born in 1720 into a French Protestant family who fled to Switzerland after the St Bartholomew's night massacre in 1572. Six generations later, the family had acquired considerable wealth. Bonnet was a member of the aristocracy of Geneva and, as he wrote in his *Mémoires autobiographiques*, the life he led was 'as regular as the orbit of the stars'.[12] He seldom travelled further than his country house on Lake Geneva. The only journey he ever embarked upon took him to the home of his friend Albrecht von Haller, a natural scientist like himself, with whom he exchanged some 900 letters. Haller lived in a village just east of Lake Geneva, while Bonnet himself lived on the northern shore.[13]

At the age of seven he was sent to school, but he left when it appeared that he was being bullied on account of his poor hearing. From then on, he was educated at home by tutors. When he was 15 he

[12] R. Savioz, *Mémoires autobiographiques de Charles Bonnet de Genève* (Paris, 1948), p. 40.
[13] *Ibid.* p. 381.

Figure 1.2: Bonnet en promenade. Engraving by G.B. Bosio (date unknown)

picked up a copy of *Spectacle de la Nature* by Abbé Pluche, a high point of the era that celebrated the pious study of nature. He was particularly captivated by the ant-lion, and from then on, he knew that he would devote his life to natural history. He corresponded with the great entomologists of his day, carried out endless observations involving aphids (one of which lasted thirty-four days) in an attempt to prove his hypothesis that reproduction was possible without copulation, did experiments involving the respiration of caterpillars, studied the process of photosynthesis in plants and the regeneration of fresh-water polyps. In 1743, Bonnet was elected to the Royal Society of London. Several years later he contracted an eye ailment which made it painful for him to look intently at an object. He also developed cataracts, and ultimately he was almost unable to read or write. This meant that a career involving microscopic research, his great passion, was out of the question. From then on, his intellectual interests were dictated by his visual constraints: he turned from insects to botany, then psychology, and finally metaphysics. The result was a 900-page manuscript entitled *Méditations sur l'Univers*, which remained unpublished.

Figure 1.3: Bonnet dictating to his secretary

Figure 1.4: A visualization of the thought experiment in which a statue is brought to life by means of sensual stimuli

In 1755, Bonnet dictated to Jeanne-Marie de la Rive a paper devoted to the subject of *amitié*, i.e., friendship or affection. The 27-year-old must have recorded his thoughts with a blush on her cheeks, for there is not a single line where the word *amitié* could not be replaced by love. Bonnet dedicated the piece to her, asked for her hand, and married her in the spring of 1756. The couple spent much of their time at the country estates of the two families. In 1757, their happiness was marred when, on a carriage ride, one of the wheels broke and Madame Bonnet suffered a miscarriage as a result. Their marriage would remain childless.

At the age of 60, Bonnet's active life lost momentum, due to various ailments and infirmities. Because of his poor eyesight, he was forced to dictate everything. His correspondence contains letters written in three or even four different hands. Severe asthma undermined his physical condition. He did all the corrections of his Œuvres himself, but they had to be read aloud, which was also problematic due to his increasing deafness. Towards the end of his life, when he was nearly blind, he began to see the strange images which his grandfather had described to him. Bonnet died in the spring of 1793, at the age of 73.

Bonnet's statue

Two figures are standing in a garden, a man and a woman. Their dress is suggestive of classical antiquity. The man's pose is passive and wooden; the woman is turned towards him and seems to be holding something up to his face. Together they are acting out a thought experiment which forms the red thread running through *Essai analytique sur les facultés de l'âme*. Bonnet is inviting his readers to create in their mind's eye the image of a statue. It is mute, deaf, blind and dead: a soul-less piece of stone. But then you endow that statue with a single sense, say the sense of smell. Through that one sense, the statue is permeated by sensations of smell, which means it is capable of smelling the rose which the woman is holding. Then open up another sense, such as the sense of sight. Now the statue is not only able to see, it is also capable of making certain associations which will connect the sensation of smell with the visual sensations. According to Bonnet, the more senses that are opened up, the richer the impressions the statue

can form of the outside world. On the basis of these sensory observations, a memory will be formed and ultimately a personality. What
began as a piece of dead stone is now a being with sensations, mental
images and conscious opinions.

Was Bonnet perhaps thinking of his summer home? In winter, the
rooms are silent behind their closed shutters. The furniture stands
motionless in the darkened room. In the spring, a servant readies the
house for occupancy. As he opens one of the shutters, a shaft of light is
beamed to the opposite wall, bathing the room in a hazy light and
revealing particles of dust floating in the sunlight. He opens the other
shutters. Ribbons of light intersect, and the room comes alive. Bonnet
and his guests can arrive at any moment. A meal is being prepared,
fragrant bouquets grace the tables, hearth fires ward off the cold,
voices are heard, and the house is alive.

The thought experiment with the statue is better known in the
version of Abbé Condillac, who made use of the same device in his
Traité des sensations (1754). Neither author held materialistic views:
the statue was intended simply to demonstrate the sensory origin of
all knowledge. The gradual activation of the senses, which formed
such a tragic contrast to what overcame Bonnet himself, opened up
the world and our ability to think about the world. But the statue was
also intended to demonstrate that psychological phenomena are
embodied in senses, nerves, fibres and muscles. For everything that
takes place in the soul, there must be a corresponding event in the
organism: for each perception a sensory impulse, for each emotion an
agitation in the body, for each memory a trace in the brain. That
precise correspondence between psychological and physiological
processes was also in evidence when his grandfather saw his images.
The origin, Bonnet tells us, must have been located in 'that part of
the brain which is connected with the organ of sight'.[14] The decline

---

[14] Bonnet, *Essai*, p. 316.

in his vision which recurred after the cataract operations points in the direction of organic change. It is not difficult to imagine, he continues, that various nerves which under normal circumstances transfer images to the soul can be stimulated by these changes 'from inside', and in this way trigger visual perceptions. If at the same time the nerves which support the powers of judgement 'are still in their natural state, then the soul will not confuse those images with reality'.[15] In modern terminology: somewhere along the pathway between eye and brain, processes take place in the nerve tissues which activate the optic nerve, despite the absence of outside stimuli.

Bonnet attributed psychological phenomena to a 'kind of agitation of certain nerves'. He could not go much further than that, given the level of neurological knowledge at the time. In the century and a half which followed, his grandfather's case regularly attracted the attention of authors who had heard about similar incidents, or had even experienced such images themselves.[16] In 1814, the mathematician Marquis Pierre-Simon Laplace referred to Bonnet in his *Essai philosophique sur les probabilités*, in a passage on the influence which imaginary or remembered images can have on one's observation. He himself was convinced that that influence can be so strong that illusory effects are created, as in the images of Bonnet's grandfather or the visions of Jeanne d'Arc. In 1826, the German physiologist, Johannes Müller, described his own images. And in 1909, the Geneva philosopher, Ernest Naville, then aged 93, used his images to demonstrate his proposition that 'an ideal scholar with expert knowledge of the fields of psychology and physiology, proceeding on the assumption that the brain is transparent, could "read" all the psychological symptoms that presented themselves in

[15] *Ibid.* p. 317.

[16] For a brief historical survey, see G. de Morsier, 'Le syndrome de Charles Bonnet: hallucinations visuelles des vieillards sans déficience mentale', *Annales Médico-Psychologiques*, 125 (1967), 677–702.

an individual, as if they were recorded in a book'.[17] This view was shared by Bonnet: a perfect correspondence between physical and psychological processes means that knowledge of one domain provides access to the other. But in 1902, when Flournoy published Lullin's notes, he was forced to conclude that ophthalmologists and psychiatrists did not have much more to go on than a suspicion that the images were due to the activation of certain nerves in an unidentified part of the brain. In other words, they were not much further than Bonnet in 1760.

The name: the baptismal text

Bonnet's description bears no trace of the pathologization which the seeing of images would later undergo. The term 'illness' is not used, nor are the images referred to as 'symptoms'; Lullin is not a 'patient' and he does not 'suffer' from the images. In fact, Bonnet refers to them not as hallucinations, but rather as 'visions'. The term 'Bonnet syndrome' does not appear until 1936. A Geneva neurologist called De Morsier published a short article on visual hallucinations in the journal *Schweizerische Medizinische Wochenschrift*.[18] It was an attempt to draw up a typology of hallucinations on the basis of six cases, and to link it to such varied conditions as brain damage, eye problems, brain tumours and psychoses. The fifth case was that of Madame R, 74 years of age. She suffered from glaucoma (elevated pressure inside the eyeball) in one eye and cataracts in the other. For about a year, she had been 'seeing' human figures which were normal in both colour and size, as well as groups of children and animals, often walking in procession. De Morsier, who was familiar with the city's history, wrote: 'We see here a syndrome which has been studied

[17] E. Naville, 'Hallucinations visuelles à l'état normal', *Archives de Psychologie*, 8 (1909), 1–8 (8).

[18] G. de Morsier, 'Les automatismes visuels (hallucinations visuelles retrochiasmatiques)', *Schweizerische Medizinische Wochenschrift*, 29 (1936), 700–3.

primarily in Geneva."[19] Towards the end of his article he christened this type of hallucinations 'Bonnet syndrome'. In view of the conflicts that later arose, it is important to record the exact wording he used: the disorder was an example of 'syndromes séniles avec lésions oculaires', or geriatric syndromes accompanied by eye injuries.[20] He would live to regret the latter addition.

Over thirty years later, De Morsier again addressed the subject of visual hallucinations.[21] In his opening sentence he notes that in 1936, he proposed that the name 'Bonnet syndrome' be given to visual hallucinations among the elderly in which the other cerebral functions remain intact. After that, he continues, the syndrome was totally forgotten by psychiatrists, for the simple reason that the elderly people in question displayed no neurological or psychiatric symptoms, and thus would not normally be admitted to institutions or clinics. This explains why the syndrome does not appear in the classifications formulated *intra muros*. It was only in the previous ten or fifteen years that there had been an increase in the number of articles devoted to Bonnet syndrome, but according to De Morsier this had resulted in a disastrous confusion. Many authors had attached the name to quite different disorders, so that the original definition was under threat. One psychiatrist had even classified the images of a demented psychopath and *'semi-clochard'* as evidence of the syndrome, while the man also had a large tumour encircling the optic nerve. Others saw the eye condition as the defining symptom, so that young people were also classed among the possible sufferers. Still others included individuals with Alzheimer's disease or chronically psychotic patients. Even the hallucinations experienced during an alcoholic delirium were associated with Bonnet syndrome. It was as if his colleagues had gone totally overboard.

[19] De Morsier, 'Automatismes', 701.　　[20] *Ibid.* 702.
[21] De Morsier, 'Syndrome de Charles Bonnet'.

For De Morsier, of course, there were several factors at issue. Any debate about the criteria of a syndrome is also a debate about the causes. Are old age and failing eyesight independent factors in the development of the images, even though they commonly appear in combination? Or is it precisely this combination which is a necessary condition? Do the images originate peripherally (in the eye) or centrally (in the brain)? De Morsier was convinced that the latter was the case, but by that time various ophthalmologists had claimed that the images were caused by processes taking place in the eye itself. Do hallucinations as a result of eye injuries also fall under Bonnet syndrome, or are they a separate category? The inclusion and exclusion criteria establish what is accidental and what is necessary, what is concomitant and what is essential. They distinguish the conditions from the consequences and the cause from the effect, bringing some kind of order to the mosaic of symptoms, side-effects and underlying factors. As long as there is no agreement on the cause of a disorder, attaching to it the label 'Bonnet syndrome' not only suggests a unity that does not exist, it also leaves the question of the name-giver unsolved. For who has the last word when it comes to Bonnet syndrome, the medical community or De Morsier? The latter begins and ends his article with the claim that it was he who proposed that the name 'Bonnet syndrome' be reserved for visual hallucinations in the elderly in the absence of other mental disturbances. This was not entirely true – the original description also mentioned the term *lésions oculaires* – but the general intent was clear: it was De Morsier who named the disorder and drew up the baptismal text, and he exhorted his learned colleagues to respect that fact. This was an understandable desire: his place in medical history was bound up with the fortunes of the syndrome, and the more the generally accepted criteria distanced themselves from his own, the more likely it was that he would go down in history as the man who gave the right name to the wrong syndrome.

In the more modern literature, the opening paragraph dutifully refers to De Morsier and his articles dating from 1936 and 1967. He is honoured as the man who gave the syndrome its name. The medical-psychiatric jargon which he introduced has also been adopted: someone who sees the images is a patient. But the exhortation to respect his criteria has been universally ignored. There are researchers who refer to young people with an eye disease as suffering from Bonnet syndrome, while others reserve the name for elderly patients with visual hallucinations, even when they are also suffering from other psychiatric or neurological conditions. Nor is there any uniformity where the terminology is concerned. The images are variously described as 'phantom images' and 'visual delusions'. The miniaturizations are referred to as 'Gulliverian hallucinations' or 'Lilliputian images', and the elongations as 'Brobdingnagian images'. Technically known as microspy and macrospy, these terms refer to distortions which may also occur at the beginning of an epileptic attack or during severe migraine headaches. The use of a common term such as 'pseudo-hallucinations' has been challenged by other researchers: hallucinations are defined by the fact that the person actually believes what he is seeing, which is not the case where the images of Bonnet are concerned. Hallucinations are by definition imaginary, and the addition of the prefix 'pseudo' makes a shadowy term even more shadowy. For this reason, some authors (like Bonnet himself) prefer the neutral term 'visions'. The most obvious choice would be simply 'Bonnet images', and yet precisely this term is absent from the professional literature.

In the past thirty years, the literature has been dominated by geriatricians and eye doctors, reflecting the two major factors which play a role in Bonnet syndrome: age and diminished vision. According to research involving larger groups (populations of patients attending eye clinics), Bonnet syndrome is not as rare as has long been assumed. One might even say: on the contrary. In the group of older patients seen by the ophthalmologist Crane in 1995, some 38 per cent displayed Bonnet-like symptoms.[22] It is as if the rarity of the syndrome is itself a case of miniaturization: people who see Bonnet images often keep that fact to themselves for fear of being thought crazy, and this leads to a sizable underreporting. However, one thing has not changed: Bonnet images are experienced as occurring outside of the individual, although over the years that experience has been described in various ways. Where Lullin wrote that the images he saw in 1759 appeared 'as in a painting', later generations used terms such as 'comme au cinéma' (1936) or 'like watching television' (1982).

The most extensive research thus far was carried out by a Dutch geriatric psychiatrist called Robert Teunisse, and in 1998 it formed the basis of his dissertation.[23] At the out-patient clinic for ophthalmology of the Radboud University Medical Centre in Nijmegen, he had at his disposal a large group of patients. In his dissertation, he first describes the neurological, psychiatric and ophthalmological characteristics of fourteen patients with Bonnet syndrome. He then reports on a detailed comparison between sixty Bonnet patients and a group of individuals in the same age group who have the same eye problems, but do not see the Bonnet images. All these patients were over the age of 64 and their vision in the better eye was 0.3 or less.

It is clear from interviews that the characteristics of those images were just as varied as their content. Most of them appeared in their natural colour, although some patients reported seeing black and white images. Occasionally, they were sharper or vaguer than in reality; some remained visible for as long as an hour, while others disappeared within a few seconds. Sometimes there was movement within the image, at other times the image as a whole moved. One

[22] W. G. Crane, 'Prevalence and characteristics of photopsias and formed visual hallucinations (Charles Bonnet Syndrome) in a low-vision population', *Southern Medical Journal*, 88 (1995), 71.

[23] R. J. Teunisse, *Concealed Perceptions: an Explorative Study of the Charles Bonnet Syndrome* (Nijmegen, 1998).

appeared to float, while the next seemed to be projected against a background. Sometimes the objects in the image were ridiculously large or small. While most people saw the images over a period of less than a year, in some cases they continued for as long as five years.

But there were also similarities. Everyone recognized the images as unreal, usually at first sight, occasionally as the result of a reality check (there are no cows in the field in the middle of winter). Everyone was able to make the images disappear, usually by simply blinking or closing their eyes. No one was able to summon the images at will, or in any way influence their content. In almost every case, the images were emotionally neutral, in the sense that they did not appear to have anything to do with the patient's own life at the time. The representations in the images were not at all threatening, although they did give rise to a certain amount of irritation or anxiety concerning one's own mental state. Only a small minority said that they would consider taking medication to get rid of the images. (In actual fact, such medication does not exist.) Three-quarters of those interviewed had not told anyone about the images, not even their partner. Those who had gone to see the GP or eye doctor were none the wiser: only rarely was the correct diagnosis made. One woman was prescribed neuroleptic medication by her psychiatrist, which did not dispel the images.

The interviews also provided information with respect to favourable circumstances. As a rule, the images appeared at dusk, in the familiar surroundings of one's own home, and at a time when the patient was not actively involved in a particular activity. Fatigue also seemed to trigger the symptoms. As a group, the people with Bonnet syndrome differed from the control group in several respects. They were more likely to be taking medication containing beta blockers. They admitted to sometimes being lonely and scored lower on an extroversion scale, indicating that they adopted a passive attitude towards new social contacts. Other factors, such as level of education, sex, living conditions, psychiatric disturbances and neurological conditions played no role.

The work of Teunisse has shed considerable light on the manner in which Bonnet images are experienced by the individual himself, the circumstances which are conducive to their appearance, and the factors which may or may not be associated with the syndrome. The prototypical Bonnet patient who emerges is someone well on in years, with severely impaired vision. Reading is almost impossible. His surroundings tend to be quiet. He lives alone, and lacks both the energy and the inclination to leave the house or to look up old friends. He receives few visitors. His days pass by calmly, each one as uneventful as the previous one. Towards dusk, when he starts to feel a little drowsy and the outside world is beginning to fade, the images appear. He does not find them disturbing, since he knows they aren't real. And he can make them disappear: all he has to do is blink his eyes and they're gone. But he doesn't talk about his experiences. After all, they are a bit strange. He doesn't want people to think he's losing his faculties.

Eye and brain

The explanations which have been put forward for Bonnet syndrome are almost as varied as the images themselves. One particularly inventive hypothesis is that the Lilliputian images are the result of regression: the individuals the patient sees are child-sized, like the characters in a children's book, and all the objects have the convenient format of toys. But macrospy appears just as often in Bonnet images as microspy. Nor does this hypothesis explain a phenomenon like autoscopy. Flynn, a psychoanalytically inspired author, has suggested that the patient's failing eyesight cuts him off from perceptible reality, thus making room for the products of his imagination.[24] In old age, the ego defends itself by creating a substitute world full of

[24] W. R. Flynn, 'Visual hallucinations in sensory deprivation', *Psychiatric Quarterly*, 36 (1962), 55–65.

entertaining scenes, which compensates for the severe loss which is beginning to make itself felt. Explanations such as regression and defence have suffered the same fate as the theories in which they originated, and have gradually disappeared from the psychiatric and neurological literature. What the hypotheses of the last thirty years have in common is the fact that they situate the cause somewhere in the neurophysiological domain. They disagree only on where the images originate, in the eye or in the brain. In most cases, Bonnet syndrome is accompanied by damage to both eyes. The cause of that damage does not appear to play a role. Conditions such as cataracts, glaucoma, infections, retinal bleeding and detached retina can all result in distorted perception. Objects may be grotesquely deformed (a single pinpoint of light is multiplied, or contours are accentuated by four or five parallel lines), while in other cases colourful auras encircle a bright spot, or amorphous specks seem to cluster and take flight. As far back as the nineteenth century, the physiologists Helmholtz and Purkinje established that electrical or mechanical stimulation of the eye produces specific subjective images, including rotating disks, stars and grids of horizontal and vertical lines. Moreover, the retina appears to be particularly sensitive to certain visual patterns, such as circles or straight lines. Even when no pressure is applied to the eye, curious optical effects may occur. Under specific lighting conditions, the eye is even capable of seeing parts of itself: objects floating around in the aqueous humour, or even a portion of the richly branched vascular system of the eye, which takes the form of a tiny tree. The physician Horowitz suggested that visual hallucinations originate in a 'process of negotiation' between eye and brain, whereby 'the eye tells the brain what it sees and the brain tells the eye what to look for, what it should and should not be seeing in what it has seen'.[25] There is no mention of Bonnet images in this article, but

---

[25] M. J. Horowitz, 'The imagery of visual hallucinations', *Journal of Nervous and Mental Disease*, 138 (1964), 513–23 (520).

later on the connection was repeatedly made: Bonnet syndrome was said to be the result of the overly free association of the brain with the severely distorted information passed on by the eyes.

This notion that Bonnet images are the result of negotiations between eye and brain is in keeping with the view of the brain as an instrument designed to recognize order in chaos, patterns in coincidence, and signals in noise, even when what it is presented with actually does consist of chaos, coincidence and noise. Since, as far as the brain is concerned, floating specks do not exist, what the eye sees must be a swarm of pigeons taking flight. In the same way, a blue haze with yellow dots that follows the movement of the eye is surely a handkerchief. At least some of the Bonnet images fit the hypothesis that the brain approaches the stimulus with a conjecture and then promptly 'sees' that conjecture. Bonnet images are regarded by some as a convincing demonstration of the law of perceptual psychology according to which the brain sees what it assumes to be there. However, the great majority of the images are too rich in pattern to be the transformation of chance. Whatever particles may be floating around in aging eyeballs, images of young men wearing silver-trimmed hats, young ladies with boxes on their heads, girls with colourful ribbons and pearl necklaces, and entire landscapes full of spouting fountains are far too complex to be regarded as a cerebral elaboration of elementary optical stimuli. And are they not very much like the images we see just before falling asleep? Is it not possible that they are generated entirely in the brain?

According to the hypothesis of 'sensory deprivation', the origin of Bonnet images lies in a protracted under-stimulation of the brain. It had been known for some time that extremely monotonous stimuli can cause hallucinations. This phenomenon has been reported by people held in solitary confinement, as well as by arctic explorers and solo sailors. It has also been reproduced under laboratory conditions, in studies devoted to sensory deprivation.[26] Experiments have shown that

[26] L. J. West (ed.), *Hallucinations* (New York/London, 1962).

blocking the senses, or 'anaesthetizing' them by subjecting them to the same stimulus over and over, does not cause the processing activities of the brain to come to a complete halt. After a while, they begin to produce sensations: sounds, images or tactile sensations which appear to come from the outside and, for that reason, are difficult to distinguish from true stimuli. The human brain cannot cope with absolute rest. The Dutch writer Rudy Kousbroek once compared the brain to a huge commercial undertaking or government ministry forced to deal with an exceptionally active, almost monomaniacal employee:

> He must constantly be kept busy, provided with enough work to fill every hour of the day, for as soon as he has an unoccupied moment, he goes to the archives and takes out all sorts of complicated cases which have been brought to a good end years ago and then, without anyone noticing, puts them back into the current administration. Invoices which have long since been dealt with have been reappearing in the bookkeeping, just as letters dispatched years ago are added to those awaiting a signature. To complicate matters still further, the employee in question was originally an archivist, and he is the only person in the company who knows his way around the enormous archives. In the cellars where they are stored, he wanders around at night, like a somnambulist. Mumbling to himself, he leafs through dossiers which everyone else in the organization has long since forgotten.[27]

Replace letters and invoices by images, the archives by visual memory, the bookkeeping by observation, the peaceful nocturnal hours by an optical system that allows almost no stimuli to pass through, and you have a graphic description of Bonnet syndrome, in the version known as sensory deprivation.

This hypothesis is supported by a number of observations. The Bonnet images usually appear under quiet conditions, at home, in familiar surroundings. When Lullin wanted to see images, he walked into an empty room and simply waited until they appeared. Bonnet

---

[27] R. Kousbroek, *Een kuil om snikkend in te vallen* (Amsterdam, 1971), p. 49.

images also have a tendency to disappear when the individual is admitted to hospital, or when the daily routine is interrupted in some other way. But there are also findings which are difficult to reconcile with the hypothesis of sensory deprivation. In the first place, the images do not resemble the 'ordinary' hallucinations which occur in sensory deprivation. Bonnet images are often fully formed, and they appear suddenly and without warning. Hallucinations generally begin as simple sensory sensations, and take some time to develop into images. Bonnet images are often clearer than real visual perceptions, while hallucinations lack that clarity. Bonnet images are usually acknowledged as imaginary, while hallucinations often lead to doubts about one's own perceptions. And the fact that most people are able to make the Bonnet images disappear at will by closing their eyes is totally contradictory to the logic of sensory deprivation: hallucinations disappear by opening one's eyes. Moreover, according to this hypothesis, both the moment that Bonnet syndrome appears and the moment that it disappears again are illogical: the images occur for the first time when the person's eyesight begins to decline, and usually disappear when total blindness sets in.

The loss of external stimuli is also at the heart of a second hypothesis which seeks an explanation in the individual's own brain activity.[28] The general mechanism is known as release and it was suggested by the neurologist Hughlings Jackson as far back as the 1860s. Jackson saw the human nervous system as a collection of hierarchically ordered units. Higher units which, from an evolutionary standpoint, appeared later were capable of making the activity of lower units invisible or inhibiting them altogether. If that control fell away due to injury or was temporarily 'switched off', then the activity of lower

---

[28] J. E. A. Bartlet, 'A case of organized visual hallucinations in an old man with cataracts, and their relation to the phenomena of the phantom limb', *Brain*, 74 (1951), 363–73.

units was released. When this is applied to Bonnet syndrome, as the ophthalmologist Cogan did, the release theory suggests that part of the visual system displays a spontaneous activity which under normal circumstances is too weak to get through to the patient's consciousness.[29] These images 'from within' remain invisible due to the unceasing supply of external images. But when that supply dries up, they are just strong enough to be discerned. Cataracts, bleeding, a detached retina – these are all examples of that curtain which darkens the hall sufficiently for the brain to project those images which it manufactures itself. You could say that Bonnet images are scenes from a silent film for the partially sighted.

But alas, the arguments against the hypothesis of sensory deprivation also hold true for the release theory. Most individuals say they see their Bonnet images with their eyes open, and that they disappear as soon as they close their eyes. Once blindness sets in and the darkness is most intense, the Bonnet images disappear. According to the release theory, they should then be at their clearest.

'Abide with me; fast falls the eventide'

Touch, taste and smell can also become dulled by age or illness. However, the literature makes no mention of hallucinations involving touch, taste or smell comparable to the Bonnet images for the sense of sight. They do, however, exist for the sense of hearing. These 'acoustic Bonnet images' are musical hallucinations experienced by people going deaf. This – as yet nameless – syndrome is less common than Bonnet syndrome, but in the past hundred years neurologists and psychiatrists have described several dozen cases of people with a history of hearing problems who, just when they were almost completely deaf, began hearing music. This was usually preceded by a

---

[29] D. G. Cogan, 'Visual hallucinations as release phenomena', *Albrecht von Graefes Archiv für klinische und experimentelle Ophtalmologie*, 188 (1973), 139–50.

period of tinnitus: a constant hissing, whistling, squeaking, humming or rustling sound in the ear.[30] As in Bonnet syndrome, most of these patients are well on in age, usually over 60, and many already have a hearing aid. The hallucinations are often so clear that the patients initially think they are hearing a very loud radio or, in the early literature, a street musician who happens to be passing. The cases reported thus far consist of four times as many women as men. It is striking that these hallucinations almost always contain music, but seldom spoken text. This points to yet another difference between these phenomena and hallucinations with a psychiatric origin: the latter are often 'voices', which say threatening or offensive things.

And just what kind of music do these people hear? Two psychiatrists described thirty patients with musical hallucinations who had been referred to a geriatric service in South Wales.[31] The group consisted largely of women (87 per cent), who were elderly (on average, 78 years old), and lived on their own (77 per cent). One out of three had hearing problems. In two-thirds of all cases, the hallucinations consisted of psalms, hymns and Christmas carols. The hymn 'Abide with Me' was mentioned six times, 'Silent Night' and 'Hark the Herald Angels Sing' twice each.[32] This hallucinatory play list also featured the national anthems of England, Wales and the United States. Secular songs were rare ('Danny Boy'), and only one title represented the popular genre ('How Much is that Doggy in the Window'). Noteworthy was the absence of more recent music. In almost all cases, the hallucinations disappeared after the administration of anti-psychotic medication. The fact that the hallucinations often featured music from the past, which was popular when the patients were children, is confirmed in another study. A man of 75

---

[30] H. Hécaen and R. Ropert. 'Les hallucinations auditives des otopathes', *Journal de psychologie normale et pathologique*, 60 (1963), 293–324.

[31] N. Aziz and V. Aziz, 'Hymns and arias: musical hallucinations in older people in Wales', *International Journal of Geriatric Psychiatry*, 20 (2005), 658–60.

[32] 'Abide with Me', by H. F. Lyte.

heard psalms he used to sing in the choir.[33] The hallucinations were so persistent that sometimes the only solution was to sing along with the music. Even turning the radio up did not help. A woman of 83 heard a medley of Irish jigs and Christmas carols in her right ear, the music, but not the words. Sometimes these hallucinations were so loud that she was unable to get to sleep. She noticed that when her heartbeat briefly accelerated after the application of eye drops, the music also went faster.

The explanations put forward for such musical hallucinations are the same as those for Bonnet syndrome, and they have given rise to similar controversies. Some neurologists place the origin of the hallucinations in the ear, others in the brain. The latter supposition is supported by the fact that musical hallucinations occasionally occur without previous damage to the individual's hearing. A woman of 66 suddenly heard the 'Star-Spangled Banner' and an 80-year-old woman Italian operas. Neither of them had hearing problems, and in both cases the hallucinations appeared to be due to neurological damage attributed to Lyme disease.[34] Treatment with antibiotics put an end to the music. Cases of musical hallucinations without deafness have also been described following infections and syphilis. As a rule, the damage was located in the right half of the brain, which seems logical, since in most people this is where the auditory associations of non-verbal stimuli originate.

The similarities between musical hallucinations and Bonnet images are obvious. They occur in elderly individuals suffering from failing sight or hearing, many of whom live alone. They do not arise gradually, but appear suddenly and continue for some time, usually several months. None of the patients involved feel threatened by the

---

[33] E. D. Ross, P. B. Jossman, B. Bell, T. Sabin and N. Geschwind, 'Musical hallucinations in deafness', *Journal of the American Medical Association*, 231 (1975) 6, 620–2.

[34] R. B. Stricker and E. E. Winger, 'Musical hallucinations in patients with Lyme Disease', *Southern Medical Journal*, 96 (2003) 7, 711–15.

hallucinations. However, there are also differences. Unlike the Bonnet images, musical hallucinations cannot be dispelled, not even by other music (while under normal circumstances it is impossible for someone listening to music to even think about other music). Bonnet images do not respond to medication, while musical hallucinations do. It is also interesting that musical hallucinations appear to be related to memories of music the individual heard in the past, while Bonnet images are usually quite fanciful. Occasionally, a patient suffers from both Bonnet syndrome and musical hallucinations. An 86-year-old woman with cataracts in both eyes began seeing children on Christmas Day 1985.[35] These were classical Bonnet images: they appeared towards dusk, the children did not speak, and she experienced no anxiety. Later, she also saw a circus, complete with ring, bright lights and performances. The scene reminded her of her childhood. At one point she also heard the music accompanying each act. She derived great enjoyment from the nightly shows. The only thing she objected to was the ringmaster: she was convinced that he was following her around. As long as the circus performance lasted, she was afraid to go to the toilet because she could see him watching her as she undressed. Upon closer examination, a distinct loss of hearing in both ears was recorded.

The brain as theatre

In 1902, Flournoy wrote that when it came to finding an explanation for the syndrome, he and his colleagues were no further than Bonnet in 1760. Another hundred years later, Teunisse concluded at the end of his dissertation that Bonnet syndrome was still largely a mystery. There is no agreement concerning the exact spot on the trajectory between eye and brain where the Bonnet images originate, nor can

[35] H. C. Patel, M. S. Keshavan and S. Martin, 'A case of Bonnet Syndrome with musical hallucinations', *Canadian Journal of Psychiatry*, 32 (1987), 303–4.

anyone say with certainty which factors or combinations of factors give rise to those images. It has proved impossible to unravel the causal, mediating or facilitating factors. The criteria for the syndrome have not been laid down. For De Morsier, old age was an essential part of the definition of the syndrome. For Teunisse, the advanced age of the patients was one of the correlating factors, a view which leaves open the possibility of young people also experiencing Bonnet images. All the explanations put forward thus far have their own drawbacks. At present, there is no grand theory on Bonnet syndrome: not in psychiatry or neurology, not in ophthalmology or the psychology of perception.

But this does not leave us totally empty-handed. There are the intriguing incidental findings which suggest the direction in which future research may be heading. One patient with damage to the visual association cortex reported seeing Bonnet-like images. As far back as 1931, it was established that electric stimulation of an area known as V19 (part of the visual association cortex) gave rise to Bonnet images.[36] Some day these images, as fleeting as they are, may come within the reach of imaging technology in the form of fMRI or PET scans, making it possible to localize the site of origin. Correlation research in large groups can bring to light relationships which point the way to new factors. To take an example, the low score for extrovert behaviour recorded by Teunisse suggests a possible link with the activation level of the brain. It has long been known that extrovert individuals tend to have a slightly lower activation level than introverted people. This finding is somewhat counter-intuitive, but the explanation commonly put forward says that extroverts are so outwardly oriented because they are seeking extra neurological stimulation; or to put it more simply: the brain of an introvert is by nature active enough, while that of an extrovert needs external stimulation. According to this hypothesis, Bonnet

[36] O. Foerster, 'The cerebral cortex in man', *The Lancet*, 2 (1931), 309–12.

images take shape in an introverted brain which is accustomed to a relatively high activation level, and in extreme circumstances (when visual stimulation has more or less disappeared), it demonstrates its natural strength by drawing upon its own resources – imagination, memories and combinations of the two – to call up one image after the other and present it for inspection.

It is a thought that would please Charles Bonnet. 'His mind makes merry with the images', he wrote of his grandfather in 1760. 'His brain is a theatre where the stage machinery puts on performances which are all the more amazing because they are unexpected.'[37]

[37] Bonnet, *Essai*, p. 317.

TWO

A tormenting round of tremors:
Parkinson's disease

On a Sunday afternoon shortly before Christmas 1824, James Parkinson suffered a stroke which paralysed him on the right side, and took away his power of speech. He was then in his seventieth year and, as a physician, he must have realized that his chances of recovery were not good. His son, John William, with whom he shared a practice in London (as Parkinson himself had done with his own father) nursed him with the utmost care, but there was little he could do. In a brief letter addressed to the Board of Trustees of the Poor of the Parish of St Leonard's, he informed them that his father had died on the morning of 21 December. In the minutes, the council expressed its appreciation for the medical services he had rendered to the parishioners. The medical societies which Parkinson belonged to duly noted the date of his death in their records. There were no extensive In Memoriams. The fact that the life of James Parkinson had come to an end was noted, but not commemorated.[1]

Everything that Parkinson had achieved in terms of fame and reputation throughout his long and active career seems to have disappeared at his passing. He was co-founder of several scientific

[1] A.D. Morris, *James Parkinson: his Life and Times* (F. Clifford Rose (ed.), Boston, 1989).

societies devoted to the study of medicine and geology (the second passion in his life). He had written handbooks on chemistry and fossils which were reprinted several times; he published works on medical care within the home for a wide audience; he was a feared pamphleteer on social and political issues; and he left behind an extensive series of books and articles on such varied subjects as gout, dangerous sports, statutory regulations for insane asylums, and how to reanimate someone struck by lightning. After his death, the collection of fossils he had amassed, regarded as one of the finest in the country, was broken up at auction. Most of the objects went to a geological museum in the United States, where they were later lost in a fire. There is no known portrait of Parkinson, the house where he was born has been demolished, and his gravestone has been removed. There is only one brief description of his person and appearance, and even that has survived almost by accident: the geologist Gideon Mantell recorded in 1850 how as a boy he had asked Parkinson's permission to view his collection of fossils. 'Mr Parkinson was rather below middle stature, with an energetic intellect, and pleasing expression of countenance, and of mild and courteous manners.'[2] Some forty years later, Mantell recalled with warmth how obligingly Parkinson had shared his knowledge, as they strolled past the cabinets.

Parkinson could not have suspected there would ever be such a thing as 'Parkinson's disease'. In 1817, he had published his *Essay on the Shaking Palsy*, in which he described most of the classic symptoms.[3] At that time he referred to the disease as shaking palsy or 'paralysis agitans': palsy referring to the weakening of the muscles, and shaking to the tremor which was such a noticeable characteristic of the disease. It was not until two generations later, in 1876, that the disease was named after Parkinson. The only eponym which bore his name

---

[2] Quoted in Morris, *Parkinson*, p. 18.
[3] J. Parkinson, *An Essay on the Shaking Palsy* (London, 1817).

in Parkinson's own lifetime was the *Parkinsonia parkinsoni*, a fossil ammonite dating from the Middle Jura, which appeared in a handbook on fossils a year before his death.

Parkinson & Son

James Parkinson's entire life was spent within the confines of a few square miles: the parish of St Leonard in the hamlet of Hoxton. His birth in 1755 is recorded in the parish registers, as is his marriage to Mary Dale in 1781 and the birth of their six children, only four of whom lived beyond childhood. His father, John Parkinson, was a dispensing physician, residing at 1 Hoxton Square. At the age of 17, James entered the practice, which remained in existence as 'Parkinson & Son, Surgeon, Apothecary, and Man-midwife' for eighty years, headed by four generations of Parkinsons.

The period between the year of James Parkinson's birth and the year of his death coincides with the era in English history known as the Industrial Revolution, a process which helped to determine the spatial and social structure of Hoxton. When James was born, the town lay just outside the northern city gates of London. It was a pleasant, leafy area, with country estates, orchards and market gardens. The arrival of dozens of factories changed all that. Anyone who could afford a carriage moved away. For those who had to travel on foot, there was little choice but to seek accommodation in the vicinity of the factory. In the next few decades, Hoxton saw the construction of endless narrow rows of working-class houses, which rapidly deteriorated into slums. While the first Dr Parkinson still had a middle-class practice, the patients that James and his son ministered to were either working-class or downright poor. The 'man-midwifery' must have kept them quite busy: between 1801 and 1811 the population of Hoxton increased from 30,000 to 50,000. It would ultimately become the most densely populated square mile in all of England, with many poorhouses and no fewer than three insane asylums, all full to overflowing. For over thirty years, Parkinson was associated with one of those asylums, Holly House, which was only a short walk from his house.

Parkinson was part of a culture of societies. He was a member of the Medical Society of London, the Medico-Chirurgical Society of London, the Society of Apothecaries, and a handful of other such bodies. Some had been founded to promote the interests of their members, such as the Society for the Relief of Widows and Orphans of Medical Men, but the functions of most of the professional organizations have since been taken over by specialist journals and conferences. During the meetings, readings were held, scientific findings exchanged, and communications from sister organizations discussed. Parkinson took part in all these activities, and even founded a number of new societies. Much of what we know about his life is drawn from the minutes and records of these learned societies.

In the annual report of the Royal Humane Society for 1777, James Parkinson was mentioned as the winner of the Honorary Silver Medal, by virtue of the resuscitation of the 29-year-old Brian Maxey.[4] His father, John Parkinson, recounted in detail the circumstances of the incident. Early on the evening of the 28 October 1777, they were called to Maxey's house. He had hanged himself. When they arrived, the body was cold and lifeless, the pupils were dilated and unresponsive to light, they could find no pulse and the jaw was fixed. He had been hanging there for at least half an hour before he was found. A neighbour had already begun blood-letting. The Parkinsons followed to the letter the instructions for such cases, which had been drawn up by the Royal Humane Society: close one nostril and then use a pair of bellows to blow air through the other nostril and into the lungs. In the meantime, others were busy rubbing the body warm. After fifteen minutes there was a weak pulse and an hour and a half later, Maxey regained consciousness. 'He expressed

[4] Morris, *Parkinson*, p. 69.

the utmost sorrow for his horrid crime', John Parkinson noted in the account, 'and the greatest gratitude to those who were instrumental in his restoration to his wife and children'.[5] The reanimation of people who appeared to be dead continued to fascinate James Parkinson. Death by drowning, freezing or asphyxiation was not uncommon, and reanimation techniques were indeed welcome tools. In 1787, Parkinson reported to the Medical Society of London on his intervention in the case of a man who had been struck by lightning and left for dead on the street. The report appeared in the *Memoirs* as 'Some account of the effects of lightning'.[6] This time wet flannels and hot brandy brought the victim back to life. In the same article, he expressed some doubt about the efficacy of electric shocks as a form of reanimation. There is something ironic about Parkinson's scepticism with regard to the latter technique (in which he had even less confidence than in the procedure which consisted in blowing tobacco smoke into the anus) given that today the 'shock treatment' is regarded as the quickest way to reactivate the vital functions.

Parkinson's medical training was somewhat checkered, which is not surprising in an era which predated official medical studies at university level. We may assume that he acquired considerable knowledge and skills in his father's practice, while from 1776 on he also attended classes at the London Hospital Medical College. In 1784, three months after the death of his father, Parkinson was awarded the diploma of the Company of Surgeons. His appointment as Fellow of the Medical Society of London followed in 1787. James Parkinson was a prolific and enthusiastic writer, although initially he wielded his pen mainly in the service of the public cause. Between 1793 and 1795, he wrote a series of pamphlets published under the pseudonym 'Old Hubert'.[7] Parkinson lived in a time of ferment.

---

[5] *Ibid.* p. 69.   [6] *Ibid.* p. 71.

[7] For Parkinson's political views, see M. D. Yahr, 'A physician for all seasons: James Parkinson 1755–1824', *Archives of Neurology*, 35 (1978), 185–8.

He was an admirer of the French Revolution and found himself in questionable company when it was followed by the Terror. With the introduction of the constituency voting system, Parliament had lost every trace of representativity. Populous industrial cities had no representatives, nor did the working class. Parkinson fought for a fairer organization of Parliament, for general suffrage (for men), and supported a campaign to combat pauperization and child labour. Looking back, these are all eminently reasonable aims, but given the balance of influence at the time, they were regarded as the views of a dangerous radical. Advocates of parliamentary reforms, Parkinson among them, had united in the London Corresponding Society, and in 1796 he found himself involved in legal proceedings against five members of the society. They were accused of plotting to kill George III. To that end, it was alleged, they had had a clock-maker fashion a kind of pop-gun from which a poisoned arrow could be fired. In the trial centring around the so-called Pop-Gun Plot, even the most peripheral involvement was dangerous, since the charge was high treason and a conviction would mean the death penalty. In those circumstances, it required courage to step forward during the proceedings, as Parkinson did, and to make an exculpatory statement, thus acknowledging that in any case he belonged to the circle of the accused.

In 1799, Parkinson published a work that was more relevant to his chosen profession: *Medical Admonitions to Families*, a kind of medical encyclopedia for laymen. Health care was sketchy and often inaccessible in those days, and people welcomed any measures to treat or prevent disease and injury that could be taken at home. The core of the book was the 'Table of Symptoms', an alphabetical list that began with 'anxiety' and 'appetite (loss of)' and ended with 'wakefulness' and 'yawning'. The recommendations were simple but sensible: in the case of contagious diseases, see that the house is well ventilated and be sure to air clothes; young children should wear protective caps; and a navel rupture can be dealt with by pressing the navel firmly back in and taping it tightly. He also advised parents to have their children vaccinated against smallpox, a procedure which had only become possible the previous year. Several years later, Parkinson published a monograph on a condition with which he was himself familiar: gout, which was caused by an acute and painful inflammation of the joints, usually in the foot. 'Nearly 15 years ago', he wrote in his foreword to *Observations on the Nature and Cure of Gout* (1805), 'I experienced the mortification of finding that I was also under the influence of this tormenting malady'.[8] The word 'also' may refer to the fact that his father before him was a sufferer. Both Parkinsons appear in the book as 'case JP', and both men experienced the initial symptoms around the age of 40. James correctly surmised that there was a hereditary factor at work. He could offer no remedy, although he did recommend consuming quantities of vegetables and abstaining from alcohol.

The previous year, Parkinson had published the first volume of his magnum opus, *Organic Remains of a Former World* (1804–1811). Today, the subject matter would fall into the category of palaeontology, but this term did not exist before 1834, and Parkinson described himself as a 'fossilist'. His son, John William, joined the practice in 1802, which no doubt allowed James more time for collecting, describing and drawing fossils. Sometimes he dug them out himself, from gravel banks and clay pits in the area, but he also bought them at auctions. In 1807, he helped found the Geological Society, and was a regular contributor to the society's *Transactions*. The period between 1790 and 1820 is known as the 'Heroic Age of Geology', and with his book Parkinson made his own contribution to those developments. It contains some 700 illustrations, mainly fossils from his own collection, and most of them drawn by Parkinson himself. The study of fossils, or 'medals of creation', was closely linked to such issues as the age of the Earth and the actual course of creation. Parkinson was a

---

[8] J. Parkinson, *Observations on the Nature and Cure of Gout* (London, 1805), p. vi.

religious man and for him the petrified marine animals and shells discovered on mountain tops or far inland were quite simply the result of the Flood. The fact that certain fossilized plants and animals later disappeared, and that the fossils were actually 'the remains of a former world' were proof that the Earth was much older than was compatible with a process of creation lasting six days. This meant that the word 'day' must be seen as a metaphor for 'certain indefinite periods'.[9]

Organic Remains established Parkinson's reputation. In 1850, the drawings were reproduced by Mantell in his 'standard work' on geology. Parkinson's conviction that marine fossils on mountain tops could be explained by the Flood, and that the seven days of Creation should not be taken literally, placed him squarely in a long and devout tradition, albeit as one of its last adherents. After Parkinson, 'modern' geology began. The three volumes of *Organic Remains*, which continued to be reprinted until 1833, marked the end of an era. By contrast, *An Essay on the Shaking Palsy* (1817), a seemingly insignificant accomplishment in comparison with his geological work, marked a beginning.

An Essay on the Shaking Palsy

Parkinson begins his *Essay* with an apology:[10] the disease which he is about to describe has not been the object of experimental research, and he has no anatomical findings to report. In effect, he has little more than conjectures to offer. But the disorder is so serious and the consequences for the patient so devastating that publication cannot reasonably be delayed. Perhaps the *Essay* will inspire anatomists to undertake new research, in memory of those 'friends to humanity and medical science, who have already unveiled to us many of the

---

[9] Morris, *Parkinson*, p. 121.

[10] *An Essay on the Shaking Palsy* is included as an appendix to Morris' biography. On the initiative of various pharmaceutical firms, it has also been published in facsimile form. The quotes are taken from the text in Morris, *Parkinson*.

morbid processes by which health and life is abridged'.[11] This appeal is followed by five short chapters devoted to the definition and the course of the disorder, the symptoms, other diseases it could be confused with, possible causes, and the prospects of finding a remedy.

Parkinson defined shaking palsy as an 'involuntary tremulous motion, with lessened muscular power, in parts not in action and even when supported; with a propensity to bend the trunk forward, and to pass from a walking to a running pace: the senses and intellects being uninjured'.[12] The first case that came to his attention, dating from several years before, had given him an opportunity to study the development of the symptoms. The patient was a man in his early fifties, who 'followed the business of a gardener, leading a life of remarkable temperance and sobriety'. He had a tremor which began in the left hand, and which the gardener himself attributed to over-exertion, being unable to come up with any other explanation. The second patient was 62 years of age, a former court attendant at a magistrate's office who had suffered from the condition for almost ten years. He had tremors in all his limbs, was almost incapable of speech, and had a tendency to fall forward when walking. He told Parkinson that the disease was a 'consequence of considerable irregularities in his mode of living', apparently a reference to excessive drinking.[13] The man was now in the poorhouse, and Parkinson happened to run into him on the street. It was the same story with the third patient, a former sailor in his mid-sixties. The agitation of his limbs was so vehement that it could scarcely be described as trembling. The body was so bowed, and the head thrown so far forward that he was obliged to go on a continued run and to employ his stick every five or six steps. By projecting the point of it with great force against the pavement, he was forced into a more upright posture. The man attributed his condition to having spent several months in a Spanish prison, where he was forced to sleep on the bare, damp earth. There were

[11] Parkinson, *Essay*, p. 152.   [12] *Ibid.*   [13] *Ibid.* p. 155.

Figure 2.1: Parkinson patient, portrayed by the physician and draughtsman Paul Richer. This drawing accompanied Béchet's dissertation on Parkinson's disease (1892)

other cases as well, which Parkinson was able to observe only briefly. One sufferer whom he only passed in the street, displayed one of the most characteristic symptoms in an extreme form. It was only with great difficulty that he set himself in motion, after which his gait went from a walk to a headlong trot. Parkinson saw him in the company of his manservant, and every few metres the servant stood in front of his master and rocked him gently back and forth. Once the man was moving again, his servant ran ahead so that he was there to catch him after a headlong dash of some twenty paces.

Parkinson's best documented account of the course of the disease focused on his sixth case, a man of 72. This patient had lived a sober life, and nothing in his past provided any indication as to the cause of the condition. About twelve years before, he had noticed a weakening of the left arm, and soon afterwards the tremor had begun. In the years that followed, it spread to the other arm and both legs. About a year later, he awoke during the night with a total paralysis of the right side, while the left side of his face drooped. The tremors on the right side subsided, but recurred after the strength in the right arm and right leg returned. Parkinson had asked him if he was fearful of falling forward when walking, and this was indeed the case. He had such difficulty lifting up his feet that the smallest object, even a pebble on the pavement, made him anxious. His wife volunteered that when he walked across the room, he would have trouble stepping over a straight pin.

In five or six sombre pages, Parkinson sketched the course of the disease. The first symptoms appear with such stealth that the patient is usually unable to say exactly when they began. The first thing he notices is a slight weakness in an arm or leg, occasionally in the head, together with a tendency to tremble. The condition inevitably spreads to the other limbs, although this may take as long as a year. The patient also notices that he has trouble remaining upright when walking, and even when seated. The hand is unsteady, 'failing to answer with exactness to the dictates of the will'.[14] Writing becomes a tiring operation, as does eating, since it is difficult to guide the fork from the plate to the mouth. The exhausting tremors are now almost continuous. Occasionally, the patient is able to halt the trembling by means of a brusque movement, but it quickly starts up again in the opposite arm or leg. In search of relief from this 'tormenting round of tremors', the patient 'has recourse to walking, a mode of exercise to which the sufferers from this malady are in general partial'.[15] But as the disease progresses, the patient is robbed of even this scant solace. The tendency to bend forward is almost impossible to suppress, so that he starts to walk on the ball of his feet. To keep from falling he must take shorter and quicker steps, until he is finally forced into a kind of trot. In this stage, the

[14] *Ibid.* p. 153.   [15] *Ibid.* p. 154.

patient's night rest is also disturbed: the tremors are so severe that he regularly awakes with a start. He is no longer able to feed himself. Due to the weakness in the muscles of the mouth and tongue, he has difficulty keeping food and saliva inside his mouth. He is now only able to walk if someone stands in front of him and provides counter-pressure by forcing his shoulders backwards. His speech is almost unintelligible. The tremors are so violent that not only the bed curtains, but also the floor and the windows shake. In the final phase, the patient loses all control over his muscles, and his chin rests immobile on his chest. 'And at the last, constant sleepiness, with slight delirium, and other marks of extreme exhaustion, announce the wished-for release.'[16]

Parkinson explained that in the past, the tremors and the tendency to go from a walk to a trot were regarded by physicians as symptoms of various different diseases. He believed that they were mistaken on this point. The tremor accompanying 'true shaking palsy' occurs at rest, while the tremor due to fatigue or alcohol abuse appears during the active use of the limbs. Similarly, the involuntary acceleration of the pace during walking differs from the compulsive movements seen in St Vitus Dance. Moreover, the latter disease strikes young people, while shaking palsy does not occur until later life. These characteristics define the disorder and serve to distinguish it from other complaints. As to the cause and location of the condition, however, Parkinson felt he could only speculate. The fact that the disease can occur in one or more limbs, as well as in the head, and that the tremors sometimes cease temporarily, suggest that it does not originate in the nerves of the affected areas but higher up in the nervous system. The place of origin cannot be the brain, since in that case the senses and the intellect would be affected. This led Parkinson to conclude that the disorder originated in the upper part of the spinal marrow, just under the brain: in the medulla oblongata. It is there

[16] *Ibid.* p. 155.

that the spinal marrow is most mobile, and thus most susceptible to damage. Since none of these patients could remember having incurred a sudden injury, Parkinson also considered the possibility that a slow infection or a pinched nerve was responsible for the symptoms. Regardless of the cause, it was clear that the steering power of the brain was affected. This is also the spot where the traditional arsenal of healing procedures was usually initiated: blood-letting high in the neck, leeches, extraction of pus from deliberately inflicted wounds and blisters. Parkinson did not expect much from restorative medications, since the disease was not the result of a general debilitation. In the face of such a slow and insidious course, during which years may pass without medical intervention of any kind, we may have to be satisfied with halting the progress of the disorder: a complete reversal would require a much better insight into the causes. In the search for a remedy, Parkinson explained, it is in one sense regrettable that the disease does not occur before the patient's fiftieth year, since both physician and patient may be inclined to regard the symptoms as the natural consequences of old age and decline.

His concluding words were addressed – indeed, almost dedicated – to Parkinson's colleagues who were then active in the field of anatomical pathology. If the cause of shaking palsy was ever identified and a remedy found, then it would be thanks to their research. He felt that the public did not realize just how much was owed to their work, work which they did out of dedication and a sense of duty, under conditions that were unpleasant, and even abhorrent.

This was quite a courageous conclusion to the *Essay*, in view of the poor reputation of anatomists. For centuries, those active in the profession had complained about the shortage of bodies.[17] From the reign of Henry VIII on, the authorities occasionally made bodies available. These were usually executed criminals (perhaps a form of post mortem punishment) and the practice was still going on in

---

[17] R. Richardson, *Death, Dissection and the Destitute* (London, 1987).

Parkinson's day. In cities with medical schools, the discrepancy between supply and demand ultimately led to the practice of grave robbing. The dirty work was done by gangs of so-called body-snatchers, also known as 'resurrection men', although they had little to do with resurrection, save for the empty grave they left behind. The body-snatchers did go about their work with a certain measure of care. After spreading a cloth on the ground next to the grave, they continued to dig until they uncovered the head of the coffin. Making an opening in the coffin, they pulled the body out, using a hook or a rope around the neck. The shroud was stuffed back into the coffin, the body disappeared into a sack, and that very night it was delivered to the anatomist or medical student. The next morning there was nothing at the grave-site to show that the body had been removed.

The reaction of the authorities to such violations was a somewhat inconsistent policy of tolerance. While anyone caught robbing a

Figure 2.2: Part of *A Tale of Two Cities* by Charles Dickens is set in London, during the final decade of the eighteenth century, when Parkinson was practising medicine and physicians had to rely on body-snatchers for their anatomical studies. Dickens portrayed two such gentlemen: the Crunchers, father and son. During the day they worked as couriers for a bank, and at night they were active in various graveyards. When Dickens wrote his novel in 1859, the Anatomy Act had long since put an end to the practice of grave-robbing

grave faced a fine or a prison sentence, the doctors who bought the bodies were never prosecuted. Thus, although the market for bodies was one of steady suppliers and steady customers, the judiciary concerned itself with the supply, but not with the demand. Nevertheless, many anatomists were afraid that their assumed involvement in criminal acts was damaging the reputation of their otherwise eminent profession. The judicial authorities, too, were becoming concerned. Why wait until the corpse of Mr Jones was buried? Indeed, why wait until Mr Jones had become a corpse? The bonuses which the anatomists were paying for 'fresh wares' were beginning to cost lives, and this was hardly in keeping with the goals of medical science. In 1832, the Anatomy Act was passed, allowing the authorities to make available those bodies which had not been claimed by their next of kin. In practice, this meant vagabonds, tramps, beggars and homeless people. Given the limited welfare provisions at the time, the shortage quickly turned into a glut.

'Maladie de Parkinson'

The calm narrative style of the *Essay* is typical of nineteenth-century medical writing. While his prose is never long-winded or rambling, Parkinson takes the time to tell his story. It is a story written with compassion, without ever becoming maudlin; it is full of imagery but never pointedly literary. The disease is discussed 'from the inside out', and his examination of what life was like for a patient suffering from shaking palsy is dignified and discreet. The aim of the *Essay* is both descriptive and comparative, and it brings to light the scope of the resources then available for medical research. Parkinson's findings are based not on experiments, but on observations and the occasional medical intervention, and even his observations are often carried out from a distance. No modern physician would present a patient he had observed from across the street as a case study.

When making such observations, Parkinson did have one demographic factor working in his favour: the enormous overcrowding in the neighbourhood where his practice was located. At a time when the life expectancy was considerably shorter than it is today, and geriatric disorders less common, the chances of being able to collect six 'illustrative cases' were far more favourable in a 'big city' environment than in the country, or in a smaller practice consisting of well-to-do patients. Even so, it takes a keen and alert clinical eye to pick out a shambling gait in the midst of a swarming metropolis.

The *Essay* was well received by the still fledgling medical press. Later authors who focused on shaking palsy had to admit that there was little they could add to Parkinson's observations. In a typical passage, taken from a clinical lesson dating from 1830, John Elliotson wrote: 'The best account of this disease which I have seen is one given by a general practitioner, now deceased, of the name of Parkinson, a highly respectable man who wrote an essay upon the subject in 1817, from which I have derived nearly all I know upon the complaint.'[18] Such references continued to surface in the English medical literature for over half a century. In a publication on diseases of the elderly written in 1863, the physician David Maclachlan stated that Parkinson had given a faithful account of the symptoms and the course of the disease, and that his *Essay* was 'still the best work on the subject'.[19] In 1860, Johann von Oppolzer, professor of medicine in Vienna, had carried out a post mortem on a man of 72 who displayed the characteristic tremor. In the medulla oblongata – the spot which Parkinson suspected – Von Oppolzer discovered an excess of connective tissue which could have been pinching the nerves. This finding attracted the attention of Jean-Martin Charcot in Paris, who in 1861 devoted several articles to the subject, together with his colleague Vulpian.[20]

[18] Cited in Morris, *Parkinson*, pp. 138–9.   [19] *Ibid.* p. 140.
[20] J.-M. Charcot and E.F. Vulpian, 'De la paralysie agitante. À propos d'un cas tiré de la Clinique du Professeur Oppolzer', *Gazette hebdomadaire*, 8 (1861), 765–7, 816–60; 9 (1862), 54–9.

Figure 2.3: Characteristic set of the hand seen in Parkinson patients: the pen grip

Throughout his career, Charcot would repeatedly return to this disease, which was still known as *paralysie agitante*.[21] As he was a physician at La Salpêtrière, there was no need for him to go in search of patients or to observe them in the street; they simply presented themselves. Indeed, *paralysie agitante* was the fifth most common ground for admission. When Charcot devoted one of his clinical lessons to the disease in 1868 (the *cinquième leçon*) he triumphantly pointed out to the gentlemen in the audience the large number of shaking women he had assembled on his ward for the occasion. 'I had a particular reason for gathering together this group of patients, all suffering from the same ailment. By means of a comparative study, I hope to help you identify certain nuances, or even marked differences, which would not be as easy to distinguish by simply observing the individual cases.'[22] Thus, unlike Parkinson, Charcot was able to demonstrate all the various stages in the development of the disease at the same time. What he shared with Parkinson was a sharp eye for detail. For example, he explained that the patient's hand displays a characteristic set: the thumb and fingers extended, so that you could slide a pen in between them. During the tremor, the thumb

[21] J.-M. Charcot, 'Cinquième leçon: De la paralysie agitante', in J.-M. Charcot, *Leçons sur les maladies du système nerveux faites à la Salpêtrière* (Paris, 1877; 5th edn, 1884), pp. 155–88; 'Appendice I: Observation de paralysie agitante', in Charcot, *Leçons*, pp. 409–13; 'II: Du tremblement dans la maladie de Parkinson', in Charcot, *Leçons*, pp. 414–20; 'III: Caractères de l'écriture des malades atteints de maladie de Parkinson', in Charcot, *Leçons*, pp. 421–2.

[22] Charcot, 'Cinquième leçon', p. 156.

moves back and forth over the fingers, as if rolling a piece of chalk or a wad of paper.[23] In some patients, the fingers move as if crumbling bread. He also noted that the individual's handwriting becomes smaller and smaller. The signature of 'Catherine Metzger, October 13, 1864' is included in his account, as an example of this 'micrographia'; it is wobbly, unsure and difficult to make out.[24] Charcot also described the gradual deceleration of all movement, the 'considerable time' that elapsed between thought and action, and the effort which it cost patients to stop once they got started, 'since they had to accelerate to a jog-trot in order to regain the balance that continued to elude them'.[25] This shuffling trot was not caused by their forward stoop, for Charcot had also discovered a remarkable symptom which he dubbed 'retropulsion': an uncontrollable tendency when walking backwards to go faster and faster, while the body is bent forward. In a note, we are told that at one point Charcot decided to demonstrate this phenomenon.[26] After asking a patient to stand up, he took hold of her skirt and gave it a sharp jerk backwards. The woman began to walk backwards, faster and faster, at a pace which would have been dangerous if no precautions had been taken. Where the tremor was concerned, Charcot noted that it was intensified by emotion and only disappeared when the patient was asleep or under narcosis. The facial muscles are immobile, resulting in a rigid, expressionless gaze. Speech is slow and articulation requires more and more effort. The patient also has a tendency to speak somewhat haltingly and finds it increasingly difficult to enunciate the words, 'like someone who finds himself astride a trotting horse before he has mastered the art of equitation'.[27] In a later stage, the patient becomes restless: if he's sitting down, he wants to stand up, and if he's standing, he wants to sit down. Charcot remarked that the nurses could tell a tale or two as well: the bed-ridden patients wanted to be turned every quarter of an hour. Although according to the thermometer their body temperature was

[23] *Ibid.* p. 166.   [24] *Ibid.* p. 167.   [25] *Ibid.* p. 163.   [26] *Ibid.* p. 176.   [27] *Ibid.* p. 168.

Figure 2.4 (a) and(b): Bourneville, one of the editors of Charcot's *Leçons*, described in an appendix the case of the 62-year-old vegetable seller Anne-Marie G. In 1872, she was admitted to La Salpêtrière with symptoms of *paralysie agitante*. The patient herself attributed the onset of the condition to her extreme dismay when one of her sons, the apple of her eye, suddenly announced that he had enlisted in the army. Not long afterwards she noticed a weakness in her right arm which spread to her other limbs, later turning into tremors. Twice, in 1874 and 1879, Paul Richer sketched the stooped upper body and the distortion of the hands

normal, some patients experienced an exaggerated sense of heat, so that they failed to dress warmly enough in the winter. But in his own view, Charcot's most valuable contribution to the clinical picture was the patient's *rigidity*. The tension in the muscles of the limbs and the neck increases; the flexors are the most sensitive, pulling both the head and the trunk forward. Ultimately, the patient becomes permanently stooped, whether sitting or standing.

As for the cause of the disease, even Charcot had little more than conjectures to offer. It was possible that prolonged exposure to cold and dampness played a role. But he was slightly more confident when it came to the role of violent emotions such as fright, fear or anger. One of his patients was married to a soldier in the municipal guard, and he was among the troops sent to quell the riots of June 1832. His wife, who was waiting for him at the barracks, saw his horse return without its rider. The tremors in her right arm began that same day, and soon spread to the other limbs. Charcot had encountered such cases before: one woman had narrowly escaped being hit by a bomb during the French-German War, another had lost a son in the hostilities surrounding the Commune. Charcot also made mention of the patient on whom Von Oppolzer had carried out his post mortem: the man's tremor first appeared following a violent fright during the bombing of Vienna in 1848.

Charcot explained that the reason he had described the symptoms in such detail was because 'even today those symptoms make up more or less the entire history of this disorder'.[28] He had carried out several autopsies himself, but had found nothing: no lesions, no abnormalities in the nervous system. 'The above considerations, *messieurs*, prove that the true lesion accompanying *paralysie agitante* has yet to be discovered.'[29] He concluded his lesson with a list of the medications which he and other researchers had tried: strychnine, opium, belladonna and silver nitrate. None of them had brought real relief. Other researchers had experimented with electric stimulation. Neither the various devices which made use of static electricity, nor the administration of electrical pulses, proved very successful, but the application of a constant current, with the aid of a battery, had a favourable effect. It was not until much later, in 1892, that Charcot came up with an instrument that actually provided relief, at least temporarily. He had noticed that Parkinson patients experienced a cessation of their symptoms after a long train journey or carriage ride. In a clinical lesson on '*médecine vibratoire*', recorded by Gilles de la Tourette, he recounted that Dr Jégu, on his instructions, had constructed an armchair with an electromotor which imitated the movement of a rocking, jolting train.[30] Unfortunately, however, Jégu died suddenly, and less than a year later Charcot followed him, having suffered a cardiac arrest during an archeological trip. This meant

---

[28] *Ibid.* p. 180.   [29] *Ibid.* p. 182.
[30] G. Gilles de la Tourette, 'Considérations sur la médecine vibratoire. Ses applications et technique', *Nouvelle Iconographie de la Salpêtrière*, 5 (1892), 265–75.

Figure 2.5: The *fauteuil trépidante* or 'shaking chair' used at La Salpêtrière for the treatment of Parkinson patients

that someone else would have to undertake the further development of this therapeutic instrument. Gilles de la Tourette agreed to continue the research, and after experimental treatments involving eight subjects, he reported that improvements were recorded after five or six sessions. Although this shaking treatment had no effect on the tremors, the stiffness disappeared, the patient's walking improved, and the *fauteuil trépidante* even made it possible for the patient to enjoy a good night's sleep. The recommended dose was half an hour a day.

It was during a lecture on 19 November 1876 that Charcot bestowed on the disease the eponym 'Parkinson'.[31] He was no longer satisfied with the designation *paralysie agitante*, for two reasons: patients did not always display signs of paralysis or debilitation, while experiments involving a dynamometer showed that even when an arm was trembling violently, the muscles retained much of their strength. Moreover, the term '*agitante*' was misplaced, since there were patients who displayed signs of the condition, such as the bent back, the facial mask and the stiffness, but did *not* have a tremor. Charcot concluded that it would be very odd to name a disease after a characteristic that was not always present. Therefore he proposed that the condition be known as 'Parkinson's disease'.

---

[31] Charcot, 'II: Du tremblement dans la maladie de Parkinson', *Leçons*, pp. 414–20.

Substantia nigra

Today, the studies of Parkinson's disease carried out in Paris would be referred to as a research programme. Indeed, several of Charcot's students devoted their doctoral thesis to the condition. The neurologist Keppel Hesselink documented the course of the research devoted to Parkinson's disease.[32] One aspect of his chronicle is particularly noteworthy: the fact that what ultimately proved to be the crucial hypotheses were formulated at an early stage, but were not confirmed until much later. As far back as 1895, Charcot's pupil Edouard Brissaud suspected that the disease was caused by damage to an area of the brain called the substantia nigra (black core), which takes its name from the dark pigmentation of the cells. But it was not until a quarter of a century later, in 1919, that Constantin Trétiakoff found evidence to support the nigra hypothesis in a series of post mortems. Although the dissertation which Trétiakoff devoted to this study was written in Paris, the centre of gravity of the research ultimately shifted to Germany, which had a considerable reputation in neuropathology. In Alzheimer's laboratory in Munich, Levy (or Lewy, as he was known after he emigrated to the United States), found in the brain of Parkinson patients the pathological protein deposits which are now known as Lewy bodies.

Since 1953, Parkinson's disease has been attributed to a lack of dopamine, which regulates the transfer of stimuli between neurons. This neurotransmitter is produced in the substantia nigra. In Parkinson patients, the cells in this area gradually become less active, and in the absence of a stimulus, the muscles stiffen and tense up, leading to the observable effects on posture and locomotion. The identification of location, substance and effect seemed to open the way to new treatment options. But half a century later, we are forced

---

[32] J.M. Keppel Hesselink, 'Some historical aspects of Parkinson's disease: the progression of insights in the period 1817–1868', Janus, 70 (1983), 263–79.

to conclude that the promise of the 1950s has not been fulfilled. It is not possible to administer dopamine directly, since it is obstructed by the blood-brain barrier, that finely branched network of vessels and cells that filter the blood before it enters the brain. During the 1960s it was discovered that the substance levodopa (L-dopa) was capable of breaching that barrier. In the brain, L-dopa is transformed into dopamine, which is now the main ingredient of much of the anti-Parkinson medication, although over time it loses some of its therapeutic effect. Other types of medicine rely on the blocking of substances that degrade dopamine, or the administration of substances which attach themselves to dopamine receptors and imitate the effect of dopamine. It appeared that a substance known as amantadine eased the involuntary movements of Parkinson patients. This was a chance discovery, after it had been prescribed as an anti-flu medication.

The surgical interventions have tended to focus on deliberately damaging the structures which govern locomotion, in an effort to halt the more violent tremors. This line of research was largely discontinued after the discovery of L-dopa, but a number of experiments have recently been carried out in patients who failed to respond to the available medication. One of the more promising procedures involved the implantation of living tissue in the brain of Parkinson patients, in the hope that this would trigger the production of dopamine. These experiments were carried out in the 1980s in Sweden and China. The fact that the tissue was derived from aborted foetuses originally resulted in a moratorium on such tests, but since 1993 they have again been permitted under certain restrictions. However, the therapeutic effect has proved limited and temporary. A more recent treatment involves the electrical stimulation of certain areas of the brain. A battery the size of a pack of cigarettes is implanted under the patient's collarbone, which he can turn on and off by means of a magnet. Stimulation of the thalamus is capable of ending a severe tremor within seconds. This effect may be due to a paralysis of the cells whose hyperactivity causes the tremor. This treatment harks back to the advice of Charcot to consider 'the application of constant current'. In 1817, James Parkinson wrote that he hoped that a substance would be discovered which 'would at least halt the progression of the disease'.[33] Now, almost two centuries later, we have even less to offer. There are medications and interventions which relieve the symptoms and slow the progression of the disease, in effect combating it without curing it.

In his collection of historic neurological studies, Keppel Hesselink says that in differentiating Parkinson's disease from the diffuse group of paralyses, the 'archetype' of the syndrome played a key role: 'Parkinson, Duchenne and Charcot saw what no one had seen before: the independent images. Images which had been hidden from view by foggy concepts.'[34] However, the metaphor of a vague image which gradually becomes more clearly defined is not applicable to the history of Parkinson's disease, nor indeed to Keppel Hesselink's own version of that history. Parkinson regarded the tremor at rest as one of the identifying features of shaking palsy. According to Charcot, however, patients without the tremor could also be suffering from the 'maladie de Parkinson', a view which was confirmed by later research: one-quarter of all Parkinson patients never develop a tremor. Parkinson did not mention rigidity, while Charcot included it among the essential symptoms. The violent emotions which, according to Charcot, were such an important factor in the development of the disease, no longer play a role in contemporary theories, although stress can aggravate the symptoms. Different neurologists, and different generations of neurologists, see a different image, rather than the same image more and more clearly.

---

[33] Parkinson, *Essay*, p. 172.
[34] J.M. Keppel Hesselink, *Beelden in de mist. De geschiedenis van de neurologie in capita selecta* (Rotterdam, 1994), p. 203.

But that variation makes itself felt mainly in medical science, i.e., in the definitions, symptoms and theories, and in the distinction between primary and secondary, essential and accidental. For the *patient*, the comparison with an archetype is well taken. It is thanks to that archetype that when the individual visits his specialist with a suspicion that he has Parkinson's disease, neurological examination generally confirms a diagnosis which had been circulating for some time in the patient's surroundings. That same archetype also means that if James Parkinson were alive, he would recognize today's patients at a glance. Their gait and their posture, their symptoms and movements have not changed all that much, despite the medication. They present the same picture as the patients he saw shuffling through the streets of Hoxton in the early nineteenth century.

It is much less likely that he would recognize Hoxton itself, now a district in London's East End. After the Second World War, a century and a half of deprivation was at last followed by progress. Almost the entire area, which was barely fit for habitation and had also suffered under the bombardments, was torn down. The new construction which replaced it was on a more spacious scale, and the parks and tennis courts recalled something of Hoxton's leafy past. The churchyard of St Leonard made way for a park laid out on the grounds: the present Fairchild Garden. It may have been during those alterations that the gravestone of James Parkinson disappeared.

THREE

Phineas Gage's posthumous stroll: the Gage matrix

In the early 1970s, a most intriguing patient walked into the surgery of the neurologist Antonio Damasio.[1] The man (Damasio refers to him as 'Elliot') was in his early thirties and had developed a fast-growing tumour in the cerebral membranes, just above the nasal cavity. The growth was pressing upwards against the two frontal lobes and had to be removed. The tumour proved benign and, medically speaking, Elliot's prospects were excellent. But after the operation his personal life began to fall apart. He was employed by a commercial firm, and when he returned to his job, he found that he had difficulty coordinating his tasks. He had lost all sense of priority. He ignored repeated warnings and offers of advice from his colleagues, and in the end he was fired. He threw himself into various business ventures and, after a foolhardy investment, was declared bankrupt. His marriage ended in divorce, as did a remarriage entered into shortly afterwards. Within a few short years he was down and out and his personal life was in ruins. Having been refused benefits, on the grounds that he was physically healthy and his mental faculties appeared to be intact, he found his way to Damasio's surgery. He hoped that the doctor would be able to

[1] A. R. Damasio, *Descartes' Error: Emotion, Reason, and the Human Brain* (New York, 1994).

establish that his condition was caused by a neurological disorder, entitling him to a disability allowance.

Brain scans showed that during the operation, the front of both frontal lobes had been damaged, the right side the most severely. However, much was still intact, including the frontal cerebral cortex, which is involved in language, memory and muscular coordination. The same pattern was seen in the neuropsychological tests which Damasio carried out on his patient. The man's intellectual powers were not affected: he scored well above normal on an IQ test. But Damasio did notice that when Elliot described the turn his life had taken, he recounted the events as if they had not happened to him, but to some third person. Divorce, bankruptcy, the loss of his job – he spoke of these things dispassionately, as if he were discussing a random acquaintance. After a test in which he was confronted with emotionally charged stimuli, such as images of people drowning or houses on fire, Elliot acknowledged that events which previously would have moved him no longer evoked any emotion.

In *Descartes' Error*, Damasio discusses various other patients with pre-frontal injuries whose intellectual powers remained intact, while the decisions they took in their personal life indicated that there was something seriously wrong with their emotional housekeeping. He bestowed on this specific pattern, consisting of pre-frontal damage, intact cognitive skills, and compromised emotional reactions, the eponym 'the Gage matrix'.[2] Among the thousands of eponyms to be found in medical science, only a handful bear the name of a patient. The Gage matrix is one of them.

'This melancholy affair'

The story has become a classic in the annals of neurology. During the summer of 1848, the 25-year-old Phineas Gage was working on the

---

[2] Damasio, *Error*, p. 56.

construction of a railroad in the American state of Vermont.[3] He was the foreman of a crew involved in clearing the roadway, to ensure a flat, straight section. Not far from the town of Cavendish, they found a large rock blocking the way and Gage prepared to blow it up. This was a standard procedure. First, a hole is drilled in the rock and filled up halfway with explosive powder. A fuse is then inserted. To ensure that the force of the explosion does not escape through the drill-hole, the powder is covered with sand, which is tamped down with an iron rod. Gage's rod was custom-made by a blacksmith: it was over a metre long, three centimetres in diameter and pointed. It weighed over 13 pounds.

In the late afternoon of 13 September, something went wrong. Gage had just poured the powder into the hole when someone behind him called out. He looked over his right shoulder, momentarily distracted. Then he began to tamp down the powder in the hole, although it had not yet been covered with sand. The charge exploded in his face. The iron rod was propelled through his left cheek and the base of his skull, almost forcing the left eye out of its socket, passed through the front part of the brain and exited through the skull, ending up 30 metres away, 'stuck in the road'.[4] To the amazement of his crew, Gage was not killed on the spot and only briefly lost consciousness. After a few moments, he was able to speak. His men helped him to his feet and into an ox-cart, and took him to Cavendish. He sat upright against the foreboard, making a few notes in his logbook. One of the men was sent ahead on horseback, to alert the local physician, Dr Harlow. On the way he met the minister, Reverend Freeman, who joined the cortege on the assumption that his services would soon be needed. They arrived at Gage's hotel at

[3] The information on the adventures of Phineas Gage is borrowed from the biography by M. B. Macmillan, *An Odd Kind of Fame: Stories of Phineas Gage* (Cambridge, MA, 2000). See also his 'A wonderful journey through skull and brains: the travels of Mr. Gage's tamping iron', *Brain and Cognition*, 5 (1986), 67–107.

[4] Macmillan, *Odd Kind of Fame*, p. 37.

5 o'clock. He got out of the cart without assistance and took a seat on the porch to await the arrival of a doctor.

The first one to arrive was Doctor Williams, from the nearby town of Proctorsville. From his carriage he could see the wound in the man's head: a hole in the crown of the skull about 4 cm in diameter, through which the throbbing brain was clearly visible. Gage welcomed him with the words, 'Doctor, here is business enough for you.'[5] He went on to explain how the accident had occurred. Williams could scarcely believe that it was possible for someone with such injuries to survive. The edges of the wound were raised, as if a wedge-shaped object had been propelled upwards through the flesh. Dr Harlow arrived around 6 o'clock and together they carried Gage up the stairs to his room. With his two index fingers, one from above and the other from below, Harlow ascertained that the object had indeed passed through the patient's skull and out the other side: his fingers touched one another. He removed several bone fragments, placed the larger pieces back on the skull and dressed the wound. According to Gage, his mates needn't bother to come by, as he would be back at work in a few days.

That optimism was not shared by the two physicians, the minister or the local coffin-maker, who came by to take Gage's measurements, so that a coffin would be 'in readiness to use'.[6] But the patient made it through the night. The following day, although he was in pain and spoke with difficulty, he recognized people and inquired who was taking his place in the work crew. The true problems did not present themselves until a few days later, when the inevitable infections and abscesses brought him to death's door. Gage became delirious and fell into a coma several days later. But he surmounted even these complications and gradually regained his strength. Two months later he was declared cured. The only visible consequences of the accident were a perceptible hollow in the crown of his skull and the fact that

[5] *Ibid.* p. 447. [6] *Ibid.* p. 30.

he was blind in his left eye. At the end of November he returned to Lebanon, where he was born.

By that time, Gage had also been reunited with his iron rod. Reverend Freeman was loath to believe that it had actually gone through the man's head, and after the doctors had ministered to Gage on the porch of his hotel, he rode out to the scene of the accident. He found the rod leaning against a smithy door. It had been found by the men on his pit team, who had rinsed it off in a nearby brook. In the written declaration which was later requested from the other witnesses as well, the minister stated that the rod was still greasy in appearance and 'was so to the touch'.[7] It was returned to Gage, together with his other tools.

The day after the accident, a piece appeared in a local Vermont newspaper which reflected the two-fold amazement which all readers must have felt. Under the headline 'Horrible Accident', the reporter recounted in detail the manner in which the rod was propelled through Gage's head, together with the dimensions of the tool down to the last inch.[8] But the most remarkable aspect of this whole 'melancholy affair' was the fact that at two o'clock on the following afternoon, Gage was still alive. In the days and weeks that followed, the headlines reflected a growing bafflement: 'an astonishing fact', 'amounts to rising from the dead', 'incredible but true'. 'We live in an eventful era', wrote someone at the *Christian Reflector and Christian Watchman* (Boston), 'but if it is true that someone has had thirteen pounds of iron in the form of a pointed rod driven through his head, taking with it a portion of his brain, and lived to tell the tale, then we may well exclaim, "What next?"'.[9] The medical world likewise took an interest in the incident. Three months later, Harlow published an article in the *Boston Medical and Surgical Journal* under the title 'Passage of an iron rod through the head'.[10] He gave an account of

---

[7] *Ibid.* p. 44.   [8] *Ibid.* p. 36.   [9] *Ibid.* p. 38.
[10] Included as facsimile in *ibid.* pp. 383–7.

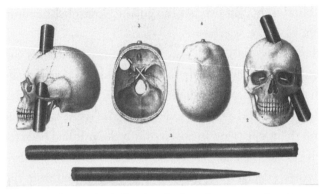

Figure 3.1: Woodcuts which Bigelow had made in 1850, showing a skull in which he himself had drilled holes in order to demonstrate the trajectory of the rod through Gage's head

the probable trajectory of the rod through the brain, the complications associated with the wounds, and the process of recovery. The scepticism among his colleagues (is this village doctor absolutely positive that the rod passed *through* the head?) was dispelled by the intervention of Bigelow, soon to be appointed Professor of Surgery at Harvard Medical School. Bigelow asked Harlow to collect as many declarations under oath as possible: from the minister, from the first physician on the spot (Williams), and from Adams, the owner of the hotel.[11] He also had the rod sent to him and later invited Gage to come to Boston. On 10 November 1849, he was presented to the Boston Society for Medical Improvement. Bigelow had two holes drilled in a skull in order to demonstrate how it was possible for the rod to travel through the brain without hitting the optic nerve. He took advantage of Gage's visit to make a plaster cast of his head, which clearly shows the presence of a depression in the crown of the skull. At Bigelow's request, Gage donated his rod to the museum at the Massachusetts Medical College. Soon afterwards, however, he asked for it to be returned. Gage had other plans for his rod.

[11] Bigelow's account in *The American Journal of the Medical Sciences* (July 1850) is included as facsimile in Macmillan, *An Odd Kind of Fame*, pp. 390–400.

Figure 3.2: Cast of Phineas Gage, made one year after the accident

Information on his subsequent fortunes has come down to us from Harlow, who in 1868 delivered a lecture to the Massachusetts Medical Society entitled 'Recovery from the passage of an iron bar through the head'.[12] Gage spent the winter after the accident at home in Lebanon. In the spring he went back to Cavendish, hoping to return to his job. However, that was out of the question. His mates noticed that his personality had altered. The previously patient and responsible foreman had become a hot-head. He used obscene language and began to curse and swear at the slightest provocation. No sooner had he set about a plan than he dropped it again. Harlow writes that in Gage 'the equilibrium or balance, so to speak, between his intellectual faculties and animal propensities seems to have been destroyed'.[13] His interests were confined to horses, dogs and, above all, to his rod, which he never let out of his sight. He left for New York, where he was one of the attractions at the American Museum of P.T. Barnum. For an extra 10 cents, visitors were allowed to lift up a lock of his hair, revealing the pulsating brain beneath a thin layer of skin. In 1851, Gage went to work in a livery stable. Then in 1852, he left for Chile, where he was

[12] Included in Macmillan, *Odd Kind of Fame*, pp. 401–21. [13] *Ibid.* p. 414.

employed as a coachman and stable hand for a stagecoach line. In the late 1850s, his health began to deteriorate. Hoping that a change of climate would do him good, Gage moved to California, where he took on a series of odd jobs. Not long afterwards he suffered an epileptic fit, the first in a series which came in ever quicker succession. Gage died on 20 May 1860 in San Francisco. He was buried on Lone Hill Mountain, with the rod at his side.

The resurrection of Phineas Gage

But Gage's body was not destined to remain there for long. Harlow had lost touch with him, but in July 1866 he obtained the address of Gage's mother. From that moment on he did everything in his power to preserve Gage's skull for the benefit of science. He sorely regretted that no autopsy had been carried out on the brain, but there was still some hope that the holes in the skull would establish exactly which parts of the brain had been damaged. When the body of Phineas Gage was disinterred in 1867, his brother-in-law saw to it that the skull and the tamping iron were sent to Harlow. In his presentation, the latter expressed his gratitude to Gage's mother and friends, for the admirable generosity with which they had put aside their personal feelings of affection and 'at my request have cheerfully placed this skull (which I now show you) in my hands, for the benefit of science'.[14] Modern readers will no doubt be struck by the word 'cheerfully'. In Harlow's perception, they considered it an honour to make their contribution to science, if only by relinquishing the remains of a loved one. The skull and rod went from Harlow's hands to the Warren Anatomical Museum at Harvard, where to this day they enjoy the status of neurological relics.

After his death and interment, Phineas Gage was to rise again, embarking on a long march through the neurological literature, with

[14] *Ibid.* p. 417.

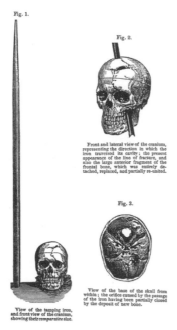

Figure 3.3: Woodcuts accompanying Harlow's article 'Recovery from the passage of an iron bar through the head' (1868)

the tamping iron under his arm. In 1851, while he was still alive, an anonymous author wrote in *The American Phrenological Journal* that after Gage's recovery 'the animal propensities' had gained absolute control over his character.[15] The choice of words is reminiscent of Harlow, who may well have been the source, although it was not until 1868 that he published his own assessment of the reversal in Gage's character. The latter's injury was a weapon in the hands of phrenologists, but also in those of their opponents. The phrenologists drew maps on plaster skulls indicating the sections which corresponded to the underlying 'brain organs'. In their topography of the brain, Gage's rod had passed through the organs of Benevolence and Veneration. Benevolence stood for compassion, sensitivity and conscience, while Veneration represented faith, devotion and obedience. Were these

[15] *Ibid.* p. 349.

not precisely the characteristics which had been lost after Gage's accident? According to the phrenologist Sizer, the man's utterances had become so vulgar that his company could no longer be tolerated by 'persons of delicacy, especially women'.[16] Critics of phrenology, including many medical men, held that the extent of the injury was the best argument against the view that the brain is divided into individual organs: if a rod can cause such damage throughout such a large area of the brain, while the patient subsequently has no difficulty speaking, remembering things, moving about and thinking, then those functions must necessarily be distributed throughout various areas of the brain. Bigelow, a vigorous opponent of phrenology, wrote that Gage's recovery was due above all to the fact that the part of the brain through which the rod passed was the area most likely to survive the injury. Perhaps the frontal lobes were not as active as previously thought?

While Gage was enjoying his brief period of funereal repose, on the other side of the Atlantic a discovery was made which would ascribe to a small area in the frontal lobes a prominent role. In 1861, the Paris neurologist Paul Broca presented the brain of a recently deceased aphasic shoe-maker. It displayed a hole in the left frontal lobe. The most obvious conclusion was that this was the site of the 'memory for words', as Broca referred to it. In the heated controversies over the location of speech which were to continue during the greater part of the 1860s and 1870s, Phineas Gage, by then resurrected, represented the counter-argument. It was incontestable that the rod passed through the left frontal lobe and equally incontestable that, after a brief interval, Gage was able to speak.

But here, too, Gage's case was incapable of settling the controversy. Perhaps the rod had just missed Broca's area? Perhaps Gage's speech centre was located on the right? Or on both sides, so that damage on

[16] N. Sizer, *Forty Years in Phrenology: Embracing Recollections of History, Anecdote, and Experience* (New York, 1882), cited in Macmillan, *An Odd Kind of Fame*, p. 348.

only one side did not interfere with speech? Was the entire notion of a speech centre not in fact contestable? In all the neurotopographical debates of the nineteenth century, the Gage case was an argument, but never the decisive argument. In 1878, the British neurologist David Ferrier cited the Gage case in support of his theory that the frontal lobes play an essential role in the psychological faculty of attention.[17] In his view, this was the site of the inhibiting mechanisms which suspend action and promote concentration. Ferrier, who was a friend of Hughlings Jackson, hoped to provide experimental proof of the latter's theory that the brain is a hierarchical system whose 'lower' parts must be held in check by the 'higher' parts. When that control falls away, more primitive evolutionary brain structures are activated. In Ferrier's view, the case of Gage confirmed this 'release theory': as a result of the frontal damage, vital inhibitive mechanisms had been lost, resulting in chaotic, impulsive behaviour. Others, however, disputed the fact that Gage acted chaotically: driving a six-span of horses, as he had done while in Chile, undeniably demanded considerable concentration. And so it was that Gage remained an impressive witness within the courts of science, although it was impossible to predict whether he would be called by the prosecutor or the defence counsel.

Phineas Gage: the Damasio version

Phineas Gage, as described above, was resurrected in exemplary fashion by the Australian psychologist, Malcolm Macmillan. With the assistance of a veritable army of local historians, Macmillan personally visited each and every location where Gage might have left behind some trace: passenger lists of ocean steamers, circus archives, museum catalogues, livery stable records, diaries, correspondence between residents of the cities on Gage's tour, local newspaper files

---

[17] D. Ferrier, *The Localisation of Cerebral Disease* (London, 1878).

Figure 3.4: Antonio Damasio

and the archives of medical societies. In *An Odd Kind of Fame: Stories of Phineas Gage*, Macmillan has not only documented the life of Gage, he has also placed his adventures, during his lifetime and posthumously, against the background of the then current neurological theories. The biography does not contain everything we would like to know about Gage, but in all likelihood everything it was possible to find.

The most recent stage in the posthumous peregrinations of Phineas Gage is his appearance in *Descartes' Error: Emotion, Reason, and the Human Brain* (1994). The author of this work is Antonio Damasio, a Portuguese neurologist who presently heads the Brain and Creativity Institute of the University of Southern California. *Descartes' Error*, which has been translated into dozens of languages, has gathered a readership well beyond the neurological fraternity. The opening is reserved for Gage. Damasio maintains that the man's mental armamentarium was still present, in the form of attention, perception, memory, language competence – everything necessary to the processes of reasoning and reflection. And yet the decisions which he took after his accident were not always prudent. It was as if he was no longer capable of learning from his mistakes. His social deterioration was the result of an inability to correctly assess the personal and social consequences of his decisions. True rationality is impossible when one's emotional household has fallen into disarray. The error which Damasio ascribes to Descartes is the notion that the intellect is capable of doing its work in the absence of feelings. A century and a half after his accident, Gage plays a supporting role in a neurophilosophical argument directed again Descartes.

In his biography, Macmillan demonstrates that many authors have tailored the history of Phineas Gage to fit the theory underlying their case. Damasio is no exception. But what is most striking is that Damasio has 'jazzed up' the accident and Gage's later adventures. No other word would be appropriate here. His version contains all manner of details which do not appear in the original documents. He has the accident take place at the end of a 'hot afternoon', while on the basis of local diaries Macmillan describes 13 September 1848 as 'quite chilly', 'clear with a cool wind', and 'pleasant but cool'. And then there was his outward appearance. There are no photographs or portraits of Gage, nothing but the cast that was made in 1849. And yet Damasio is able to tell us that he was 'like a young Jimmy Cagney, a Yankee Doodle dandy dancing his tap shoes over ties and tracks, moving with vigor and grace'.[18] And towards the end of his life, in 1860, when he finds himself in San Francisco, it is not in one of the more affluent neighbourhoods: 'We would probably find him drinking and brawling in a questionable district, not conversing with captains of commerce.'[19] Even more radical is Damasio's portrait of Gage as a jack of all trades and master of none, suggesting that he never made a wise decision after the accident, and wherever he was taken on he ultimately quit or was fired. In actual fact, this was only true of the last year of his life, after his health had begun to deteriorate. Before then he remained in one job for a year and a half and another for seven years. It is interesting to note that, several pages before, Damasio compliments Harlow on his 1868 account: 'It is

---

[18] Damasio, *Error*, p. 3.   [19] *Ibid.* p. 9.

a trustworthy text, with an abundance of facts and a minimum of interpretation.'[20]

'A modern Phineas Gage'

Which theory was this version of Gage designed to fit? Damasio has a considerable reputation in the field of research into pre-frontal injuries, and in his account he trots out a procession of patients from the neurological literature and his own practice, each of whom represents a link in the line of reasoning which concludes that loss of emotionality can lead to irrational behaviour. Damasio devotes one of his most detailed case studies to the patient named Elliot, mentioned in the opening paragraph of this chapter.[21] And just as in Gage's case, the problems began after his physical recovery.

Upon first acquaintance, Elliot made an engaging, if somewhat inhibited impression. He was invariably polite and retiring, even when the subject under discussion was painful for him. Damasio decided to begin with a so-called frontal lobe test, known as the Wisconsin Card Sorting Test. The cards are categorized according to various criteria, such as the colour, shape or number of the signs. The examiner can alter the criterion, and the subject must then identify the new criterion as quickly as possible. Patients with pre-frontal damage tend to cling too long to the criterion they have just discovered. But the results recorded for Elliot were in no way inferior to those of healthy subjects. Damasio could only conclude that the origin of the change in his subject's behaviour could not be identified by means of the traditional neuropsychological instruments.

Then Damasio began to notice something peculiar: Elliot discussed the turn his life had taken with a detachment which was hardly in keeping with the tragic facts of the situation. Damasio says that, listening to Elliot's stories, he suffered more than Elliot himself.

[20] *Ibid.* p. 7.   [21] *Ibid.* pp. 34–51.

Family members recounted that in his daily life, too, he was consistently neutral and moderate in all his emotional utterances. Damasio: 'He tended not to display anger, and on the rare occasions when he did, the outburst was brief; in no time he would be his usual new self, calm and without grudges.'[22]

In a later phase of his research, Damasio focused on subtle anomalies in Elliot's powers of judgement, in the hope of finding a testable parallel for the impulsive and unstable behaviour of Phineas Gage. In a series of 'gambling experiments', Elliot and other patients with injuries to the frontal area were more likely than the healthy control group to choose cards that provided short-term gain but were unfavourable in the longer term. The most paradoxical element in his behaviour was the fact that towards the end of the experiment, Elliot *knew* which was the best choice, and yet continued to opt for higher short-term rewards. According to Damasio, 'This is the first laboratory task in which a counterpart to Phineas Gage's troubled real-life choices has been measured.'[23]

The chapter in which we are introduced to Elliot is entitled 'A modern Phineas Gage' – much to the astonishment of the reader, for whether we opt for the version put forward by Harlow or that of Damasio himself, Gage is almost the direct opposite of Elliot. He is impulsive, coarse and easily frustrated, while Elliot is calm, even-tempered and retiring. Whereas following his accident Gage appeared to be somewhat disinhibited, Elliot became increasingly moderate after his operation. But what the two men have in common, according to Damasio, is the fact that although they both retained their cognitive skills, they were incapable of setting out the course of action most favourable for them. Apparently, both of them had lost the ability to take sensible decisions in the social or personal sphere. On the basis of his findings in the case of Elliot and a dozen or so other patients with pre-frontal damage, Damasio identified a pattern

[22] *Ibid.* p. 45   [23] *Ibid.* p. 214.

of symptoms which he referred to as the 'Gage matrix'. Patients in this category display 'flattened emotions', while their other functions remain intact.

However, it soon becomes clear that this single matrix is capable of accommodating highly diverse categories of patients. The series opens with several historical cases. From 1932: a stockbroker with a brain tumour, who after the operation became passive and emotionally superficial. From 1940: a 16-year-old boy who sustained serious damage to the frontal lobes as a result of an accident, and whose social development subsequently stagnated. From 1948: a patient who suffered frontal damage during birth and subsequently led an emotionally vapid life, devoid of initiative. To these individual cases, Damasio added the large number of psychiatric patients who during the 1930s underwent pre-frontal leucotomy, an operation developed by the Portuguese neurologist Egas Moniz, whereby nerve bundles in the frontal lobes were severed. As a result, their anxiety and agitation disappeared, together with all other emotions. (Lobotomy is a notorious later variant of this operation.)

And then, Damasio continues, there is 'another neurological condition that shares the Phineas Gage matrix', namely anosognosy, the inability to recognize one's own disease.[24] Patients in this category may be paralysed on the left side and yet have no awareness of the fact. The same thing can occur in the case of blindness and aphasia. It is noteworthy that these patients respond with indifference to their often serious condition or prognosis. Anosognosy is the result of a specific brain injury which occurs exclusively on the right side, and further back than the pre-frontal injuries which Damasio had initially entered into the Gage matrix. Shortly afterwards, it appeared that such conditions as bilateral injuries to the amygdala, deep within the brain, also fit the Gage matrix. To recapitulate: the Gage patient is now linked to left frontal injury (Gage), predominantly right frontal

---

[24] *Ibid.* p. 62.

injury (stockbroker, 1932), both right and left frontal injury (16-year-old boy, 1940), the bottom of the frontal lobes (leucotomy), the back of the right frontal lobe (anosognosy), and not in the frontal lobe at all (amygdala). This is a considerable degree of variation for a single matrix. It was at this point that the reviewer in *The Lancet*, the neurologist Blau, began to feel 'intellectually uncomfortable'.[25] The phrasing is both British and collegial. In fact, the neurological conditions lumped together in the Gage matrix are a bit of a silly list.

The somatic marker

The next step in the argument against Descartes is the hypothesis of the 'somatic marker'.[26] Each dilemma which we face confronts us with decisions which branch off into new dilemmas. Each option is accompanied by its own consequences, both intended and unintended. If we had to go on calculating and recalculating all the branches and all the branches of branches, the result would be a kind of combinatory explosion, an impenetrable thicket of possibilities and outcomes. In such cases, the somatic marker functions as a pruning knife. In most dilemmas of a personal or social nature, such as an intended marriage or a career change, the weighing of certain options automatically calls up a bodily sensation, an attendant feeling, either pleasant or unpleasant. These somatic markers bestow on each of our options a kind of emotional value, which automatically eliminates some of those branches. In effect, somatic markers reduce the number of alternatives to manageable proportions. Cost-benefit analyses take care of the remaining options, which have already been sorted and graded by means of somatic markers.

Damasio suggests that what patients with the Gage matrix are suffering from is a condition whereby the mechanism responsible for

---

[25] J. N. Blau, 'Review *Descartes' Error*', *The Lancet*, 346 (1995), 38–9 (38).
[26] Damasio, *Error*, p. 196.

placing a somatic marker on the various options under consideration has broken down. When they weigh their options, they must do so without the encouragement of a pleasant connotation or the warning of an unpleasant one. They blithely enter into risky adventures which a sinking sensation in the stomach would previously have warned them against.

And even beyond the fairly broad group of patients assumed to be suffering from the Gage matrix, Damasio sees symptoms which he attributes to a lack of somatic markers. For example, the cold indifference of sociopaths and psychopaths may be caused by disturbances in the mechanism of somatic markers. This enables them to commit the most ghastly crimes 'in cold blood', crimes which are, moreover, to their own detriment. The latter consideration plays an important role in Damasio's argumentation: the sheer egocentricity of people whose somatic markers are not functioning leads them to take decisions which in the long term have disastrous personal consequences. It is precisely the lack of emotion which makes their decisions so curiously irrational. According to Damasio, it is even possible for a 'sick culture' to decommission the marker mechanism, with fatal consequences for entire population groups.[27] He points to the example of China during the Cultural Revolution and Cambodia under Pol Pot. This is a neuropolitical analysis which is reminiscent of the political asides of Hughlings Jackson and (once more) gives rise to a certain intellectual disquiet. In any case, Damasio has now strayed quite far away from the pre-frontal cortex, be it right or left, front or back, upper or lower.

Descartes' dream

But what exactly was *Descartes' error*? It is only towards the end of the book that Damasio addresses this question. Actually, there appear to

---

[27] *Ibid.* p. 178.

be two errors. The first is contained in his *cogito ergo sum*. This proposition – 'I think, therefore I am' – expresses the very opposite of Damasio's own view: where Descartes suggests that being or existence follows thought, the biological reality is that being precedes thought. It was not until quite late in the evolutionary process that organisms developed into rational beings. 'For us then, in the beginning it was being, and only later was it thinking.'[28] The second of Descartes' errors is described by Damasio as 'the abyssal separation between body and mind', the consequence of which is 'the suggestion that reasoning, and moral judgment, and the suffering that comes from physical pain or emotional upheaval might exist separately from the body'.[29] There are also several minor errors, such as Descartes' representation of the circulation of the blood, as well as lesser mistakes which he later helped to promote, such as the mechanistic orientation of Western medicine, and the view that mind and brain are related to one another as software to hardware. But for Damasio they all pale into insignificance alongside the dramatic error of *cogito ergo sum*.

Had Descartes been aware of Damasio's reproach, he might have raised an eyebrow in surprise (or disdain?), as in the portrait that Edelinck did of him. And he would have every right to do so. To make this clear, however, we must first embark on an examination of Descartes' contention – one that focuses not on his error, but on his vision.[30]

The most famous dream in the history of philosophy was dreamt by René Descartes on the eve of the feast of St Martin, 11 November 1619. He was then 23 years old. He had served for a time in the army of Prince Maurice of Nassau, and was now a mercenary in the service of the Duke of Bavaria. The army had made camp in the town of Ulm, on the banks of the Donau. Winter had set in early that year,

---

[28] *Ibid.* p. 248.   [29] *Ibid.* pp. 249–50.
[30] G. Rodis-Lewis, *Descartes: biographie* (Paris, 1995).

Figure 3.5: René Descartes, engraving by Edelinck

and the military operations had come to a standstill, so that for several weeks Descartes was able to devote himself to his studies without distraction.

Early on the evening of 10 November, after another long day of intense concentration, he sensed that he had succeeded in formulating the essence of his 'methods', i.e., those principles which are arrived at through mathematical argumentation and are best suited to address philosophical and scientific issues. It was not until much later, in 1637, that he would describe those methods in his *Discours de la méthode*, but the breakthrough of his insights induced a state of feverish excitement. In his enthusiasm, he believed that the answers to his questions had been revealed to him by divine intervention in a blinding flash of light. Following that vision, he retired and spent a restless night. Descartes later recorded the events of that night, an account which after his death was found among his personal papers.[31]

First, he dreams that he is surrounded by ghosts and finds himself being spun round by a whirlwind, which pins him against the wall of a

---

[31] These papers were later lost, but the first biographer of Descartes, *abbé* Adrien Baillet (*La vie de Monsieur Des Cartes* (Paris, 1691)), had access to them. He copied portions of them, which were later used to reconstruct Descartes' notes. They now form part of his *Œuvres philosophiques* (Paris, 1973), vol. I, pp. 53–61.

church. To his amazement he sees that the other people in the street are not bothered by the wind, while he barely manages to remain standing. A man presents him with a melon from a strange far-away land. Then Descartes wakes up, prays to God to protect him against demons, and turns over on his right side. He starts to dream again. This time a loud clap of thunder awakens him with a start. The room is filled with a shower of sparks. Opening first his left and then his right eye, he realizes that they are not sparks, but rather flashes of light striking his retina. Reassured, he falls asleep again.

The third and last dream is detailed and serene. There is a book lying on the table. Descartes notes to his satisfaction that it is a dictionary. In the same moment he sees a second book, a collection of poetry. He opens the book to a random page and finds a poem by Ausonius entitled 'Quod vitae sectabor iter?' ('What road in life shall I follow?'). A stranger appears from nowhere and places before him a verse that begins with the line 'Est & Non' ('Yes and No'). Descartes recognizes the verse and searches for it in the collection. When he cannot find it, he tries to look up 'Quod vitae sectabor iter?'. The man then disappears from his dream as suddenly as he appeared. The books are likewise nowhere to be seen.

This time Descartes does not awake. He is aware that he is dreaming and, while still asleep, he begins to clarify his dreams. In the first two, with their ghosts and whirlwinds, he was being urged to seek more worthy goals in life than he had hitherto done. The dictionary no doubt stood for the whole of science, the book of poetry for the marriage of philosophy and wisdom. In the lines of poetry, Ausonius provides advice on living a virtuous life, while the line Est & Non no doubt refers to what is true and false in human knowledge. The flash of lightning and the accompanying peal of thunder that awakened him were a sign that the spirit of truth had taken possession of him. In short, Descartes interpreted the events of that night as a divine sign that he was predestined to bring about the unification of all science.

That enormous project was initiated in the Netherlands. In 1629, he enrolled as Renatus Des Cartes, Gallus, Philosophus, at the university in Franeker, then the second university town in Holland. With the exception of a few brief journeys, Descartes never left the Netherlands again. In order to give shape to his philosophy in peace and quiet, he chose 'to withdraw here to a country where the long duration of the war has established such discipline that the armies maintained there seem to serve only to ensure that the fruits of peace are enjoyed with the maximum of security; and where, in the midst of a great crowd of busy people, more concerned with their own business than curious about that of others, without lacking any of the conveniences offered by the most populous cities, I have been able to live as solitary and withdrawn as I would in the most remote of deserts'.[32] In the ten years between 1630 and 1640, Descartes was indeed able to work undisturbed on the task he had taken upon himself at the age of 23. The interest on a legacy enabled him to devote himself to research and study. He carried out experiments on the refraction of light, dissected animals, and devoted himself to mathematics and meteorology, and did all the above at a leisurely pace, in deference to his rather weak constitution. He received few visitors and usually slept until around 11 o'clock, except when (as one acquaintance recalled) he sat straight up in bed in order to record some flash of inspiration.

I think, therefore I am

In 1637, Descartes had the Leiden publisher Jean Maire print a tract entitled *Discours de la méthode*. It was published anonymously, but anyone who was anyone in the republic of letters knew that Descartes was the author. The *Discours* elaborates on Descartes' method for acquiring true knowledge in the fields of science and philosophy, and

---

[32] R. Descartes, *Discourse on Method and Other Writings* (F. E. Sutcliffe (trans.), 1968), pp. 51–2.

also includes a number of *essais* in which this method is applied to such subjects as the refraction of light, geometry and the anatomy of the eye. Instead of royalties, Descartes received 200 complimentary copies of the book. These were presented to King Louis XIII, Cardinal Richelieu, and several of his former teachers, as well as other *personnes de qualité*.[33]

As a literary text, the *Discours* has lost nothing of its freshness in the intervening three and a half centuries. Descartes has adroitly interwoven his 'doctrine' with an account of his life which is part philosophical tract and part autobiography. Sometimes pedantic, at other times modest, it is written in the deceptively transparent style which has guaranteed him a place in the annals of French literature. The *Discours* opens with an aphorism: 'Good sense is the most evenly shared thing in the world, for each of us thinks he is so well endowed with it that even those who are the hardest to please in all other respects are not in the habit of wanting more than they have.'[34] It is unlikely, Descartes continues, that everyone is mistaken on this point. More probably, the ability to distinguish true from false is present to the same degree in all of us. The fact that we sometimes disagree cannot be blamed on the instrument which we employ – reason – but rather on the manner in which we employ it. Reason must be guided. This requires rules, precepts and points of departure, in short, a *method*, which Descartes, your humble servant, is willing to provide for the benefit of the reader.

In developing his method, Descartes did not build upon what his predecessors had written concerning knowledge and science. Had he been obliged to rely on the book learning of those who had gone before, his own work would have resembled an old city which started out with just a few houses, but has slowly expanded through the addition of winding, irregular streets. This former legionnaire under

---

[33] Th. Oegema van der Wal, *De mens Descartes* (Brussels, 1960), p. 159.
[34] Descartes, *Discourse*, p. 27.

Prince Maurice compared his own method to one of the new, harmoniously constructed fortresses 'which an engineer designs at will on some plain'.[35] Indeed, this association with the austere, mathematical design of a seventeenth-century fort was eminently appropriate. In his design Descartes was inspired by the long deductive chains which geometricians use, and the self-evident axioms which, via strict definitions and proofs, lead to complicated propositions. That process consists of various steps and is deductive in nature. Descartes took as his first principle 'never to accept anything as true that I did not know to be evidently so: that is to say, carefully to avoid precipitancy and prejudice, and to include in my judgements nothing more than what presented itself so clearly and so distinctly to my mind that I might have no occasion to place it in doubt'.[36] In this way, Descartes situated the criterion for knowledge and truth in the judgement of the individual, in what personal intellect recognizes as clear and distinct. Reason, rather than the authority of tradition, is the arbiter for what counts as knowledge.

There is a question contained within the first principle of the method, for when is knowledge truly indisputable? Is there anything so certain that it can serve as the starting point of the deduction, the philosophical equivalent of a mathematical axiom? Descartes' discussion of this question has given us one of the most famous passages in the philosophical literature. He begins by asking himself whether that certainty can be found in sensory knowledge. Apparently not: place a straight stick in water and you will see a bend. Thus, the sense of touch and the sense of sight contradict one another. If our senses sometimes deceive us, then they are not capable of providing absolute certainty. Reasoning is not conclusive, for people can easily be mistaken, even in the case of simple geometric problems. Nor can we rely on our perceptions or thoughts, for we sometimes experience those same perceptions and thoughts in our dreams, none of which can

---

[35] *Ibid.* p. 35.   [36] *Ibid.* p. 41.

possibly be true. Philosophical doubt, when strictly applied, appears to eliminate all certainty. The operative word here is *appears*, for Descartes then gives his argumentation an exhilarating twist: 'But immediately afterwards I became aware that, while I decided thus to think that everything was false, it followed necessarily that I who thought thus must be something; and observing that this truth: *I think, therefore I am*, was so certain and so evident that all the most extravagant suppositions of the sceptics were not capable of shaking it, I judged that I could accept it without scruple as the first principle of the philosophy I was seeking.'[37] With this 'Je pense, donc je suis', one half of Cartesian dualism was formulated.

As a rational thinking being, I have a conception of the outside world. I see, smell, hear, feel and taste, my senses provide me with information about the material world. If thought is the essence of my mind, what then is the essence of the material world? Let us begin by considering something quite ordinary, Descartes proposes in the second of his *Meditations*: for example, a piece of wax which has just been removed from the beehive.[38] The wax is lying on the table in front of me. It is soft and still retains the scent of the flowers from which it was gathered. It has a colour and a taste, as well as a certain hardness, size and shape. But as I speak, someone places it near a flame. And suddenly all the characteristics mentioned above begin to change: the wax starts to melt, its taste and smell are altered, and it takes on a different shape and size. Is what now lies on the table the same object which was lying there a few moments ago? This is something that cannot be denied. And yet everything that we know about the wax on the basis of our senses has changed. Apparently it was not the scent, the consistency, the colour or the shape which determined our representation of the wax. The only characteristic which has *not* altered is the fact that the wax still occupies space. This, then, appears to be the essence of material objects: they occupy space. All that is

[37] *Ibid.* pp. 53–4.   [38] *Ibid.* pp. 108–11.

material exists as extended thing, or *res extensa*. Now we realize clearly and distinctly (still according to Descartes) that there are two substances. One, *res cogitans*, does not occupy space, is indivisible and has as its essence thought, while the other, *res extensa,* is divisible and has as its essence extension.

Thus, with one stroke of the sword which, as a nobleman, he was accustomed to wear, Descartes slashed reality in two. Something is either thought or extension. Nothing is both, nothing is neither. Cartesian dualism is a division without remainder.

Passions of the soul

This elegant conclusion marked the beginning of a great many difficulties. With his two substances, Descartes was trying to make it clear that, for the rational intellect, body and mind are separate. This is an epistemological dichotomy: in a philosophical sense, any interaction between body and mind is incomprehensible. And yet, Descartes never denied the existence of that interaction. Everyone knows from personal experience that body and mind influence one another. In the *Discours* Descartes says that he wanted to devote himself to medicine. 'For even the mind depends so much on the temperament and on the disposition of the organs of the body, that if it is possible to find some means of rendering men as a whole wiser and more dexterous than they have been hitherto, I believe it must be sought in medicine.'[39] The mind dependent on temperament and organs? This is not the view of a dualist.

On other occasions, too, Descartes defended himself against the charge that he denied the interaction between body and mind. On 16 April 1648, he was questioned by Frans Burman, the 20-year-old son of a Leiden preacher. Burman had marked over seventy different passages on which he required enlightenment. Descartes received

---

[39] *Ibid.* pp. 78–9.

him at home, in Egmond-Binnen, and the discussion lasted an entire day.[40] In the course of their conversation Burman brought up the subject of the relationship between body and soul. He presented Descartes with a passage from his *Méditations*: 'For nature teaches through the sensations of pain, hunger, thirst, etc. that I am not only present in my body as a sailor is present in a ship, but that I am very closely joined and, as it were, intermingled with it.'[41]

Burman: 'But how can this be, and how can the soul be affected by the body and vice versa, when their natures are completely different?'

Descartes: 'This is very difficult to explain; but here our experience is sufficient, since it is so clear on this point that it just cannot be gainsaid. This is evident in the case of the feelings and so on.'[42]

In the comparison which Descartes makes between the helmsman and his ship, he maintains that we do not register an injury to our body in the same way that a helmsman registers damage to his ship, i.e., externally. Pain is experienced internally, because our mind is bound up with our body.

This is a position he had previously adopted in his correspondence with Elizabeth, the daughter of the banished elector of the Pfalz, whose court was then installed in The Hague. He had dedicated his *Principia philosophiae* to her (Descartes combined a reputation for being a recluse with the talents of a networker) and sent her a complimentary copy upon publication in 1644. During their intensive correspondence, the princess repeatedly revisited the subject of the relationship between body and soul. Her questions focused on a single issue: how interaction can take place between two substances which have nothing in common with one another. His standard reply is that the relationship may well be incomprehensible, that God created us as a union of body and soul, that while it is not granted to us to understand that union, the interrelationship between them cannot

---

[40] J. Cottingham (ed.), *Descartes' Conversation with Burman* (Oxford, 1976).
[41] Descartes, *Discourse*, p. 43.   [42] Cottingham, *Descartes' Conversation*, p. 28.

be denied.[43] But Descartes went further: he wrote a splendid little tract for her on 'the passions of the soul' entitled *Passions de l'âme*, which contains dozens of examples of that interaction.[44] He discusses love, which makes the pulse race and the heart swell; and passion, which moves the heart more violently than all the other emotions and sharpens the senses; about hate, which heightens the pulse rate and causes a stab of heat in the chest; about sorrow, which slows the pulse and makes us feel as if the heart is constricted and 'frozen by icicles that pass on their cold to the rest of the body'.[45] He also deals with facial expressions, turning pale, blushing, trembling, fainting, the welling up of tears and the difference between tears of pain and tears of sorrow, why some children turn pale instead of crying, why we sigh or moan, why children and old people cry so easily. The inner life of a human being is physical, bodily. Whoever follows the trail leading from present-day theories on the biology of human emotions to those of the past, including Damasio's, will be led to *Passions de l'âme*, published in November 1649 by Elsevier in Amsterdam.

Damasio's panorama

Descartes' Error was reviewed by no small number of professional philosophers.[46] Regardless of the ultimate verdict delivered by each of them (reserved, on the whole, and somewhat aggrieved by the author's serene neglect of all that philosophers had thus far put forward on the subject of emotions and thought), the almost universal reaction was a desperate cry: 'And what about the *Passions de l'âme?*' That single brief tract would have saved Damasio from publishing a caricature in which Descartes is heard to declare that body and

---

[43] Descartes, 'Lettre à Elizabeth', 28 June 1643, *Œuvres*, vol. III, pp. 43–8.

[44] R. Descartes, *Les passions de l'âme*, *Œuvres*, vol. III, pp. 941–1103.

[45] *Ibid.* p. 1028.

[46] See, e.g., R. de Sousa, 'Prefrontal Kantians: a review of *Descartes' Error*', *Cognition and Emotion*, 10 (1996) 3, 329–33.

soul are separate entities, thus holding him responsible for a medical science which views the body as a defective machine and ignores the psychological origin of certain physical conditions or, conversely, for the psychological consequences of disease. Poor Descartes: as the object of Damasio's attention, he has fared no better than Phineas Gage. According to the philosopher De Sousa, it is a presentation of Descartes which paves the way for the 'discovery' that body and mind are not separate at all and that this fact has just been verified in the laboratory. *Breaking news!* In his view, neurological stories have become the Aesop's Fables of our day: 'Through the almost incredible wonders revealed to the high priests of brain research, we hope to fathom the deepest truths about our nature and our destiny.'[47]

But there are many such high priests, even if not all of them are involved in brain science. The pattern is always the same. The author has a well-earned reputation in a specific area: DNA, language, genetics, the pre-frontal cortex, etc. This is the spot where the fulcrum comes to stand, the site of the miracle in which that one man or woman lifts up the world. Their books bear titles like *The Astonishing Hypothesis: the Scientific Search for the Soul* (Francis Crick, co-discoverer of the structure of DNA) or *How the Mind Works* (Steven Pinker, linguist). Characteristic of these works is the wide grasp, the broad brush, the far reach: from the pre-frontal lobe it is only a few steps to a philosophy of emotion, an aside on the regime of a Mao or a Pol Pot, the relationship between body and soul, nature and culture, heart and reason. These are panoramic works, the literary equivalent of those created by nineteenth-century panorama painters: you follow the author up the narrow, winding stairs leading to a platform; you look around you, your glance spans a space of 7 or 8 metres, and there is sand at your feet. You turn full-circle. You cannot see where sand ends and paint begins. From your tiny podium, you gaze kilometres into the distance, your eyes rove across the beach and the sea, the dunes and

---

[47] De Sousa, 'Prefrontal Kantians', 329.

the polders, the fishing villages and the cities on the horizon, astounded at the illusion created by a painted reality rising at a 90-degree angle out of the sand.

No doubt Descartes would have shrugged his shoulders at the philosophical accusations made against him by Damasio. Neither Princess Elizabeth nor the young Frans Burman entertained the notion that body and soul were separate entities. They were inquiring into the *how* of the interaction, not questioning its existence, and thus scrupulously avoiding Damasio's error. But no doubt Descartes would have delighted in the material which Damasio and his colleagues collected in their clinics and laboratories. Descartes had a vibrant sense of curiosity. On one occasion he ordered cow's eyes from the butcher in order to trace the trajectory of the visual stimuli between pupil and retina, and developed a theory on how the images on the retina are processed by the brain. When it came to the study of the brain, in Descartes' day one could do little more than weigh it, measure it and transect it, while the instruments available to today's neurologist – from neuropsychological tests, lesion studies, EEGs, and surgical and pharmacological interventions to electric stimulation of the cortex and imaging techniques – have opened up worlds that were inaccessible to Descartes. Indeed, many of the above techniques were developed thanks to the mechanistic orientation of which Damasio accused Descartes.

In his *Méditations*, Descartes wrote about what he found when he turned his gaze inwards. Damasio could have used the outcome of this introspection as a motto for the chapter on somatic markers: 'But what, then, am I? A thing that thinks. What is a thing that thinks? That is to say, a thing that doubts, perceives, affirms, denies, wills, does not will, that imagines also, and which feels.'[48] Damasio's error was that he failed to see Descartes as an ally.

---

[48] Descartes, *Discourse*, pp. 106–7.

The philosophical unease brought about by Damasio's treatment of Descartes will not affect the acceptation of the Gage matrix as an eponym. The majority of neurologists do not read philosophical works, and the philosophers who have read Damasio were probably alerted by the title. Whether or not an eponym becomes part of the scientific vocabulary depends on other factors. It is one thing to propose a name, but getting the scientific community to accept that name requires powers of persuasion, allies and a degree of influence on the part of the person proposing the eponym. Various circumstances which increase the chances of success are related to the person of Damasio himself. He has a considerable reputation in the area of prefrontal lesions, and his work has been translated into numerous languages. Such factors enhance his starting position. The fact that the nomination was followed by a fierce debate on whether this eponym refers to a clearly defined pattern of neurological and behavioural abnormalities is not necessarily a drawback – indeed, this is quite common. In the case of Parkinson, Gilles de la Tourette and Alzheimer, there were similar controversies over the exact boundaries of the disease. A total lack of discussion, by contrast, would be fatal. The Gage matrix is long past that stage. In fact, various reviewers have asked themselves whether the boundaries of this eponym are not too elastic to be truly useful in the formation of neuropsychiatric theory.[49] Ironically, this public scepticism has facilitated rather than hindered the introduction of the Gage matrix. Each new term must first acquire a certain dissemination, and criticism is just as effective as approval in bringing this about. Not until twenty or thirty years from now, after examining the handbooks of neurologists and psychiatrists, will we know whether the Gage matrix has been accepted.

Meanwhile, the biographer of Phineas Gage saw to it that the 150th anniversary of the 'horrible accident' was commemorated in suitable

---

[49] See, in addition to Blau, 'Review *Descartes' Error*', D.N. Robinson, 'Review note', *Theory and Psychology*, 6 (1996), 356–8.

fashion. In 1998, Macmillan chose Cavendish as the venue of a John Martyn Harlow Frontal Lobe Symposium. On that occasion, in the presence of the Rev. Edward Williams IV, the great-great-grandson of Doctor Williams, the first physician to arrive on the scene, a memorial plaque was unveiled featuring a portrait of Gage, a chronology of his life, and a drawing of the damage to his skull.[50]

[50] M. Macmillan, 'Commemorating the 150th anniversary of Phineas Gage's accident', *Journal of the History of the Neurosciences*, 9 (2000) 1, 90–3.

FOUR

The Celestine prophesy: Broca's area

Like Columbus before him, the discoverer of 'Broca's area' was not sure exactly what he had discovered. The anatomical facts seemed clear enough. In April 1861, in the Bicêtre Hospital in Paris where Broca practised as a surgeon, the death was recorded of a man who had lost the power of speech. When Broca carried out an autopsy on the brain of the deceased, he found severe damage to the lower part of the left frontal lobe. Some of the brain tissue had disappeared, and what remained was pulpy in structure. The conclusion seemed obvious: this must be the part of the brain involved in the production of language. It is a reconstruction favoured by many neurological handbooks: Broca discovered the link between a speech disorder and damage to a specific location in the left half of the brain, thereby becoming the name-giver of 'Broca's area' and the related 'Broca's aphasia'. And yet this representation of the facts is misleading. Broca believed he had discovered something quite different. Not until two years later did he realize that he had set foot on land not in Japan, but in the New World. The discovery was not a cause for rejoicing.

Figure 4.1: Pierre Paul Broca (1824–1880)

Monsieur Tan

In 1841, the 17-year-old Pierre Paul Broca left for Paris to study medicine. He did so well in the comparative exams and the competitions leading to a registrarship that he abandoned the idea of returning home after his studies to take over his father's general practice.[1] In 1848, he was appointed professor of anatomy at the medical faculty of the University of Paris, and secretary of the Société d'Anatomie, the youngest in the society's history. At the age of 23 he authored his first scientific article (on the anatomy of club foot) and from that moment on he produced a steady stream of *mémoires*, *observations*, *études* and notes dealing with a wide variety of subjects, ranging from pathology, anatomy and surgery to anthropology, biology, neurology and archaeology. Between his first and his last publication (the speech he made at the graveside of his colleague Périer on 15 May 1880, two months before his own death), we find some 500 articles dealing not only with aphasia, tumours, blood

[1] The most important biography of Broca is R. Schiller, *Paul Broca: Founder of French Anthropology, Explorer of the Brain* (Oxford, 1992).

transfusions, hypnosis, nymphomania and hospital hygiene, but also with the bones discovered in the cave of Mont Maigre, the skull of the German poet Schiller, the skin colour of negroes at birth, the skull and brain matter of the murderer Lemaire, the art of making a fire, the dissemination of the Basque language, and the origin of the Celts.[2] Over the years, his interest shifted towards physical and cultural anthropology, but in the early 1860s his reputation was still based largely on his medical work.

On 18 April 1861, at a meeting of the Société d'Anthropologie, Broca presented the brain of the man who had lost the power of speech.[3] A few hours before, it had been removed from the skull of a 51-year-old shoe-maker named Leborgne. In a detailed autopsy report published later that year, Broca recorded that in the Bicêtre Hospital, Leborgne had long been known as 'Monsieur Tan'.[4] 'Tan tan' was his standard reply to all questions, but when angered he would shout 'sacré nom de Dieu!', thereby exhausting his entire vocabulary. He did understand what was said to him, since he was capable of carrying out a task provided it was explained verbally, and when he wanted to make something clear, he would gesticulate with his left hand. Tan, as Broca, too, referred to him, had an unhappy medical history. As a child he had been prey to epileptic seizures, and at the age of 30 he had lost the power of speech. Ten years ago, first his right arm and then his right leg became paralysed, and he was confined to his bed. Broca acknowledged that the care he received in the Bicêtre Hospital left

[2] Most of these articles appeared in society bulletins. For a bibliography, see Schiller, *Broca*.

[3] P. Broca, 'Perte de la parole, ramollissement chronique et destruction partielle du lobe antérieur gauche du cerveau', *Bulletin de la Société d'Anthropologie*, 2 (1861), 235–7. The most important publications dealing with the localization of language have been reprinted in H. Hécaen and J. Dubois (eds.), *La naissance de la neuropsychologie du langage 1825–1865* (Paris, 1969).

[4] Quoted from the translation: 'Remarks on the seat of the faculty of articulate language, followed by an observation of aphemia', in G. von Bonin (ed.), *Some Papers on the Cerebral Cortex* (Springfield, 1960), pp. 49–72.

much to be desired. The bed linens were only changed once a week, and infections in the leg which had no feeling in it were not discovered until after they had become gangrenous. In fact, this was the reason he had been transferred to Broca's surgical ward. But the man was dying and Broca could do nothing for him.

In the few days that Tan had to live, Broca was loath to burden him with lengthy interrogations. But it was clear from a cursory examination that Tan's mind was still clear. When asked how long he had been in the hospital, he opened his left hand four times and then held up one finger. And indeed, he had spent the last 21 years in the Bicêtre. Broca repeated the question the following day, and again Tan held up his open hand four times and then one finger. On the third day, when Broca asked the question again, the reply was a frustrated 'sacré nom de Dieu!'. When asked about the sequence in which his complaints had manifested themselves, he pointed first to his tongue, then to his right arm, and finally to his right leg. Broca established that there was nothing wrong with his tongue. It was not paralysed, the timbre of his voice was normal, and what little he was able to say sounded normal. Tan appeared to be capable of all the movements of tongue, lips and vocal chords required for speech. And yet he could not speak.

Tan died on 17 April and the autopsy was carried out the following day. Broca had the skull carefully sawed open and began by assessing the general condition of the brain. Judging by the large quantity of pus between the cerebral membranes, it had lost much of its original size. After draining off the brain fluid, he was left with a brain weighing 987 grams, some 400 grams lighter than the average weight for a man of around 50. On the left side of the frontal lobe, the cerebral membrane sagged inward, covering a cavity 'about as large as a hen's egg'.[5] Although no part of the brain was completely intact, the lesions were particularly severe in the third convolution. Broca cut a hole of the same size from a healthy brain and weighed the piece

[5] Von Bonin, 'Remarks', p. 66.

he had extracted: he estimated that some 50 grams of Tan's brain tissue had disappeared. The rest of the weight loss could be explained by general atrophy. In Broca's view, it was a miracle that someone with such severe brain damage had survived so long. During the reconstruction, it became clear that the injury which had caused the speech disturbances twenty-one years before had begun on a spot at the imaginary centre of the cavity (the third frontal convolution), while the paralysis of the right limbs was a consequence of the ongoing softening of the brain. Broca decided against excising any more of the tissue: this brain belonged in a museum. After the autopsy, he slid it into a jar of alcohol. Tan's brain was subsequently transferred to the Musée Dupuytren, where it was added to the collection under catalogue number '55a, Nervous System'.

A neuropolitical minefield

Broca's public life was dictated by the rhythm of society gatherings. On Friday there was the Société d'Anatomie; Tuesday afternoon was reserved for the Société de Chirurgie and Saturday afternoon for the Société de Biologie. All these meetings were organized according to a schedule which took no account of vacations, and those who absented themselves were subject to a fine. In 1859, Thursday afternoon was added to the list, when Broca co-founded the Société d'Anthropologie. He was to serve as its secretary until his death. Two years before, he had married Adèle Augustine Lugol, eleven years his junior, who bore him three children.

Although the Société d'Anthropologie was not founded on political principles, almost every topic that came up for discussion had political implications. The differences between 'races', to mention just one of the subjects that regularly featured on the agenda, might have consequences for one's standpoint on slavery, while differences between men and women were relevant to the question of whether women should be admitted to institutions of higher learning. The activities of the society were closely monitored by the authorities, and each meeting was attended by a plain-clothes policeman. Anyone who ventured to speak on the subject of the human brain, even when the topic was as ostensibly theoretical as the representation of language, found himself on the edge of a neuropolitical minefield.

The controversy surrounding the question of whether psychological functions such as memory, speech and perception correspond to specific locations in the brain was rooted in phrenology, a theory formulated by the Viennese physician Franz Joseph Gall. Within the annals of neurology, phrenology is generally regarded as a curiosity. It holds that the brain consists of a collection of organs whose size corresponds to their level of development. A talent for language or mathematics, and such characteristics as courage and vanity, were thought to be reflected in bumps on the skull. Gall himself once encountered a patient who had lost the power of speech: as a soldier, he became mute after a sabre entered the left eye socket, penetrating the frontal lobe. Phrenologists believed that this spot, directly behind the eyes, was the seat of memory, and Gall concluded that his patient's memory for words had been deactivated as a result of the stab wound. But the medical establishment in France would have nothing to do with phrenology. During the 1820s, the Parisian physician Pierre Flourens introduced a new neurological technique known as extirpation, whereby parts of an animal's brain were removed and its subsequent behaviour observed. Flourens established that perception, memory and locomotion were distributed much more widely throughout the brain than Gall had found. He was unable to locate any separate 'faculties'. In Flourens, the neurologist and the devout Catholic found one another in the comforting conviction that the human spirit is a harmonious and indivisible entity, the seat of which is an integrated brain. Flourens dedicated his *Examen de la phrénologie* to Descartes.[6]

---

[6] P. Flourens, *Examen de la phrénologie* (Paris, 1824).

Some thirty years after Gall's death in 1828, phrenology could claim only one significant adherent within French medical science: Jean-Baptiste Bouillaud, founder of the Société Phrénologique. Bouillaud, a member of the Académie de Médecine and dean of the Medical Faculty, was a force to be reckoned with. As far back as 1825 he had published observations which appeared to indicate that speech loss was the result of damage to the frontal lobes.[7] He had sought confirmation for this theory in a rather grisly experiment which involved drilling a hole in the skull of a dog, thereby damaging the side of the frontal lobe. According to Bouillaud, the dog was noticeably less smart than before, and it no longer barked.[8] In 1839, he reported on a demonstration experiment: a patient had shot himself in the head, whereby a portion of the skull had disappeared. Bouillaud: 'Curious to know what effect it would have on speech if the brain were compressed, we applied to the exposed part a large spatula, pressing from above downwards, and gently from front to back. With moderate pressure, speech seemed to die on his lips; by pressing harder and more sharply, speech not only failed but a few words were suddenly cut off.'[9] The distinction made by Bouillaud was one which Broca himself would later repeat, namely that between 'internal speech', the instrument of thought, and 'external speech', the articulation of thoughts. In 1825, he wrote that both forms of speech were located in the frontal lobes, and in 1860 he still believed that to be the case.

In February 1861, a few months before the memorable presentation of Tan's brain, Ernest Auburtin, a physician as well as Bouillaud's son-in-law, spoke at a meeting of the Société d'Anthropologie. He maintained that speech disturbances are reflected in damage to the frontal lobes. At this time, Broca, like Flourens, was convinced that the

---

[7] J.-B. Bouillaud, *Traité clinique et physiologique de l'encéphalite ou inflammation du cerveau, et de ses suites* (Paris, 1825).

[8] F. Bateman, 'On aphasia, or loss of speech in cerebral disease', *Journal of Mental Science*, 15 (1869–70), 367–93.

[9] Cited in Schiller, *Broca*, p. 173.

representation of higher functions is distributed throughout the brain. While he acknowledged the possibility that the frontal lobes played a role of some importance in those functions, this could not be attributed to the phrenological 'organs'. And he certainly had no desire to be associated with the brain theories of Gall. When the patient known as Tan appeared on his ward in April, Broca saw his chance. Several days passed between the first clinical examination of Tan and the autopsy on his brain, and it was during this period that he invited Auburtin to come to the Bicêtre. Did the honoured colleague not agree that this was a clear case of speech loss? And if the autopsy were to reveal no damage to the frontal lobe of the patient, would he (Auburtin) then be prepared to permanently disassociate himself from the views of Bouillaud and Gall? Following a brief examination of the patient, Auburtin agreed to Broca's proposition. Tensely, the two men awaited the death of the shoe-maker.

Agreeing to the experiment clearly required more courage on the part of Auburtin and his father-in-law. After all, they risked witnessing the unequivocal refutation of a theory which had already made them an object of ridicule among their colleagues. The discovery of the cavity in Tan's frontal lobe must have been most welcome. But Broca was a good loser. He explained to his audience that his observations corroborated the views of Bouillaud, although he added that it had not yet been established whether the entire frontal lobe was involved in spoken language or only certain groups of convolutions. He proposed that the loss of speech be christened 'aphemia', but received little support. Several years later, the medical community opted for the term 'aphasia', literally 'without speech'.

Broca's discovery was not well received. The notion that language, which is associated with reason and judgement, is represented in a relatively limited area of the brain was greeted with scepticism. Fortunately, the fact that this area (if it existed) was located in the frontal lobe did fit in neatly with the prevailing views: after all, what distinguishes us from animals is not only our command of language, but also a much larger frontal lobe. This, then, is what Broca believed he had discovered in 1861: that the seat of language is in the *frontal* lobe – not that the site is the third convolution, or that it is unilateral, let alone that it is always on the *left* side. On this point, Bouillaud and Broca were in total agreement: language could not possibly be represented on one side only.

Later that year, Broca was examining the brain of an 84-year-old man named Lelong who had lost the power of speech when, to his astonishment, he discovered an injury in precisely the same spot as in the case of Tan. The area affected was smaller, about the size of a one-franc coin, but it was in the same frontal convolution, and likewise on the left side. He reported that he was inclined to see this as pure coincidence, but to be on the safe side, this brain was likewise dispatched to the museum. In the years that followed, Broca carried out autopsies on eight new cases of speech loss. In each case the injury was on the left side. For Broca, this was a most aggravating development. He regarded it as an infringement of the anatomical law of symmetry formulated by the French physician Xavier Bichat: 'Harmony is to the *functions* of the organs what symmetry is to their *conformation*; it supposes a perfect equality of force and action, as symmetry indicates an exact analogy in the external forms and internal structure.'[10] The fact that organs with an identical structure serve an identical function was so self-evident that it was never questioned: kidneys, lungs, eyes, ears and other paired organs all have the same function. It was unthinkable that the two halves of the brain, precise mirror images of one another, were an exception to that rule. Broca was disturbed by the gradual proliferation of documentation on patients with speech loss who displayed lesions on the left side of the brain. 'A breach of symmetry', he wrote, 'would be a veritable

[10] Cited in L. J. Harris, 'Cerebral control for speech in right-handers and left-handers: an analysis of the views of Paul Broca, his contemporaries, and his successors', *Brain and Language*, 40 (1991), 1–50, 6.

subversion of our knowledge of cerebral physiology.'[11] And: 'I hope that others, more fortunate than I, will finally find an example of aphemia caused by a lesion of the right hemisphere. Up until now, it is always the left third frontal convolution that has been affected.'[12] However, in July 1863, the very reverse of what Broca was hoping for occurred: a colleague reported the details of a patient with a severely damaged third convolution in the *right* frontal lobe. His power of speech had been unaffected.

In actual fact, Bichat's law of symmetry was a departure point for research rather than a result. Symmetry was associated with beauty, equilibrium and order, values which science also claimed for itself. Whatever deviated from symmetry – lop-sided growth, instability, one-sidedness – appeared to open the way to chaos and pathology. The appeal of symmetry is evident from the derisive reactions to the suggestion that the loss of spoken language was due exclusively to lesions on the left side. This was a notion that could not possibly be taken seriously, as the physician Briquet told his colleagues during a session of the Académie de Médecine. Surely no one would claim that we hear 'do, re, me, fa' with the right ear, and 'sol, la, ti' with the other ear? Or that we smell pleasant odours with the right nostril and unpleasant ones with the left? But slowly, and grudgingly, the growing number of cases of aphasia in combination with damage on the left side of the brain were propelling Broca in the direction of what he would later refer to as his 'discovery'.

Dax's area

In March 1863, the Académie des Sciences and the Académie de Médecine received a letter from a general practitioner, a certain

---

[11] Cited in A. Harrington, *Medicine, Mind and the Double Brain: a Study in Nineteenth-Century Thought* (Princeton NJ, 1987), p. 52.

[12] Harrington, *Medicine*, p. 52.

Gustave Dax, who lived in Sommières, a small town near Montpellier. He enclosed a report said to have been presented in 1836 by his father, Marc Dax, likewise a GP.[13] Gustave Dax wished to have it recorded that, well before Broca, Marc Dax had discovered that the loss of speech is related to left-brain damage. This marked the beginning of a controversy which would rapidly turn not only on the question of priority, but also on the issue of what actually counts as a scientific 'discovery'.[14]

In 1800, Marc Dax met a former cavalry officer who had experienced serious memory problems after suffering a sabre wound to the head. After the man's death, Dax asked the family where exactly the man had been wounded. It appeared that the sabre had entered the middle of his left temple. In the years that followed, Dax saw a number of similar cases, in his surgery and in the literature. The renowned botanist Broussonet lost the power of speech in 1806, and after his death Dax happened to read that an autopsy had revealed a large abscess in the left hemisphere of the brain. By 1836, Dax had collected over eighty such cases of speech loss, and without exception the injury was located in the left hemisphere. This had to be evidence of an organic law. Why an injury on the left side affects the patient's memory for words, while other forms of memory remain intact, was a mystery to Dax, but the link was clear and he had put these insights to good use in his practice. A female patient of his had fainted and fallen out of her chair. She related that after coming around, she had briefly been unable to utter a word. When two days later she again lost consciousness, Dax was called to the scene and established that this

---

[13] Dax's report was reprinted in Hécaen and Dubois: M. Dax, 'Lésions de la moitié gauche de l'encéphale coïncidant avec l'oubli des signes de la pensée' in *Naissance*, pp. 97–101. Quoted from the translation in R. Joynt and A. L. Benton, 'The memoir of Marc Dax on aphasia' in A. L. Benton (ed.), *Exploring the History of Neuropsychology* (Oxford, 2000), pp. 167–73.

[14] S. Finger and D. Roe, 'Gustave Dax and the early history of cerebral dominance', *Archives of Neurology*, 53 (1996), 806–13.

time she had completely lost her power of speech. As he himself said, 'I had no need for reflection to know the nature, the site or the treatment of this illness. I promptly applied a large number of leeches to the left temple and in a few minutes, as the blood flowed, her speech was gradually restored.'[15] Dax recorded his findings in a brief *mémoire* which he intended to present at a congress held in Montpellier in 1836. But apparently nothing came of the plan. Thus, not only is there no proof whatsoever that Dax actually presented his paper, there is also no trace of it in the form of references in the literature. He himself was unable to publish it, as he died in 1837.

His son Gustave also went into private practice in Sommières after completing his studies. Dax Jr made the left-sided origin of speech loss into a family affair, ultimately collecting an additional 140 cases drawn from the literature and his own practice (87 involving speech loss following lesions in the left hemisphere, and 53 instances in which there was no speech loss following lesions in the right hemisphere) and added them to the dossier compiled by his father. By 1858, Gustave Dax had drawn up an extensive account of their combined findings. Unfortunately, like his father, he was somewhat lax when it came to publication. Gustave passed around a few copies among colleagues, but in the end did not submit his findings to a journal.

It was not until 1861, after the publicity surrounding the presentation of the brain of the shoe-maker Tan, that Dax finally took action. His faith in the two Académies was considerable, and perhaps somewhat naive. Initially, the sole result was the installation of two committees. Flourens served on the one initiated by the Académie des Sciences, which was never heard from again. The physician Lélut was on that of the Académie de Médecine and, after an interval of a year and a half, he issued a scathing report, declaring that he could see nothing in the work of father and son Dax but an attempt to breathe

---

[15] Joynt and Benton, 'Memoir', p. 170.

new life into phrenology.[16] If the 'honourable author of the memoir' was right about his 140 cases, 'then each of the two hemispheres, and even each part of these hemispheres, could be the seat of a different function. This same principle would then hold true for the other paired organs of the body.'[17] This was as far as Lélut was prepared to go. But he warned that before long someone would stand up and announce: 'Thus one could be led to think that there is only one eye, the left, for instance, that sees, whereas the right eye is used for other purposes.'[18] And although Dax *père* and Dax *fils* had piled up one example after the other, Lélut himself maintained that some thirty years ago he had seen solid proof of the contrary, in the person of an epileptic patient whose speech was normal, despite the fact that, on autopsy, the left half of his brain proved to be nothing but a pulpy mass. Another patient had a tumour in the cerebellum, accompanied by a speech defect, even though there was no abnormality at all in the left hemisphere. In closing, he expressed to the Académie his fervent wish never again to be accosted on this particular subject.

As the report was not calculated to provide Dax with any form of redress, he resolved to do what he should have done at a much earlier stage: publish. On 28 April 1865, the article by Marc Dax finally appeared in the *Gazette Hebdomadaire de Médecine et de Chirurgie* followed by a 'Sur le même sujet' by Gustave Dax.[19]

Meanwhile, Broca learned that Gustave Dax had submitted a report to the Académie de Médecine which established that as far back as 1836, Marc Dax had described the role which the left hemisphere plays in speech loss. Broca's definitive version of his own insights appeared six weeks *after* the publication of the articles by

---

[16] Lélut's report appears in translation in Finger and Roe, 'Gustave Dax'.

[17] Finger and Roe, 'Gustave Dax', 809.   [18] *Ibid.* 809.

[19] M. Dax, 'Lésions de la moitié gauche de l'encéphale coïncidant avec l'oubli des signes de la pensée', *Gazette Hebdomadaire de Médecine et de Chirurgie*, 2 (1865), 259–60. G. Dax, 'Sur le même sujet', *Gazette Hebdomadaire de Médecine et de Chirurgie*, 2 (1865), 260–2.

father and son Dax in the *Gazette*.[20] Broca had little choice but to begin by addressing the chronology of the discoveries. 'I do not like the discussions on priority, and I would have avoided indicating that the discovery of Mr Dax, unpublished as it was, was a non-event from the viewpoint of history, if several people had not given me to understand that I ought to have cited the opinion of Mr Dax (the father), when I, in turn, pointed out the special influence of the left hemisphere of the brain on the faculty of speech.'[21] It was abundantly clear that he did not intend to do so. Broca wrote that no one in Paris was aware of the existence of the account put forward by Dax. In fact, it was even unknown in Montpellier, where it was purportedly delivered in 1836. Broca had searched the local newspapers and even written to the librarian of the medical faculty, a certain Monsieur Gordon, who had likewise been unable to find any mention of the lecture. He personally contacted some twenty physicians who had attended the conference, none of whom could remember a presentation by a certain Marc Dax. Broca did not question the authenticity of the report: 'But I wish to establish that it was impossible for me to guess the existence of the paper that was brought to light two years after my first publications on the subject of *aphémie*.'[22]

In effect, this neatly restored the chronology. Broca made no mention of the fact that in his 'first publications on the subject of *aphémie*', he was still claiming that the power of speech was represented *bilaterally*. In his later articles on the brain and language, he made no reference to the work of Dax. The fact that the celebrated neurologist had quietly antedated the discovery of left-sided dominance for language from 1863 to 1861 (and that his colleagues in France

[20] P. Broca, 'Sur le siège de la faculté du langage articulé', *Bulletin de la Société d'Anthropologie*, 6 (1865), 337–93. Reprinted in Hécaen and Dubois, *Naissance*, pp. 108–21. Quoted from the translation in E. A. Berker, A. H. Berker and A. Smith, 'Translation of Broca's 1865 report', *Archives of Neurology*, 43 (1986), 1065–72.

[21] Berker, Berker and Smith, 'Translation', 1066–7. [22] *Ibid.* 1067.

and beyond had quickly followed his example) caused Dax considerable agitation, a state which continued until his death in 1893, and from time to time compelled him to write fruitless letters to the editor.

Should Broca's area actually have been christened Bouillaud's area or Dax's area? Or would a combination have been more appropriate, such as the Dax-Broca area? The answer depends on exactly what the eponym is designed to honour. In 1825, Bouillaud was the first person who, on the basis of a more or less systematic collection of cases, made it plausible that spoken language was localized within a relatively limited area, namely the frontal lobes. But since he believed that language was represented on both sides, it is impossible to attribute to him the discovery of the left-sided dominance for language. In 1836, Marc Dax became the first researcher to point to the left hemisphere as the brain-half which, when damaged, can give rise to speech disturbances. But much of his material was second-hand, taken from newspaper articles or 'In Memoriams'. He himself never carried out an autopsy or designated a specific section of the left hemisphere. He also failed to publish his discovery. His findings sank without a trace, and it was only thanks to the efforts of his son in 1863, and the belated publication of his original account in 1865, that Dax can still be regarded as a candidate. What befell Marc Dax is reminiscent of the fate of numerous discoveries dating from a time when it was possible to establish reliably the geographical latitude (the north-south position) but not the longitude. In the case of some small island, this meant that after the discoverers sailed away, the island could only be located again by exploring a sizable stretch of ocean from east to west. Columbus is said to have remarked disconsolately that little is gained by discovering new countries if they are 'mislaid' immediately thereafter. Marc Dax had sailed away without recording the coordinates of his discovery in keeping with the conventions of the day.

Broca, by contrast, took care to follow each and every step dictated by those conventions. He kept the scientific community informed of his findings by means of publications in society journals, and in compiling those findings he employed a convincing method: autopsies. The more the better. Broca was also fortunate in having an established reputation. It was as if every new thought he put forward echoed his earlier work, lending him an authority which was not granted to father and son Dax. And yet, one can hardly give him credit for discovering that the dominance for language lies in the left hemisphere, and certainly not for having done so in 1861. In a sense, the fact that he discovered the damage to the precise spot which is now known as Broca's area is a bizarre coincidence: where Broca was concerned, the cavity could just as easily have been on the other side. And even the second case (Lelong), where the damage was in exactly the same spot, was described by Broca as 'purely accidental'. It was not until two years and eight autopsies later that it began to dawn on him that the fact that it was on the left was actually the essence of his 'discovery'.

Not long ago, the historians of neurology Finger and Roe came up with yet another candidate.[23] Although he had been in the vicinity the whole time, he could easily have been overlooked: Gustave Dax. Finger and Roe state that in the wake of Broca's presentation in 1861, he was probably the only physician who understood that if the crux of the matter was the neurological representation of speech, then Bichat's symmetry thesis was plainly wrong. But what was more important, Gustave Dax situated the locus of speech disturbances not in the frontal lobe, as Broca did, but further back, in the temporal lobe. It is a cruel twist of fate that in the history of neurology, *that* particular discovery has become associated with a young German neurologist named Carl Wernicke, even though Gustave Dax

[23] S. Finger and D. Roe, 'Does Gustave Dax deserve to be forgotten? The temporal lobe theory and other contributions of an overlooked figure in the history of language and cerebral dominance', *Brain and Language*, 69 (1999), 16–30.

published in 1865 and Wernicke not until 1874. But then, priority had not helped his father either.

Broca's Rule

Broca's 1865 article has gone down in history as the first convincing formulation of cerebral asymmetry. But contained within that asymmetry were several other hypotheses which betray how difficult it was to break the habit of thinking in terms of symmetry. Broca maintained that at birth the left and right halves of the brain are totally equivalent and equally suitable for carrying out the language function. Thus, in its rudimentary form, the brain is a symmetrical organ. However, because the left frontal lobe experiences a slight growth spurt in the early years, most individuals are right-handed and their representation of language is located in the left frontal lobe. In a minority of cases, Broca goes on, the reverse is true: these individuals are left-handed and right-brained. At the time, Broca had little or no evidence to back up this 'mirror image theory' of the relationship between hand preference and the precise spot where the language centre is located, and there was little if any statistical evidence available. Up until then, no one had had any reason to suspect that there was such a connection, and the hand preference of patients was not recorded. Further on in his article, Broca did to some extent play down the relationship between language centre and hand preference, but that could not prevent neurologists from adopting 'Broca's Rule': the centre of language is located on the side opposite the preferred hand, i.e., in left-handers on the right.[24] Apparently, the appeal of symmetry was so great that the possibility that in a number of left-handers the language centre was on the left

---

[24] P. Eling, 'Broca on the relation between handedness and cerebral speech dominance', *Brain and Language*, 22 (1984), 158–9. See also L. J. Harris, 'Broca on cerebral control for speech in right-handers and left-handers: a note on translation and some further comments', *Brain and Language*, 45 (1993), 108–20.

did not occur to them. Broca's Rule remained in sway for almost a century. To correct this misconception would have required a research population of a magnitude which was simply not available, at least not in peacetime.

However, following the demobilization of the armies which had been deployed during the Second World War, new armies entered the neurological literature. They had survived their wounds, but the price they paid was invalidity and handicaps. These armies no longer marched: they lay in bed or hobbled around on crutches. They were aphasic or blind, paralysed or spastic, epileptic or deaf. Much of our knowledge concerning the neurological topography of functions was collected as a result of the penetration of the head by bullets and shrapnel. Within a relatively brief period of time, theories were refuted or corrected, some of which had been part of accepted neurological knowledge for as long as a century. In the period 1943–1945, the German neurologist Klaus Conrad examined over 800 patients in an army hospital for men with brain damage.[25] In almost all cases, the injuries were caused by bullets and shrapnel, which made it possible to localize the neurological damage by means of x-rays. Over 200 of these patients had been rendered aphasic by their injuries: in some this state was temporary, while in others it persisted. With the exception of a few cases which were unclear, most of the aphasic *right*-handers displayed brain damage on the left side. To Conrad's surprise, however, it appeared that in just over half of the aphasic *left*-handers, the injury was likewise on the left, which contradicted Broca's Rule.

In Conrad's population, aphasia due to brain damage was recorded in only one-quarter of cases. Left-handedness was considerably less common (under 6 per cent). Because the *combination* of aphasia and left-handedness is extremely uncommon, a great many instances of

---

[25] K. Conrad, 'Über aphasische Sprachstörungen bei hirnverletzten Linkshändern', *Der Nervenarzt*, 20 (1949), 148–54.

injury are needed in order to detect an interesting neurological pattern. During the war years, those cases were available. Conrad published his results in 1949, putting an end to the mirror image theory. Today the rule of thumb is that in about 70 per cent of left-handers the seat of language is located on the left, in 15 per cent on the right, while in the remaining 15 per cent it is divided between left and right.

The splendid seventies

Broca's work spawned new neurological expeditions. In 1870, the German physicians Gustav Fritsch and Eduard Hitzig used a weak galvanic current to stimulate the exposed cortex of dogs, and discovered what we now know as the 'motor projection area', a strip of the frontal lobe just in front of the central groove which is involved in muscle movement. In 1873, the Englishman David Ferrier employed this same method to stimulate monkey brains and discovered the 'sensory projection area' and its role in the processing of sensory information. It was Ferrier who in 1876 proposed honouring Broca by means of the designation 'Broca's area'.[26] But the most important development in the study of aphasia after Broca was the work of the German Carl Wernicke. Inspired by the discoveries of Fritsch and Hitzig, this 26-year-old medical intern at the Allerheiligen Hospital in Breslau devised a theory of language disorders which he published in a short monograph in 1874.[27] Wernicke did not base his theory primarily on studies of injuries, as Broca had done, but rather on what had by then been learned about the neurological representation of functions. According to Wernicke, a spoken word evokes an 'acoustic image' which, through association, then becomes bound up with the meaning of that word. The representation of the meaning of the word

---

[26] D. Ferrier, *The Functions of the Brain* (London, 1876), p. 126.
[27] C. Wernicke, *Der aphasische Symptomen-Komplex* (Breslau, 1874).

then evokes a 'motor image'. Since we know that the portion of the brain in front of the central groove is responsible for motor tasks, while the portion behind it processes sensory information, there must be two types of aphasia: motor or expressive aphasia, which Broca discovered, and sensory or receptive aphasia. While studying this second type of aphasia, Wernicke pinpointed the area in the left temporal lobe that would come to bear his name. To this day, it is acknowledged as one of the main types of aphasia. A patient with Broca's aphasia understands what is said to him and can formulate a reply in his head, but lacks the capacity to express that reply. A patient suffering from Wernicke's aphasia is still capable of producing language, but is no longer able to understand it. The sign language used by the deaf likewise reflects this classification: damage to Broca's area does not affect the motor system involved in signing, but rather the meaning of the gestures. In clinical practice, a 'pure' Broca or Wernicke is rare: mixed forms are the rule.

In the field of neurology, the 1870s came to be known as the 'splendid seventies'. The identification of two 'language centres' raised the issue of whether functions such as reading, writing and arithmetic also had their own 'centres'. Schemas and diagrams were devised in an effort to link a variety of disturbances to a neurological substrate. In 1871, the loss of the ability to move parts of one's body in order to perform an action was referred to as 'apraxia', and it was soon followed by 'alexia' (reading), 'agraphia' (writing'), 'amusia' (music) and 'acalculia' (arithmetic). Like aphasia, these disturbances have an expressive and a receptive variant, although here, too, they tend to appear in a combined form. A well-known case of amusia is that of the composer Maurice Ravel. In 1932, he was involved in an automobile accident and sustained brain damage which gradually worsened, ultimately resulting in a combination of aphasia and amusia.[28]

---

[28] The neurologist who was treating Ravel devoted a publication to this case: T. Alajouanine, 'Aphasia and artistic realization', Brain, 71 (1948), 229–41.

Ravel's ability to recognize and assess music remained intact, but his musical expression was severely affected. He was unable to compose and could no longer play the piano from sheet music. His case was particularly interesting from a neurological standpoint. It was long thought that listening to or playing music was governed largely by the right hemisphere, but in the case of the right-handed Ravel, the damage was to the left side of the brain. In his case, the specific pattern of areas affected or spared suggests that, to a degree, the expression of music involves the same processes as language. Both music and language require precise coordination in time, a faculty which is regulated by the left hemisphere.

Civilized asymmetry

Boulevard Henri IV in Paris was once the site of the convent of the Celestines, of the order of St Benedict. During the eighteenth century, the community fell into decline and was ultimately dissolved. The convent was vacated in 1785 and four years later, after the French Revolution, it was torn down. In 1847, during the construction of the boulevard, a number of sarcophaguses dating back to the twelfth century were found in the grounds of the old churchyard. Broca, then a 23-year-old medical intern at the Hôtel-Dieu hospital, became interested in the skeletons which had accumulated there over the previous seven centuries. He succeeded in obtaining an appointment as supervisor at the excavation site, which gave him an opportunity to measure the skulls. This was the beginning of a lifelong craniometric campaign which bordered on the obsessive. For Broca, the painstaking work of measuring skulls and brains held out the promise of one day being able to formulate a theory concerning Man's proper place in the universe, in society, in his personal life, and in history. Broca was convinced that in the course of centuries the human brain had increased in size, together with, and thanks to, the rise of European civilization. In 1862, he reported the results of an extensive study in which the 116 skulls found in the Celestine cemetery were compared with skulls from an eighteenth-century and a nineteenth-century cemetery.[29] In 1981, the palaeontologist Stephen Jay Gould, in his turn, delved into Broca's research in order to demonstrate that the Frenchman had consistently interpreted his craniometric findings in such a way that they could only reinforce his theory of a steadily enlarging European brain. Gould referred to this as 'the great circle route': the conclusions came first, determining the interpretation of the facts, and were then supported by those facts.[30]

Broca had painstakingly measured the capacity of the skulls and arrived at the following averages: twelfth century, 1426 cc; eighteenth century, 1409 cc; and nineteenth century, 1462 cc. The problem is obvious: it was not the oldest skulls, but those dating from the eighteenth century which were the smallest. How was this to be explained? Broca's answer goes back to a dichotomy within the group of nineteenth-century skulls. Some of these (ninety to be precise) came from individual graves, the other thirty-five from a mass grave. The difference in size was noteworthy: 1484 cc as opposed to 1403 cc, in favour of the on-average more prosperous and thus presumably more intelligent deceased who were buried in individual graves. This would explain the curious discrepancy between the skulls from the twelfth century and the smaller specimens dating from the eighteenth century: only the elite could afford to bury their dead in a sarcophagus. But this raised a new problem. How was it possible that the skulls from an eighteenth-century mass grave were larger (1409 cc) than those from a nineteenth-century mass grave (1403 cc)? Again the answer is bound up with social class. In the eighteenth century, before the French Revolution, one had to be wealthy to end up in a cemetery. In other words, when it came to skull size, the poor of the

---

[29] P. Broca, 'Sur la capacité des crânes parisiens des diverses époques', *Bulletin de la Société de l'Anthropologie*, 3 (1862), 102–16.

[30] S. J. Gould, *The Mismeasure of Man* (New York, 1981), p. 85.

nineteenth century found themselves on a level with the rich of a century before. The conclusion of this far more extensive exercise was that, provided one looked closely and was not deterred by the semblance of contradiction, the series 1426–1409–1462 cc was indeed numerical proof of ever bigger skulls. For Broca, it was an objective and incontestable fact that the people of Paris had gradually acquired larger and larger brains.

Broca was a past master at 'correction'. Gratiolet, a fellow member of the Société d'Anthropologie, had established by means of measurements that German brains were on average some 100 grams heavier than French brains. He then submitted this fact as a decisive argument against the theory that there is a positive relation between brain size and intelligence. Broca set up a detailed comparative study based on assessments accurate to the last gram, supplemented by corrections for age differences and national differences in body weight. The conclusion was that although lighter than German brains, French brains were – in the final analysis – nevertheless heavier.

In his day, Broca was honoured as the man who had taken physical anthropology and turned it into a science of size and number. In a standard work on anthropological methods and techniques which appeared in 1888, forty instruments and measurement methods were discussed, nineteen of which were attributed to Broca.[31] The eponyms 'Broca's area' and 'Broca's aphasia' are part of what was once a much longer honours list. Most of the other accolades, such as 'Broca's angle', 'Broca's stereograph' and 'Broca's plane', reflect his acknowledged position as the leading researcher in the field of physical anthropology. Measurements should be devoid of any form of subjective human judgement: the more the process of registration could be left to the instrument itself, the better. Broca's stereograph is the concrete expression of that striving. The skull was anchored by screwing plugs into both auditory channels. The anthropologist

---

[31] E. Schmidt, *Anthropologische Methoden* (Leipzig, 1888).

Figure 4.2: 'Broca's stereograph' made it possible to establish the circumference of the skull in the flat plane

then passed a holder with a stylus over the skull, so that the shape was copied onto the paper mounted behind it. In this way, various measurements could be taken in the flat plane. Depending on the position of the skull in the clamps, it was possible to determine the distance between the front and back of the head, the height and slant of the forehead, and the size of the jaw in relation to the forehead. These and various other measurements were employed as quantitative arguments in controversies centring on the differences between individuals, generations and races. The most essential requirement was that the registration should involve as little personal intervention as possible: once the skull was anchored in the stereograph, it basically projected itself onto the paper. This concept of intervention-free measurement was widely adhered to, even in the catalogues of instrument-makers.

There can be no doubt that in all these measurements, as well as in the statistical techniques used to record them, Broca was striving for objectivity and, moreover, that he firmly believed he had been successful in that striving. In almost every article he stressed that observations are more important than theories, and it was in this spirit that even such issues as the intellectual powers of women and the brain size of 'primitive' peoples were addressed. What Broca expected cephalometers, cranioplagiometers, cranioscopes, endometers, endographs, tachycraniographs, goniometers and tropometers to do was to exclude prejudice. In actual fact, each measurement became a delicate game of precision and margins of tolerance, culminating in an outcome which lent objective scientific backing to existing views.

This same pattern is evident in Broca's research into differences between the left and the right hemisphere. The fact that one or two years after birth, language migrates to the left half of the brain is the result of a minor growth spurt in the left hemisphere. But after that, we ourselves give that half of the brain an increasing advantage by means of our education. In this sense, asymmetry is the hallmark of development, training and civilization. This distinction was even made between wild and domesticated animals. The brain of a fox, Broca wrote, is almost perfectly symmetrical. That of a dog, for centuries under the tutelage of Man, is asymmetrical. (As a Lamarckian, Broca had a firm belief in the heredity of acquired characteristics.) However, not all human brains were equally susceptible to this development in the direction of asymmetry. In 1869, the Société d'Anthropologie was informed that white European males displayed the highest degree of asymmetry, women somewhat less, and 'primitive' peoples and lower animals the least. The historian of neurology, Anne Harrington, has documented how in the late nineteenth century anthropologists, marching steadfastly in the direction indicated by Broca, declared the left hemisphere to be the dominant hemisphere, where all human, social and scientific virtues come together, from moderation and reason to logic and will power.[32] The right hemisphere was subordinate, and a good thing, too, since it was seen as the seat of animality, intuition, instinct, criminal

---

[32] Harrington, *Medicine*, pp. 70–104.

leanings, impulsiveness and a susceptibility to mental disturbances. It is almost superfluous to note that the left hemisphere was henceforth seen as the 'masculine' brain-half and the right hemisphere as the 'feminine' brain-half. Many of the findings used to support this distribution of roles were provided by Broca.

It is too simplistic to conclude that Broca was a victim of the prejudices of his day, considering that he was himself one of the architects of those prejudices. Over the years, he held literally thousands of skulls and brains in his hands before measuring and weighing them, and time after time he discovered in the data on volume, weight and circumference precisely those relationships which confirmed the current views pertaining to the intelligence of men and women, and between 'higher' and 'lower' races. In those 12 or 13 ounces of brain tissue, Broca found the neurological arguments which restricted the possibilities for women to enter higher education, and discouraged self-government for 'primitive' peoples. His findings came full circle: by means of the dominant left hemisphere and docile right hemisphere, he reproduced at the cerebral level the existing social relationships between men and women.

Society of Mutual Autopsy

Today, a century and a half later, it is difficult to assess Broca's political and social views, and any attempt to do so using modern coordinates such as 'left' or 'right' is doomed to failure. To begin with, there is the discrepancy between the nature of his findings and his own liberal views: in 1848, the same man who relegated women and 'primitive' peoples to a lower rung of the developmental ladder, founded a society of free-thinkers, and that same year he welcomed the Republic, which took shape literally from one day to the next. From 1870 on, he saw to it that registrarships in his hospital were open to women, and when he was appointed to the Senate in 1880, he showed himself to be a reformist, calling for better health care for the poor, and an educational system for women and girls which was independent of the Church. Broca, who was stridently anticlerical, became the victim of bitter hate campaigns because of his views on the origins of Man. In his own secular manner, he believed in progress driven by biological factors. The fact that the brains of women and uncultured peoples were smaller had been irrefutably demonstrated, but that did not mean that they were not capable of growing in the course of evolution. Civilization – European civilization, at any rate – was capable of promoting that process: the higher the demands placed upon our brains by education and training, the faster they develop. If between the twelfth century of the Celestines and the present day, some 20 or 30 cc had been added to the human brain, and if, moreover, we now knew which factors stimulate its growth, then clearly it was sciences such as neurology and physical anthropology which pointed the way towards true civilization. While there was perhaps no direct line leading from autopsy to utopia, Broca saw in his study of 'the contents of Parisian skulls during various periods' much more than a simple increase in volume. That increase reflected the rise of art, literature, jurisprudence, science, commerce and whatever else distinguished a Parisian of his day from a fellow citizen during more primitive eras. It is a sign of Broca's personal involvement that his signature appears on the charter of yet another society, but one which would not play a role of any importance until *after* his death. The members of the Société d'Autopsie Mutuelle pledged to donate their bodies to science, *in casu* to their colleagues.[33]

No doubt it was a source of pride to Broca that within the science of physical anthropology a Parisian school had formed around his person. But what Broca saw as the secret of this success (exact measurements, where possible performed mechanically, followed by a disinterested, impartial interpretation) is now regarded by Gould

[33] J. M. Hecht, *The End of the Soul: Scientific Modernity, Atheism and Anthropology in France* (New York, 2003), p. 5.

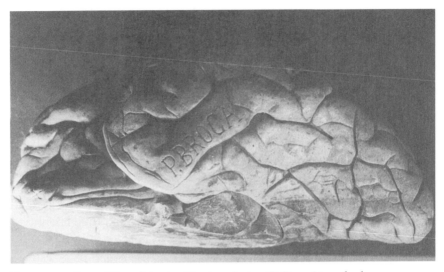

Figure 4.3: Cast of Broca's brain. The inscription 'P. Broca' is etched across the area that bears his name

and other critics as the prime factor behind his failure. There was no such impartiality. Even before the skulls had been anchored in the stereograph or craniograph, the wording of the question was clouded by the bias of the researcher. Is the frontal lobe of women as large as that of men? Is a lower level of civilization reflected in smaller frontal lobes? Through a mysterious gravitational process, the answers to these questions were invariably in line with what the cultured, scientifically enlightened citizen already believed to be the case.

In his analysis, Gould repeatedly points to the methodological errors which, in his view, Broca was guilty of: no 'blind' measurements and no control conditions. This is a reproach which does not entirely do justice to Broca's efforts to ensure that his measurements were as free from human influence as possible. It was by delegating the registration function to instruments that he hoped to exclude every form of bias. It is a tragic footnote to his life's work that such bias managed to creep in elsewhere. Gould, himself a child of the Enlightenment, maintained that as soon as researchers succeed in avoiding methodological errors, their results will no longer confirm prejudices, but rather refute them. Ironically, that was precisely what Broca had expected of his science.

Paul Broca died on 7 July 1880 of heart failure, having just turned 56. In the previous few years, he had encountered several fellow members of the Société d'Autopsie Mutuelle on his dissection table. Now it was his turn to render one final service to anthropology. Broca's laboratory assistant Chudzinski removed the brain of his chief from the skull and made a cast of it. The brain itself was placed in formalin. The cast, with the letters P.BROCA etched across the third convolution of the left frontal lobe, found its way into the collection of the Department of Anatomy at the University of Paris. Seven years after his death, a statue of Broca was erected in the Place de l'École de Médecine: in one hand he held a skull and in the other a pair of callipers. In 1941, the German occupiers had the statue melted down, together with 129 others 'not representing any true artistic or historic interest'.[34]

---

[34] Schiller, *Broca*, p. 291.

FIVE

Sparks from a Leyden jar: Jackson's epilepsy

It would perhaps be an exaggeration to say that John Hughlings Jackson regarded constitutional law as a branch of neurology, but it is not far off the mark. In his version of the human brain, the balance of power between the higher and lower parts mirrored the public order which reigns in a state with a powerful central authority. The government has its seat in the convolutions of the frontal lobes, the part of our nervous system that thinks, takes decisions, and monitors the activities of the lower parts of the brain. As long as the upper parts are able to exert their authority undisturbed, we remain unaware of the activities of the lower parts. When that order is undermined, however, the consequences are disastrous. In an epileptic seizure, for example, the loss of control causes the disinhibition of lower brain parts, resulting in spasms and convulsions. Jackson saw epilepsy as the neurological equivalent of rebellion and anarchy.

Jackson was a Victorian, and very much so. In an article dating from 1884, he compared the upper parts of the brain to the twenty-four admirals who constituted the Navy Board, presiding over a fleet which helped to maintain control over the British Empire.[1] An epileptic seizure, he explained, is like an order given by an admiral who has suddenly lost his mind: chaos breaks out among his subordinates.

[1] J.H. Jackson, 'Evolution and dissolution of the nervous system', *The Lancet*, 1 (1884), 649–52 (649).

Figure 5.1: John Hughlings Jackson (1835–1911)

Thinking in terms of hierarchies was second nature to Jackson, and for him it was self-evident that the hierarchy in our brain was evolutionary in origin. In 1859, the same year that Jackson moved permanently to London, Darwin's *On the Origin of Species* appeared, and the philosopher Herbert Spencer published his theory that higher and more complex brain structures evolve from lower structures, exercising supervision over them. In a healthy brain, order and authority reign.

Six horses abreast

John Jackson was born in 1835, the son of Samuel Jackson and Sarah Hughlings.[2] He grew up in Green Hammerton, Yorkshire. At the age of 15, he was taken on as a pupil by William Anderson, who had a practice in York. He became familiar with the various tasks which were part of a general practice: hand-rolling pills, crushing powders, mixing salves, binding up wounds, splinting broken bones and

---

[2] Until now only one biography of Jackson has been published: M. Critchley and E. Critchley, *John Hughlings Jackson: Father of English Neurology* (Oxford, 1998). See also G. Holmes, 'John Hughlings Jackson (1835–1911)' in K. Kolle (ed.), *Grosse Nervenärzte* (Stuttgart, 1956), vol. I, pp. 135–44.

assisting at deliveries. Two years later, he entered York Medical School. In the middle of the nineteenth century, it was possible to prepare for a medical career by entering a university, but most aspiring physicians attended one of the 'medical schools' which were affiliated with a hospital. In York, Jackson spent many long days bending over a dissecting table. He took courses in chemistry, obstetrics, anatomy and physiology, as well as botany and forensic medicine. Much of his schooling was informal in nature. For example, he learned a great deal from attending the discussions of the Post-Mortem Club in York, where he was a member. Examinations were administered by medical societies: in Jackson's case, the Royal College of Surgeons and the Worshipful Society of Apothecaries. Acceptance as a member was the equivalent of certification. Jackson never studied at a university, and never regretted the fact.

By the time Jackson moved to London in order to continue his training, his interests had broadened to such a degree that he considered devoting himself to a study of literature and philosophy. A lifelong friend, Jonathan Hutchinson, advised him against this course: he would be of more benefit to the world if he became a philosophizing doctor instead. And Jackson followed that advice. His wide-ranging interests were fed by a long career in medical journalism. In 1861, he joined the staff of the *Medical Times and Gazette*, where he reported on important operations, medical discoveries, developments in forensic medicine, and any other subject he deemed of interest to his colleagues. He contributed to this journal for close to half a century. Jackson never authored a handbook, opting instead for short pieces, and a great many of them.[3] His bibliography encompasses over 300 articles, and the list is almost certainly incomplete, since Jackson wrote mainly for smaller journals which are

---

[3] A selection of these pieces appears in J.H. Jackson, *Selected Writings of John Hughlings Jackson*, 2 vols. (J. Taylor (ed.), London, 1931–1932). Part 1 focuses on epilepsy, Part 2 on aphasia and the 'evolution and dissolution of the nervous system'.

today difficult to trace. That his style was verbose is something on which both friend and foe agreed. Jackson was a writer who, having embarked on a sentence, was almost immediately seized by a new association, which was promptly parked between dashes. Shortly after he embarked on the parenthetical phrase, another association presented itself, and was duly ensconced between parentheses, thereby exhausting the conventional punctuation marks designed for embedded phrases. When another association arose during the writing of the phrase in parentheses – which was invariably the case – it was presented in the form of a footnote. But shortly after the beginning of the footnote ... etc., etc. Jackson once confided to a friend that when he was writing, he felt as if he was 'driving six horses abreast, each of which needed continuous attention'. The hapless reader seated in the carriage could only hope and pray that he would reach his destination in one piece.[4]

Jackson's first hospital appointment was at Moorfields Eye Hospital in London, where he developed a lifelong passion for ophthalmology. In 1851, he introduced the ophthalmoscope, recently invented by Helmholtz. Over the years, Jackson discovered that many neurological conditions are reflected in defects of the eye. In 1863, he joined the staff of the National Hospital for Nervous Diseases as assistant physician, with an extra appointment at the National Hospital for the Paralysed and Epileptic. It was around this time that he came to the conclusion that there were a great many John Jacksons around, and decided to take his mother's maiden name as well. His tasks originally included home visits, but these were soon discontinued. Patients were not at ease with Jackson and the feeling was mutual. He was shy and reserved, and never succeeded in refining his bedside manner. For example, he made no effort to remember names: patients were always referred to as 'the man behind the door' or the 'woman with the hammer toe'. As he did his rounds, he avoided patients

---

[4] Quoted in Critchley and Critchley, *John Hughlings Jackson*, p. 48.

for whom he could do nothing and, according to a colleague, he appeared to be somewhat afraid of insane patients.[5]

In 1865, Jackson married his cousin Elizabeth Dade Jackson. They had known each other all their lives and as children had lived next door to one another. Their marriage remained childless, and she died after eleven years. Jackson never remarried, and no one was ever allowed to occupy 'her' chair at the dining table. When his brother and his family dined with him, his wife and children were seated in a long row on one side of the table, leaving Elizabeth's chair empty. It is ironic that Elizabeth suffered from a form of epilepsy which is now known as 'Jackson's epilepsy'.

The brain as battery

In the 1860s, it was assumed that the origin of epilepsy (popularly known as 'falling sickness') lay in a disturbance of the brainstem.[6] That disturbance interfered with the motor system, and led to loss of consciousness and involuntary muscular contractions. Robert Bentley Todd, a neurologist of the generation before Jackson, likened the brain to an electric battery.[7] Epilepsy could be seen as the result of a sudden discharge, comparable to the way sparks sometimes flew from a Leyden jar charged with galvanic energy. He had tested that theory on live rabbits. By inserting wires into the brain and briefly charging them, Todd was able to call up the precise symptoms which were characteristic of an epileptic seizure: convulsions and rolling of the eyes. Jackson was familiar with the work of Todd, but possibly not with this particular experiment. In all probability he

---

[5] G. Savage, 'Dr John Hughlings Jackson on mental disorders', *Journal of Mental Science*, 63 (1917), 316.

[6] O. Temkin, *The Falling Sickness: a History of Epilepsy from the Greeks to the Beginnings of Modern Neurology* (Baltimore/London, 1971).

[7] E.H. Reynolds, 'Todd, Hughlings Jackson, and the electrical basis of epilepsy', *The Lancet*, 358 (2001), 575–7.

developed his own theory on the relationship between electrical discharges in the brain and various types of epilepsy without ever having heard of Todd's rabbits.

But even Jackson's account of the type of epileptic seizure that begins with spasms in a specific part of the body and, following a more or less fixed course, spreads throughout one half of the body, was not the first. As far back as 1827, the Frenchman Louis-François Bravais had published an article on 'unilateral epilepsy'.[8] Jackson always acknowledged the priority of Bravais, and referred to seizures with a focal onset as 'Bravasion seizures'. Jackson's true contribution lay in the fact that he was able to incorporate the electrical source of epileptic attacks and the wide-ranging symptoms of those attacks into a theory which encompassed the functional structure of the nervous system. That structure was tripartite. The spinal cord, the medulla and the pons made up the lowest part and were the seat of simple, reflexive movements. The motor cortex, located in the middle of the brain, guided the more complex movements. The prefrontal cortex was responsible for voluntary, complex movements and such higher functions as thought and consciousness. The hierarchically higher parts 'supervised' the lower parts. According to Jackson, epilepsy was the result of sudden, excessive and rapid discharges of the grey matter on the surface of the brain. When these discharges take place in the pre-frontal cortex, the functions governed by this part of the brain, such as maintaining consciousness, shut down. In addition, the lower parts, which are no longer blocked, become active. Every epileptic seizure, therefore, displays a combination of negative symptoms, such as loss of function, and positive symptoms, such as involuntary muscle contractions.

Jackson's epilepsy is accompanied by discharges on the middle level. The seizure often begins with automatic spasms or a tingling

---

[8] L.-F. Bravais, *Recherches sur les symptômes et le traitement de l'épilepsie hémiplégique* (Paris, 1827).

sensation in one hand, usually near the thumb or index finger. While the discharges continue along the motor strip of the cortex (the 'Jacksonian march'), spasms also occur in other parts of the body. They are restricted to one half of the body. Jackson wrote that autopsies had shown that this type of epilepsy is accompanied by damage to the cortex of the opposite half of the brain. His first publication on the type of epilepsy which would later bear his name appeared in 1863.

Seven years later, Fritsch and Hitzig, the discoverers of the motor strip, noticed that excessively strong stimulation of the brain surface of a dog produced symptoms suggestive of epilepsy. In experiments with apes, the Englishman David Ferrier found that a different type of current, transmitted by an induction wire, evoked specific movements similar to those of epilepsy, such as biting, grabbing or scratching. It appeared that a wide variety of motor reactions were projected onto the surface of the cortex. Ferrier regarded his results as a confirmation of what Jackson had concluded from his own clinical observations, and in 1876 he dedicated his book *The Functions of the Brain* to him.[9] Later EEG studies showed that Jackson's epilepsy did indeed begin with a sudden, spontaneous 'firing' of a cluster of neurons in the motor strip of the cortex, and that this activity spread to neighbouring areas.

Dreamy state of Dr Z

Jackson wrote at length on a variant of epilepsy which is accompanied by what he had heard a patient describe as a 'dreamy state'.[10] Before an imminent seizure, the patient has the feeling that he has entered an altered state of consciousness, from which he cannot

[9] D. Ferrier, *The Functions of the Brain* (London, 1876).

[10] R.E. Hogan and K. Kaiboriboon, ' "The dreamy state": John Hughlings Jackson's ideas of epilepsy and consciousness', *American Journal of Psychiatry*, 160 (2003), 1740–7.

escape as long as the seizure lasts. Jackson located the origin in the temporal lobe. In drawing up his clinical description, he made use of the account of a colleague whom he had been treating for epilepsy since 1877, and whom he referred to as 'Dr Z'.[11] This patient was later identified as Dr Arthur Thomas Myers, associated with Belgrave Hospital in London.[12] Myers came from a prominent English family. His elder brother Frederic was one of the founders of the Society for Psychical Research, a study group devoted to para-normal research. Arthur Myers himself regularly published in the proceedings of the SPR.

In 1870, under the pseudonym Quaerens, Dr Z had briefly described what such a 'dreamy state' felt like.[13] He sought inspiration in the works of contemporary poets and writers, including the following verses from Tennyson's poem 'The Two Voices':

> Moreover, something is or seems
> That touches me with mystic gleams
> Like glimpses of forgotten dreams –
> Of something felt, like something here;
> Of something done, I know not where;
> Such as no language may declare.

In *David Copperfield* (1850) we find Dickens' famous description of what in the 1890s would come to be known as *déjà vu*: 'We have all some experience of a feeling, that comes over us occasionally, of what we are saying and doing having been said and done before, in a

---

[11] J.H. Jackson, 'On a particular variety of epilepsy (intellectual aura); one case with symptoms of organic brain disease', *Brain*, 11 (1888), 179–207. This article contains a detailed account of Z himself, who appears as Case 5. It forms part of a series of neurological accounts involving doctor-patients: N. Kapur (ed.), *Injured Brains of Medical Minds* (Oxford, 1997).

[12] D.C. Taylor and S.M. March, 'Hughlings Jackson's Dr Z: the paradigm of temporal lobe epilepsy revealed', *Journal of Neurology, Neurosurgery, and Psychiatry*, 43 (1980), 758–67.

[13] Quaerens, 'A prognostic and therapeutic indication in epilepsy', *The Practitioner*, 3 (1870), 284–5. From Kapur, *Injured Brains*, p. 360.

remote time – of our having been surrounded, dim ages ago, by the same faces, objects, and circumstances – of our knowing perfectly what will be said next, as if we suddenly remembered it.'[14] Z wrote that as a boy he had experienced such sensations, but that they had become more intense and more frequent during a long period of overwork. On two occasions the sensations were followed by an epileptic seizure, and since then he had interpreted them as a warning that it was time to take things easy. While Dickens seemed to think that everyone has had such experiences, according to Z they were an indication of a disturbance in the brain, the precursor of an imminent attack.

After the *déjà vu*, Z drifted into a passive mental state in which there was a sense that something had occurred to him which he had long been trying to recall; this was accompanied by the sense of relief which such an experience usually evokes. At the same time, there was a vague realization that what had suddenly been 'recalled' was not really a memory, but only something that felt like a memory. Shortly afterwards, the memory of the retrieved 'memory' faded away. Z also noticed that it had become almost impossible to think about something in a focused manner. There was memory loss for familiar names and faces that could last several minutes. Friends told him that in this state he answered every question, no matter how absurd, with a resolute 'yes!'. Once, during a seizure, he had attempted to continue with the text he was working on. When he later reread it, he found that it contained all sorts of strange words which he did not remember writing down. Others told him that during the onset of one attack, he had stamped his right foot several times and made smacking noises, as if he was tasting something. During a vacation in Switzerland, he had had a seizure while hiking across a glacier. Afterwards he realized that he had travelled quite a distance without

[14] For a discussion of theories on *déjà vu*, see D. Draaisma, *Why Life Speeds Up as You Get Older* (Cambridge, 2004), ch. 12.

any recollection whatsoever of having done so. Another time, during a game of tennis, he had had a seizure which went unnoticed by his opponent (his shots were 'no worse than usual') and here, too, several minutes had simply disappeared from his memory.[15] In 1887, Z went to visit a friend. He planned to go by Metropolitan Railway, get off at the fourth stop and walk the last half a mile. At the second stop, a conversation between two fellow passengers gave rise to a *déjà vu*. The next thing he remembered was standing at the door and taking a house key out of his pocket. It was a quarter to one, the exact time that he expected to arrive at his destination. While in the 'dreamy state', he had apparently got off at the fourth stop and walked the rest of the way, just as he had planned. He had no memory of having done so. Once an attack occurred as he was about to examine a young man who suffered from a lung complaint. He had just asked the boy to open his shirt when he felt the attack coming on. After it had passed, he found himself back at his desk, talking to someone else. A little later he remembered the boy and asked what had happened to him. It appeared that he had listened to the boy's lungs, made the diagnosis (pneumonia of the left lung) and immediately confined the patient to bed. A while later, Z visited him and repeated his examination. The diagnosis which he had made during his 'dreamy state' was correct.

On 10 January 1894, Z took an overdose of the tranquillizer chloral hydrate and died.[16] The seizures had become increasingly severe, and in the autumn of 1893 Z was forced to give up his practice. At the age of 42, he saw a once promising medical career come to an end. His interests had been transferred to neuroses and hypnosis, subjects which, according to the 'In Memoriam' in *The Times*, were perhaps

[15] Jackson, 'Particular variety'; Kapur, *Injured Brains*, p. 357. As regards the remark 'no worse than usual', it should be noted that Arthur Myers was on the Cambridge tennis team.

[16] The suicide rate among patients with temporal lobe epilepsy is extremely high, Taylor and March, 'Hughlings Jackson's Dr Z', 759.

not calculated to improve his own mental health. The result was 'a fine intellect in ruin and confusion'.[17] Jackson had witnessed that decline from close by: he and Z were neighbours in Manchester Square.

At Jackson's request, his colleague, Walter Colman, carried out the autopsy. In one of the left convolutions, Colman found a spot where the brain tissue was soft. Together, they drew up a report in which Jackson revisited the peculiarities of the 'dreamy state'.[18] On one occasion he had had an opportunity to observe such a seizure, as Z was at that moment sitting in his surgery. He had suddenly fallen silent, and shortly afterwards he slid onto the floor, then got to his feet holding a thumbtack and pretended that he was trying to prick Jackson with it, after which he appeared to be himself again. To make sure Z was safe, Jackson then accompanied him back to his house. On the way they talked about Jackson's plans to add a room onto his house. The next day Z said he had no recollection of anything which had passed from the moment he entered Jackson's surgery. The fact that immediately thereafter he found himself in his own house led him to conclude that a part of his memory was missing. Jackson also quoted from notes that Z had made during a consultation when he had been overcome by the 'dreamy state'. They resemble the incoherent mumblings of someone talking in his sleep: 'For the last 18 mos years there has been some decided indefinite on R side in dress circle.'[19]

These symptoms fit in with Jackson's theory on the hierarchy within the brain.[20] Dr Z displayed negative symptoms, such as the loss of conscious, concentrated thought, which as a result was not

[17] The 'In Memoriam' appeared in Taylor and Marsh, 'Hughlings Jackson's Dr Z', 760–1.

[18] J.H. Jackson and W.S. Colman, 'Case of epilepsy with tasting movements and "dreamy state": very small patch of softening in the left uncinate gyrus', *Brain*, 21 (1898), 580–90. Included in Kapur, *Injured Brains*, pp. 361–6.

[19] Jackson and Colman, 'Case of epilepsy', 585.

[20] G. York, 'Hughlings Jackson's evolutionary neurophysiology' in F. Clifford Rose (ed.), *A Short History of Neurology: the British Contribution 1660–1910* (Oxford, 1999), pp. 151–64.

stored in his memory. But that same loss also released the positive symptom of actions carried out automatically, such as Z's apparently undisturbed resumption of his trek across the glacier, or his routine-based examination of a patient. In some cases, the loss of inhibition went so far that the patient displayed conduct which in a healthy individual would be downright criminal. This is also known to have occurred during the sickness of Z. Jackson diplomatically refrained from recording exactly what form that conduct took, but in fellow-sufferers an attack was regularly accompanied by a maniacal aggression. The suggestion is clear: without the supervision and control exercised by the higher centres, little good can be expected from the lower ones. Over a century later, it became clear that such aggression and frenzy, the *furor epilepticus*, is often the result of well-intentioned efforts on the part of bystanders to subdue the patient, which due to his confusion are experienced as threatening.[21]

'Pig, brute, stupid idiot!' Mrs B asks if you will please sit down

Again and again, Jackson's research into the neurological substrate of language led him to what seemed to be an inevitable conclusion: the emanations of the brain become base and dangerous when all control from on high falls away. In the 1860s, when Broca was publishing his studies on aphasia, Jackson began collecting case histories of neurological patients with speech disorders. As in Broca's case, these examples ultimately served as arguments in a debate on hemispheric dominance. Jackson would continue to write on this subject for the next thirty years.[22] He shared Broca's conviction that language disturbances are accompanied by damage on the left side, but over

[21] P. Fenwick, 'The nature and management of aggression in epilepsy', *Journal of Neuropsychiatry*, 1 (1989), 418–24.

[22] For a survey of Jackson's views on language disorders, see chapters 12–14 in Critchley and Critchley, *John Hughlings Jackson* and H. Head, 'Hughlings Jackson on aphasia and kindred affections of speech', *Brain*, 38 (1915), 1–27.

the years he had also developed a theory on the neurological representation of language which constituted a radical departure from that of Broca. We know that in 1868, both men took part in a symposium held in Norwich, but there are no surviving reports on a debate between the two leading neurologists of the day, or even a personal meeting.[23] Broca appeared with a diagram and a plaster cast of the brain, so that he was able to point to the exact location of the damage which causes aphasia. Jackson presented conclusions based on over thirty cases of aphasia accompanied by paralysis on the right side. The fact that in a large majority of cases the damage was on the left side did not necessarily mean that this was also the seat of language. In Jackson's view, that particular spot was no more than a kind of gateway leading to the expression of language. While it might well be the site of the obstruction, what had to exit through that gateway was prepared in other parts of the brain, including the right half. Locating the damage which causes the loss of speech is quite a different thing from locating the seat of speech.

Jackson's own theory focused on the language which was *spared* in cases of aphasia. He was intrigued by speech utterances which under certain circumstances were capable of breaking through the barrier thrown up by aphasia. One severely aphasic patient had suddenly turned to his son and asked 'How is Alice getting on?'. Another patient, whose entire vocabulary consisted of 'no!', said to his wife just before he died, 'Five nights, six nights, seven nights, and then five nights out of seven.'[24] Jackson suspected that such utterances were not *caused* by the injury, but rather *were permitted to emerge*. In all probability they originated in the right half of the brain, which for Jackson was the seat of automatic and emotional language. Focused thought takes place on the left, while the emotional charge

---

[23] R.J. Joynt, 'The great confrontation: the meeting between Broca and Jackson in 1868' in F. Clifford Rose and W. F. Bynum (eds.), *Historical Aspects of the Neurosciences* (New York, 1982), pp. 99–102.

[24] Jackson, *Selected Writings*, p. 124.

is added by the right. One of his patients could utter only the word 'no', and even then only when he became excited. If Jackson asked him to say 'no', he was unable to, but when the children started acting up, he would suddenly call out 'no!'. Only once did Jackson get him to utter the word 'no', and that was in answer to the absurd question 'Are you a hundred years old?'. Immediately afterwards the sole remaining word in his vocabulary was again inaccessible.[25] The same held true in the case of an aphasic woman who took fright when she saw a fire in the street across from London Hospital, where she had been admitted, and in panic shouted 'Fire!' – a word that she was only capable of uttering in the agitation of the moment.

But even more often, the word that was spared consisted of a curse or a term of abuse, a phenomenon familiar to French physicians. Jackson recalled the neurologist Jules Baillarger, who in 1865 had noted that in cases of aphasia, 'conscious' reactions are destroyed, while 'spontaneous' reactions are sometimes spared. Another French physician, Armand Trousseau, described the case of Mrs B: 'When visitors were shown in, she stood up and greeted them with a friendly smile. Then pointing to a chair, she said: "Pig, brute, stupid idiot!" A relative then added, "Mrs. B asks if you will please sit down", thus interpreting the wishes of the patient, which had been expressed in such a remarkable fashion.'[26] A portion of the vocabulary appears to be located in a spot in the brain which is not affected by an injury in Broca's area. Jackson claimed that when someone who is healthy begins to curse or swear, he is not actually using language, but rather reinforcing a speech act. A swear word is comparable to raising your voice, or waving your hands around. As an intellectual product, language was primarily the output of the left hemisphere, the brain-half which Jackson saw as the 'elder twin', the one in charge. In view of what the right hemisphere was able to produce under its own steam when there was a disturbance, it was a good thing the left hemisphere had the reins firmly in hand.

[25] Ibid. p. 131.   [26] Cited in F. Bateman, On Aphasia (London, 1890), pp. 201–2.

Dissolution

In the same way, there existed a healthy hierarchy between the two hemispheres of the brain: on the left side order, intelligent thought and control, and on the right side emotions, simple reflexes and other calamities that had to be carefully kept in check. Damage to the brain, the consequences for behaviour and the way in which they were experienced by the patient were regarded by Jackson as a window on the evolutionary history of the nervous system. What could be learned from neurological patients, whether aphasic or epileptic, suggested that the healthy brain was a delicate system of components which alternately block and restrain one another. In cases of disease or damage, Jackson wrote, we see a process of 'dissolution', i.e., the opposite of evolution: when the higher functions are affected, the brain regresses to a more primitive level of functioning. Jackson borrowed the term dissolution from the philosopher, Herbert Spencer.[27] His formulation meanders in inimitable fashion between neurology and politics:

> The higher nervous arrangements evolved out of the lower keep down those lower, just as a government evolved out of a nation controls as well as directs that nation. If this be the process of evolution, then the reverse process of dissolution is not only 'a taking off' of the higher, but it is at the very same time a 'letting go' of the lower. If the governing body of this country were destroyed suddenly, we should have two causes for lamentation: (1) the loss of services of eminent men; and (2) the anarchy of the now uncontrolled people. The loss of the governing body answers to the dissolution in our patient (the exhaustion of the highest two layers of his highest centres); the anarchy answers to the no longer controlled activity of the next lower level of evolution (third layer).[28]

From whence this obsession with control and command? In his masterly study of the concept of 'inhibition', the historian of science,

---

[27] H. Spencer, *Principles of Psychology* (London, 1855).
[28] Jackson, 'Evolution and dissolution', 651.

Roger Smith, demonstrates that Jackson's manner of reasoning is typically Victorian.[29] Evolution was seen as the development of higher life forms out of lower, so that 'new' automatically meant 'higher'. This biological hierarchy was described in the same terms and metaphors as social and political hierarchies, with higher centres that lead, guide and control. Moreover, that hierarchy was seen as the ordering structure *within* organisms, given that the human nervous system also had parts which, in an evolutionary sense, were either old or new. This made the most recent component, the pre-frontal cortex, the seat of the highest psychic functions. It was the 'organ of the mind', a delicate instrument which was easily disturbed, and one that was indispensable to the mental equilibrium of the individual. In the field of neurology, hierarchies, whether high or low, dominant or subordinate, represented the authority of modern science. After a lifetime of clinical studies, all of which seemed to indicate that an infringement of the hierarchical relationship leads inevitably to pathology, confusion, rage, aggression, swearing or, as in the case of Dr Z, criminal actions, Jackson had no choice but to conclude that both the brain and society would benefit from what was already a deep-rooted Victorian ideal: discipline.

Fabric of language

While Jackson enjoyed reading about neurological experiments, such as the electrical stimulation of the brain surface of dogs or apes, he always managed to suppress the urge to experiment himself. In the same way, he was happy to leave microscopic research to others. His strength lay in clinical observation, case studies and, occasionally, if permitted by the moment of death, attendance at a post mortem examination of the brain. This has in no way diminished the universal respect for his work. In 1878, he was made a Fellow of the Royal

[29] R. Smith, *Inhibition: History and Meaning in the Sciences of Mind and Brain* (London, 1992).

Society, and in that same year he co-founded *Brain*, which is still a leading neurological journal. When the Neurological Society was founded in 1886, Jackson was elected president.

A number of his observations, diagnostic signs and explanatory principles are part and parcel of modern neurology. The 'release phenomenon', the notion that a process can be activated when control or restraint from above is withdrawn, is still in general use, even beyond the field of epilepsy research. The visual images accompanying the Bonnet syndrome and the acoustic variant of the condition have been described as release phenomena, as have the tics and cursing which are characteristic of Gilles de la Tourette syndrome. Dreams have also been explained as a product of the nocturnal disinhibition of primitive parts of the brain, such as the brainstem. A macabre release phenomenon is the erection of hanging victims: under normal circumstances, the activity of the nerve structure which regulates swelling is blocked by hierarchically higher structures. Jackson himself regarded automatisms such as those of Dr Z as a prime example of actions which result from loss of control. And yet even after the advent of EEG and imaging techniques, it is still unclear whether they are indeed due to the release of mechanisms which would otherwise not be active, or to the direct activation of neurological circuits.[30] What is clear from that same research is that 'dreamy state'-like symptoms are indeed customarily associated with temporal lobe epilepsy.

In many respects, modern research on aphasia would appear to be closer to the work of Jackson than to that of Broca. According to the historian of neurology, Israel Rosenfield, during the era of Broca and Wernicke something went very wrong in the theorizing on the brain and the mind.[31] With the discovery of the location of all sorts of functions, the myth took shape that the brain is a mosaic of 'centres',

---

[30] Hogan and Kaiboriboon, 'Dreamy state', 1745.
[31] I. Rosenfield, *The Invention of Memory: a New View of the Brain* (New York, 1988).

each connected with a specific function or memory, such as that for words or movements. That myth has promoted a mechanical representation of the brain which, a century later, lives on in the computer metaphor: the brain as an apparatus with fixed circuits and programs. Everything we think and experience is stored in the database of our brain, like a collection of bits in a neural register. Rosenfield attempted to explode this myth by reanalysing several famous case studies, such as that of Broca on 'Monsieur Tan'. He cited details which actually suggest that the disturbance of someone who is, say, unable to read what he has just written is due not to the loss of an isolated function, but rather to the patient's inability to *coordinate* his functions. The conclusion to be drawn from all these revised case studies is invariably the same: it is not a specific 'centre' that has been lost, but the ability to integrate words, images and sounds into a whole which has meaning within the emotional context of, for example, a conversation. Rosenfield sought, and found, support for this view in Jackson and his swearing, cursing aphasic patients. If aphasia was actually the result of a blotting out of the memory for words, then it is a mystery why precisely words like these manage to survive. Like Jackson, he believes that the explanation lies in the fact that the meaning of curses and swearwords is independent of the context: we swear for the sake of swearing, not in order to express a particular thought, which means there is no need to combine the words with a meaning before we utter them. In the case of the woman described by Jackson, who shouted 'Fire!', it is unlikely that out of her entire vocabulary precisely that one word had survived the ravages of her brain damage. It is far more likely that the emotions and the excitement temporarily provided the context in which the woman was able to integrate word and meaning. Once she had calmed down, the word 'fire' was just as inaccessible as it had been before. For Rosenfield, Jackson's interpretation of language as a fabric of thoughts, emotions, sounds and movements is a welcome argument against an all too mechanical representation of the human brain.

Unwittingly, these examples from the work of Jackson also reflect the arbitrariness with which neurologists have made use of the theories and findings of their predecessors. Present-day applications of the release phenomenon are invariably accompanied by a reference to Jackson, but divorced from the social and political associations which he attached to the processes of inhibition and disinhibition. In the same way, the strict moral qualifications which Jackson associated with the activity of 'higher' brain structures, as well as the calm, reasonable control of the left hemisphere over its other half, prone to irrational emotional outbursts, are universally ignored. Neurologists still play politics with their profession (a subject which will be further explored in the final chapter), but they borrow from the work of Jackson only what fits in with the tastes and preferences of the day. It is the fate of all great oeuvres from the past: sooner or later they turn into a pick-and-choose buffet.

Mr Jackson of London

In France, a controversy had raged since the middle of the nineteenth century over the relationship between epilepsy and hysteria. Both disturbances began with a sudden attack, and many of the symptoms were the same, such as loss of consciousness, spasms and frenzy. Jackson himself once maintained that what patients do after a seizure could easily be mistaken for hysteria. Perhaps there was such a thing as 'hystero-epilepsy' after all, a combined form in which the two syndromes could not be distinguished from one another. In Paris, the neurologist Paul Richer, a pupil of Charcot, devoted a brilliant, self-illustrated monograph to this *hystéro-épilepsie*.[32]

Charcot himself attempted to isolate epilepsy from hysteria: he recounted how hysterical patients on his ward tended to imitate the

---

[32] P. Richer, *Études cliniques sur l'hystéro-épilepsie ou grande hystérie* (Paris, 1881).

Figure 5.2: Jean-Martin Charcot. In the background, several of the poses which hysterical patients adopt when imitating an epileptic seizure

seizures of the epileptic patients. He was convinced that Jackson had identified a purely neurological disorder and was deserving of a suitable accolade. That accolade was bestowed on him in 1887. Like many men who enjoy an unassailable position of power, Charcot tended to adopt an air of nonchalance at moments when that power was most visible. This was the case on the occasion when the name 'Jackson epilepsy' was awarded. In one of his *Leçons de Mardi*, he presented an epileptic patient and said:

> Lately, an English savant, M. Jackson of London, has raised this subject and has treated the subject so thoroughly that it has repeatedly happened that I spoke of this disorder as Jacksonian epilepsy and the name has been perpetuated. Such was just. I do not regret it. I have done Bravais a little injustice but in fact the work of M. Jackson is so important that truly his name deserves to be attached to that discovery. If one could link Bravais and Jackson,

the Frenchman and the Englishman, and speak of Bravais-Jacksonian epilepsy that would be more correct; it is true that this would be a little lengthy.[33]

These are seemingly casual words, as if he were simply musing aloud, weighing various possibilities. And yet everyone in the room knew with certainty that at that moment the name of Jackson was permanently attached to the disorder which he had described.

Jackson made use of this honourable eponym on only one occasion, in 1908, in private correspondence.[34] John Hughlings Jackson died three years later, 76 years old. A nephew who had been designated his executor was instructed 'to destroy with his own hands all my letters and diaries and all my case books and all correspondence relating thereto'.[35] He carried out the task assigned to him with the greatest respect for the neurologist, and with no consideration whatsoever for neurology. Almost nothing of a personal nature has survived. Even the casebooks in which Jackson noted his observations have disappeared.

[33] J.-M. Charcot, *Leçons du Mardi à la Salpêtrière*, 2nd edn (Paris, 1892), Part 1, p. 12. Cited from Critchley and Critchley, *John Hughlings Jackson*, p. 65.

[34] Critchley and Critchley, *John Hughlings Jackson*, p. 64.   [35] *Ibid.* p. 188.

SIX

Siberian brandy: Korsakoff syndrome

In the Western world, little is known about the life of Sergei Korsakoff. He never got around to writing his memoirs (he died of heart disease at the age of 46) and the biographical sketches which have appeared outside Russia are brief and lean toward hagiography.[1] The image they call up is that of a much-loved master, excellent teacher and fatherly counsellor, set against a background of overflowing lecture halls and waiting rooms still full of patients close to midnight. The information which is available pertains mainly to the public marks of his career: the dates and locations of his education, training and appointments – all in all, little more than the contents of a modern CV. What remains of Korsakoff in the collective memory of Western history of science consists of a handful of fragments and a gaping void: as if historians had been told to reproduce the memory of a Korsakoff patient.

Sergei Sergeivich Korsakoff was born in 1854 in Guss-Chrustallny, a small town some 250 kilometres east of Moscow. It was named after

[1] A. W. Snjeshnewski, 'Sergej Sergejewitsch Korsakow (1854–1900)' in K. Kolle (ed.), *Grosse Nervenärzte* (Stuttgart, 1963), vol. III, pp. 86–94. See also S. Katzenelbogen, 'Sergei Sergeivich Korsakoff (1854–1900)' in W. Haymaker (ed.), *The Founders of Neurology* (Springfield, 1970), pp. 311–14.

the glass and crystal factory which provided work for many of the inhabitants, including Korsakoff's father. At the age of 10, Sergei left home to study at a secondary school in Moscow. He must have had excellent language teachers, for several of his articles on what came to be known as Korsakoff syndrome were written in flawless German and English. After completing his medical studies, Korsakoff spent his entire career in neurological and psychiatric clinics. It was as a hospital physician that he was awarded a doctorate in 1887, for his dissertation on 'alcohol paralysis' and the other physical and mental effects of alcoholism. When a psychiatric clinic was opened at the University of Moscow the following year, Korsakoff, by then professor of neurology, accepted an invitation to take over as director.

There is an odd tension between his psychiatric and his neurological work. In Russia, his reputation is based not only on the syndrome that bears his name, but also on his pioneering attempts to humanize the care of psychiatric patients. He advocated a form of nursing which did not include bars on the windows, straitjackets, or any other physical restraints. He was not a proponent of sleep therapy or rest cures. Patients were better off living in small communities in the country, under the supervision of psychiatrists. Sedatives should be used to calm patients, not to keep them in a permanent soporific state. Such views met with resistance among doctors and nurses: the lack of physical restraints meant that greater demands were placed upon those caring for patients.

At the same time, Korsakoff believed that all forms of mental illness can ultimately be traced to a disorder of the nervous system, and that patients can only be cured by following a neurological trajectory. The specific memory disorder which he had observed in many of his patients, not only alcoholics, but also people who had never touched a drop, was in his eyes yet another confirmation of the theory that psychological disorders can always be traced to damage to the nerves.

The first publication devoted to this disorder appeared in a Russian journal in 1887, under the title 'On a polyneuritic psychosis with a singular disturbance of concentration and pseudo-reminiscences'. According to Korsakoff, polyneuritis caused both acute confusion and pseudo-reminiscences, due to the patient's tendency to mistake his fabrications for actual memories. This initial description of the condition was followed in 1889 by an extensive article in the *Revue philosophique*.[2] In 1890 and 1891, three more articles appeared in German psychiatric journals.[3] These platforms were all well chosen, for at the time it was not English, but rather French and German which predominated in the fields of psychiatry and neurology. Moreover, the *Revue philosophique* was edited by the neurologist, Théodule Ribot, which meant that Korsakoff was almost assured of a favourable assessment. In 1881, Ribot had published his monumental monograph on memory disorders, *Les maladies de la mémoire*.[4] No doubt Korsakoff felt he could count on a warm welcome for an article which he entitled 'Étude médico-psychologique sur une forme des maladies de la mémoire'. And, more importantly, one which contained a clinical confirmation of Ribot's own conclusions. The article opened with a case history.

[2] S. Korsakoff, 'Étude médico-psychologique sur une forme des maladies de la mémoire', *Revue philosophique*, 28 (1889), 501–30.

[3] S. Korsakoff, 'Über eine besondere Form psychischer Störung, combinirt mit multipler Neuritis', *Archiv für Psychiatrie und Nervenkrankheiten*, 21 (1890), 669–704; S. Korsakoff, 'Eine psychische Störung, combinirt mit multipler Neuritis (Psychosis polyneuritica seu Cerebropathia psychica toxaemica)', *Allgemeine Zeitschrift für Psychiatrie und psychisch-gerichtliche Medicin*, 46 (1890), 475–85; S. Korsakoff, 'Erinnerungstäuschungen (Pseudoreminiscensen) bei polyneuritischer Psychose', *Allgemeine Zeitschrift für Psychiatrie*, 47 (1891), 390–410. An English translation of the second German article dating from 1890 appeared in 1955 in M. Victor and P. I. Yakovlev, 'S. S. Korsakoff's psychic disorder in conjunction with peripheral neuritis: a translation of Korsakoff's original article with brief comments on the author and his contribution to clinical medicine', *Neurology*, 5 (1955), 394–406.

[4] Th. Ribot, *Les maladies de la mémoire* (Paris, 1881).

Figure 6.1: Sergei Sergeivich Korsakoff (1854–1900)

Really nothing wrong

On his travels to Siberia, a 37-year-old Russian writer had got into the habit of drinking large quantities of brandy. Alcohol abuse, Korsakoff hastened to add, was one of the major causes of polyneuritis. Friends noticed that his memory was deteriorating, and that each morning he had to be reminded of his plans for the day. They also saw that his gait was becoming unsteady. On 25 June 1884, the man drastically curtailed his intake of alcohol. He gave no reason for this decision, and his friends speculated that his memory was now so poor that he even forgot to drink. That night he slept badly: he was agitated, repeated his questions over and over, and did not want to be left alone. In the days that followed, his agitation increased and it was clear to those around him that he could no longer remember anything. He barely slept.

Korsakoff saw the patient on 30 June. The first thing he noted was that the patient had absolutely no recollection of things which had just happened. He did not know if he had eaten or not, or whether he had had any visitors that day. Everything that happened more than five minutes before was immediately erased. When reminded of something that had just taken place, he remarked that he had always had a poor memory. However, memories of events before his illness were still intact. For example, he recalled that in June he had started a short story. He had got over half-way, but could no longer remember how he had planned to end the story.

Later, when the crisis had subsided, the writer became adept at pretending that there was really nothing wrong. His reasoning was perfectly logical, and he conversed with friends on a wide range of subjects, relying on the 'intellectual capital which he had acquired over the years'.[5] In actual fact, Korsakoff wrote, the circle of his thoughts had become quite narrow. If he was interrupted, he immediately lost his train of thought, and often repeated what he had just said, with the identical phrasing and the identical intonation. It struck Korsakoff how stereotypical his sentences were: a particular impression always evoked the exact same cliché, presented in a tone which suggested that it had just occurred to him.

And Korsakoff saw something else. Despite his memory loss, the man appeared to have stored traces of his experiences, 'no doubt in the unconscious sphere of psychic life'.[6] The patient had never met Korsakoff before he fell ill, and claimed at each visit that he did not know him, neither his name nor his face, but from the beginning he was aware that he was talking to a doctor. Equally striking was the fact that the patient could give a detailed description of events which had never taken place. He described exactly where he was the day before, and if someone pointed out to him that those details were a figment of his imagination, he refused to believe them. It was not long afterwards that paralysis of the limbs and the respiratory muscles set in, ultimately leading to the death of the patient.

Korsakoff had recorded the same pattern of symptoms in a number of other patients. It was invariably the 'old' memories that were preserved. This sometimes gave rise to bizarre situations: one patient

[5] Korsakoff, 'Étude', 503. [6] Ibid.

was very good at checkers, but only minutes after the board was removed, he denied that he had just played checkers, and even claimed that it had been ages since his last game. Another patient, a former anatomist, was capable of describing, in almost pedantic detail, the exact structure of the vascular system in a particular part of the body, and yet had no recollection of an event which had taken place 15 minutes before. These patients also had a poor memory when it came to their own mental processes: they forgot what they had just said, and embarked on the same rambling story for the tenth time in the space of an hour. One of them would sit for hours with the same page of the newspaper in front of him, and every few minutes he was struck by the same amusing item, which he promptly read aloud: 'Écoute donc, maman.'[7] 'During a session of electrotherapy lasting less than ten minutes', Korsakoff wrote, 'another patient told me at least five times that at secondary school he was afraid of electricity and always fled from the physics laboratory. Each time this information was repeated, in the same stereotypical wording, it was as if he was telling me something new. I knew beforehand that as soon as I placed the electrode on his skin, he would say, "Oh, electricity! I've always been frightened of electricity", etc., etc.'[8]

Another characteristic symptom, especially in the early stages of the disease, is the habit of confabulating: patients would fill in the gaps in their memory with made-up stories. Although bedridden for months, they cheerfully recounted where their walk had taken them the day before. Due to the disorientation in time and the absence of any recent memories, patients had no idea how long they had been in the institution, and often underestimated their own age. Because they took their reminiscences for recent memories, they lived in the past, referring to the people around them by the names of old friends or family members long since deceased.

[7] *Ibid.* 509.   [8] *Ibid.*

Korsakoff's patients themselves were largely unconcerned. They dismissed their memory problems, did not consider themselves ill, and did not grieve over the loss of so many memories. Most of them viewed their problems with indifference, although there were those who were afraid they might have said something unpleasant or improper.

Once the fearful agitation of the early stages had passed, the patient gradually regained the ability to think calmly and logically. But there was little or no restoration of memory. Initially, some patients would read the same passage again and again without realizing they had read it before. 'Recovery' usually meant that they finally recognized the passage, but were unable to recall the contents. One of Korsakoff's patients, a lawyer, recovered sufficiently to work as a corrector for a newspaper. He had no trouble locating the errors, but had to mark carefully each line in pencil, since otherwise he would have read the same line over and over. He later returned to the law, where he managed to cope by relying on commonplaces and past routine.

Korsakoff's explanation for the peculiar selectivity of this memory disorder – the disappearance of recent experiences and the survival of 'old' memories – was in keeping with the description given by Ribot in *Les maladies de la mémoire*. When cells are activated by a stimulus, they undergo a change which ensures that the following activation of those cells is not only faster, but also evokes the original experience. Memories are connected by 'association paths', and the more paths there are leading to a particular memory, the greater the likelihood that that memory will be reproduced. According to Korsakoff, the poisoning of the nerves weakens the fixation powers of nerve cells, but in his view the root of the problem lay in the damage to the association paths. In many cases, the memories have been recorded, but the ability to access them has been lost: they are still present as fragile, latent traces which are capable of influencing behaviour without entering the consciousness of the patient. 'Old' memories escape this fate, because they were recorded via numerous associations, have been repeated more often, and are more automatic, making them easier to recall. But these memories, too, are difficult for the patient to interpret, because his powers of association are impaired. He is unable to give them a place within his present experience, he doesn't know which period or situation they pertain to, whether the event or situation is something which he experienced, or dreamt, or made up. They become ghostly snatches of events which float in and out of his consciousness. In one of his Russian articles, Korsakoff referred to a woman who was fond of describing a trip to Finland she had taken before she became ill, but intertwined with this description were her recollections of a journey to the Crimea. As a result, she described a Finland populated by Tatars, whose diet consisted mainly of lamb.

Following his article in the *Revue philosophique*, Korsakoff published several German-language pieces on the medical aspects of the psychological disorder which he had identified. The fact that they were all submitted to psychiatric journals was no coincidence, as the condition was scarcely known among psychiatrists. General practitioners and gynaecologists, by contrast, were familiar with it, as it often occurred as a complication of other maladies, such as poisoning or childbed fever. This also explains why the disorder had not been described in detail: physicians focused on the primary illness and failed to notice the secondary one. The psychological symptoms present together with the physical complaints arising from polyneuritis: paralysis, cramps, oedema, atrophy of muscle tissue, unstable gait, double vision and reflex paresis. The disease begins with a crisis:

> The patient cannot rid himself of obsessive, anxious thoughts; he expects something terrible to happen – either death, or some kind of seizure, or a catastrophe he cannot give a name to. He is afraid to be alone, constantly entreats people not to leave him, while groaning and lamenting his fate. At times there are wild shouts, near-hysterical episodes during which the patient is capricious, upbraids the people around him, throws things at members of the household, and beats

his chest. The agitation is particularly severe at night; patients are usually sleepless and disturb the sleep of others; they constantly call for help, demanding that someone stay with them, help them to change position, entertain them, and so on.[9]

Korsakoff wrote that other physicians had occasionally drawn attention to this memory disorder, the first of whom was Magnus Huss.[10] This Swedish physician had introduced the term 'alcoholism' back in 1849, and described the memory disorder as one of the complications of that condition. What Korsakoff first brought to the attention of physicians was the fact that the disturbance also occurs as a side-effect of or together with polyneuritis, which is *not* due to alcoholism. He himself had already described fourteen cases in which the nerve damage was caused by other diseases, such as typhus, tuberculosis and childbed fever, and various forms of poisoning, including arsenic, lead, tainted grain and carbon monoxide. Even a foetus in a state of decomposition had caused a young woman to suffer from this type of memory loss. Korsakoff suspected that in all these cases the poisoned blood had given rise to neuritis, often in the brain. He gave this psychological disturbance a name which neatly sums up the causal course of the condition: cerebropathia psychica toxaemica: brain disease as a result of blood poisoning. In his own Moscow clinic, a female patient suffering from this disease had just died, and the autopsy revealed that almost all the nerves were inflamed.

All the strings that have ever vibrated

A nervous system ravaged by inflammations was still able to retain memories from the past. What it could not do was to store new experiences. Korsakoff's patients found themselves on the edge of

---

[9] Quoted from the translation by Victor and Yakovlev, 'Korsakoff's psychic disorder', 397.
[10] Korsakoff, 'Psychische Störung', 483.

an empty plain, where each subsequent footprint would immediately be erased. And those memories that did surface from the patients' past were no longer reliable. The things they thought they remembered, which *seemed* to be memories, were often fabrications. Apparently, these patients had lost the ability to identify the source of their thoughts and ideas. Things they had once dreamt, read, heard or imagined returned to their consciousness in the guise of personal memories. These 'pseudo-reminiscences', as Korsakoff dubbed them, varied from patient to patient, but were almost always of an ominous or morbid nature. Korsakoff noticed that they often had to do with death. Patients said that someone had just passed away or that they had recently attended a funeral; they mentioned the name of the deceased and the church where the services had taken place. Pseudo-memories of this type were often recounted by patients who had been, or still were, close to death. Such memories could develop into a delusion, causing intense agitation. In the autumn of 1889, Korsakoff was called in for a consultation on just such a case.

P was a 53-year-old businessman.[11] He had a strong constitution, was a moderate drinker, and his health was good up until 21 August 1889, when he caught typhus. For three weeks he ran a high fever. When on 15 September the fever finally subsided, he was disoriented, his speech was incoherent, and his memory, which had previously been good, was seriously affected. He almost immediately forgot whatever was said to him. Until late September he lay in bed, subdued and silent. After he had recovered some of his strength, the family noticed that his memory began to improve, but also that he began to relate things that could only have sprung from his imagination. P told them that someone had died, that somewhere there was the body of a man, and that it had to be buried. He returned to the subject again and again. As long as he was too weak to even leave his bed, the family listened to him and tried to put his mind at rest. But as he began to

[11] Korsakoff, 'Erinnerungstäuschungen', 395–9.

recover, the stories became increasingly agitated and insistent. There was a young man who had once done him a favour and now he was dead and he felt obliged to see that he was given a decent burial. Initially, he thought the deceased was somewhere in the house. Later the story changed, and P said that he was sure the body was in Medynzeff's house on Pokrovski Boulevard, and that arrangements had to be made for the funeral. The family was faced with a dilemma. P's memory had largely recovered, he was lucid, and his condition was much improved. However, that one isolated delusion remained, and there was no way they could talk him out of it. At their wits' end, they decided that the only solution was to go to the house in question, so that he could see for himself that there was no body there. When they arrived, P called the concierge over to the carriage and inquired about the deceased. Korsakoff: 'Naturally, the concierge was quite surprised and said that no one in the house had died. The patient returned home, and for a long time remained sunk in thought. He then proceeded to adjust his delusion. He now claimed that the dead man had already been buried and it was his duty to take care of the cost of the grave and the funeral expenses. This thought likewise took possession of him, and every day, especially towards evening, he began to insist that his family go with him to pay the amount that was due.'[12]

All this took place around the middle of October. On 21 October, Korsakoff had an opportunity to examine the patient himself. His first impression was that P had made a complete recovery. He knew where he was and that a physician had come to see him. He knew which doctor had treated him, and also that he had been seriously ill. It was only after the interview had gone on for some time that it became clear that his memory was still quite deficient. During the conversation he repeated himself on several occasions, and had no idea what he had done earlier that day. Korsakoff, too, was treated to an account of the unpaid bill. P had rented the house himself, there was some

[12] *Ibid.* 396–7.

relationship between the young man and his children, and he felt obliged to pay the funeral expenses, which came to such and such an amount. All these details were recounted calmly and quietly. The situation at home, however, was quite different, as Korsakoff heard from the family. When the man started going on about the bill, he became so agitated that it was difficult to calm him down. They also told Korsakoff that P's delusion might be related to an event that had taken place some eight years before. The patient's children had contracted some deadly disease and had to be nursed in a special house, which P had rented himself and which was not far from Medynzeff's house. The children survived the disease, and returned home.

Shortly after Korsakoff's visit, the situation became intolerable. P had recovered to such an extent that he could not be deterred from carrying out his plan. The family then devised a ruse: the concierge at the Medynzeff house agreed to tell P that the person he was looking for had moved away. He would then give him the address of the physician who was treating him. There, too, the residents were aware of the ruse. When P left Medynzeff's house and arrived at the physician's door, he was told that the man he was looking for was not at home, but had left instructions for him to accept the money. P paid him and returned home quite satisfied. After a few days, however, he became restless again. He insisted on going back to Medynzeff's house just one more time: he had left some of the young man's belongings there and had to see to them. After several visits, he was informed that Medynzeff had gone abroad and would not be returning in the foreseeable future. It was only then, in January 1890, that the delusion was laid to rest. Apparently P had concluded that his story contained a number of inconsistencies, and he did not return to the subject. In fact, he would not allow anyone else to discuss the matter either. The only reminder of his delusion was a burning desire to travel abroad. The destination which he had in mind was the city where Medynzeff was supposedly living.

Korsakoff believed that P's delusion was an indication that memory traces never entirely disappear. In the depths of one's memory, beyond consciousness, they form associative links with other traces. In P's case, the mortal danger in which he found himself may have become bound up with memories of the life-threatening illness from which his children had suffered. This strange construct of erroneous associations, together with one or two realistic fragments, then took shape in his consciousness, at a time when it was too weak to correct the misrepresentation of the facts. Here was proof that the vibrations of neurological traces never totally die out. In this light, Korsakoff concluded, no matter how serious the memory loss, in every patient there is something that is characteristic of him, something in which, despite all the damage, he remains himself: 'In his soul, there is the quiver of all the strings that have ever vibrated, a gentle echo of every thought he ever had. They are not all equally strong, and – keeping to the metaphor – unlike sounds may emerge, or different melodies, but the timbre of the melodies remains the same.'[13]

Thiamine

In 1897, Korsakoff organized the Twelfth International Medical Congress in Moscow. In the section Neuropsychiatry, he was the recipient of fraternal praise from Friedrich Jolly, professor and director of the Berlin mental hospital the Charité.[14] Jolly observed that the mental disorders accompanying polyneuritis had on occasion been described, but nowhere as systematically and graphically as by Korsakoff. After Korsakoff, any institutional physician was capable of recognizing a syndrome which previously had barely been noticed. Apparently, this also held true for Jolly himself. In December 1891,

[13] Ibid. 405–6.
[14] F. Jolly, 'Über die psychischen Störungen bei Polyneuritis', Charité Annalen, 22 (1897), 579–612.

shortly after the appearance of Korsakoff's German articles, he began keeping a record of all the patients admitted to his institution with a diagnosis of polyneuritis. Between then and September 1897, he recorded a total of sixty such patients. Many of them had a history of alcoholism, but there were also four cases of acute arsenic poisoning following a suicide attempt. Some twenty-two patients were found to be suffering from a delirium. After the disappearance of the delirium, they reported no memory problems. In nineteen patients there were signs of the memory disorder described by Korsakoff. But there were also nineteen patients *without* any memory problems. This was hardly a clear picture: polyneuritis could present with or without a memory disorder, and in exactly the same number of patients. Moreover, Jolly had two patients without neuritis who did have the memory disorder. Apparently, all combinations were possible, so that at this point it was difficult to draw any conclusions about the cause of the neuritis or the memory disorder, or the relationship between them. In such cases, Jolly maintained, it is better to formulate the description in as neutral a manner as possible: 'If the proposal is accepted to refer to this state as the Korsakoff complex of symptoms or – even shorter – the syndrome of Korsakoff, then we now have a simple term for a characteristic syndrome, a term which is not bound up with an attempt at a hypothetical explanation, thereby simplifying the subsequent discussion.'[15] Thus, the name of the condition was not to be cerebropathia psychica toxaemica, but rather the Korsakoff syndrome. After Jolly, Korsakoff syndrome became increasingly detached from the neuritis and is now generally confined to the memory disorder.

As regards the probable cause, Jolly and Korsakoff were in agreement. The memory disorder was not a direct consequence of alcohol, arsenic, lead, or any other poisonous substance. It seemed more likely that poisonous substances had brought about some metabolic change, producing a secondary, as yet unidentified, substance which

[15] Jolly, 'Psychischen Störungen', 595.

was responsible for the self-poisoning. Jolly could simply not conceive of any other explanation. And no doubt this was quite literally the case, for physicians who trained in the 1870s were totally unfamiliar with the concept of a deficiency disease. There was only one exception, and that was scurvy, which could be cured by means of sauerkraut or fruit. Given the symptoms which Korsakoff had identified, it was more logical to think in terms of an infection or a poisoning rather than a deficit.

That same inability to think in terms of a deficiency played a role in the investigation of a disease which in certain respects tallied with the symptoms recorded by Korsakoff and which, moreover, had an interesting connection with the Dutch Indies.[16] With the advent of steampowered mills in the 1870s, it became possible to remove the so-called silver skin surrounding each rice kernel. In the course of time, the native population, who were dependent on rice, developed a disease which they referred to as beriberi. In 1879, the Dutch physician Van Leent noticed that Indonesian sailors suffered from beriberi, while the Dutch members of the crew were spared.[17] He concluded that rice contained a poisonous substance which became concentrated in the body and ultimately gave rise to the disease. No such substance has ever been found. But in the 1890s, the bacteriologist Christiaan Eijkman discovered that the silver skin which was removed during polishing contained a substance which *prevented* the occurrence of neuritis. By feeding chickens polished rice, he succeeded in generating polyneuritis experimentally, and then curing it by feeding them unpolished rice. In 1911, the physiologist Funk isolated a substance which cured polyneuritis in birds: by combining the words 'vita' and 'amine', he characterized this substance as essential for life. In 1936, thiamine, one of the vitamins of the B group, was synthesized. In clinical studies, Korsakoff patients responded well to high doses of

---

[16] B. A. Blansjaar, *Alcoholic Korsakoff's Syndrome* (Leiden, diss., 1992), p. 1.
[17] F. J. van Leent, 'Über Beri Beri', *Allgemeine Wiener Medizinische Zeitung*, 24 (1879), 446.

thiamine. It appeared that Vitamin B1 was for Korsakoff's disease
what vitamin C was for scurvy, although thiamine supplementation
could not entirely cure the memory disorder.

The critical role of thiamine was also borne out by research involving patients who were not getting sufficient vitamin B1 as a result
of conditions other than alcoholism or disease. In 1947, a study was
published focusing on the symptoms of prisoners of war in southeast
Asia, who had contracted beriberi as a result of malnutrition.[18] They
were admitted to a Singapore hospital, where it was determined that
they had begun to suffer from serious memory problems some six to
fourteen weeks after being taken captive.

Today, Korsakoff-like symptoms have been described in connection with a whole series of conditions associated with a thiamine
deficiency, including excessive vomiting during pregnancy, diseases
of the digestive tract, and anorexia. Korsakoff syndrome may also
present as a complication of a hunger strike or even a stomach
reduction. The human body is incapable of storing vitamin B1.
When it does not enter the body or cannot be absorbed, memory
problems can occur within a matter of months. The Russian author,
the woman who thought Finland was full of Tatars, the Moscow
businessman searching desperately for the body of his friend, and all
Korsakoff's other patients, whether alcoholics or not, were simply
suffering from a lack of vitamin B1.

During the 1980s in Australia, various initiatives focusing on prevention were considered.[19] The fact that the typical Korsakoff patient
was a beer drinker led physicians to consider the practical solution
of adding thiamine to beer. However, they never succeeded in raising
the necessary support for this move. Dieticians were against the
suggestion on principle: it was simply wrong to add something good

---

[18] H. E. de Wardener and B. Lennox, 'Cerebral beriberi (Wernicke's encephalopathy): review of 52 cases in a Singapore PoW hospital', *The Lancet*, 1 (1947), 11–17.

[19] A. S. Truswell, 'Australian experience with the Wernicke-Korsakoff Syndrome',
Addiction, 95 (2000) 6, 829–32.

to a substance you want people to consume less of. Beer brewers were afraid it would alter the flavour and pointed out that because of their poor memory, Korsakoff patients were not the most reliable inform- ants with respect to their alcohol consumption. It was decided to add thiamine to bread, a step which had already been taken in most developed countries. This was not done specifically for the benefit of Korsakoff patients: it was found that the processing of wholemeal flour to white flour was accompanied by a vitamin loss that had to be compensated for. The result was a drastic reduction in the number of new Korsakoff cases. It is unlikely that we can rid the world of Korsakoff's disease by means of bread alone. As long as brewers see no future in beer containing thiamine, an Australian physician reflected, there can be no focused prevention.

Wernicke-Korsakoff

In the medical literature dating from before Korsakoff, there are easily ten or twelve different descriptions of patients who would today be diagnosed as Korsakoff patients. None of those authors have ever been honoured with an eponym. There is no syndrome of Hooke (1680), or D'Assigny (1697), or Lawson (1878).[20] Priority is an over- rated factor when it comes to discoveries. Of these three, the most promising candidate is Robert Lawson, a physician at the Lunatic Hospital in Exeter.[21] He published an article in the newly founded journal *Brain* which focused on three separate types of mental disor- ders traceable to chronic alcohol abuse. One of these is a form of 'dementia' accompanied by an 'almost absolute loss of memory for recent events'.[22] Even on the doctor's third visit of the day, the

---

[20] These candidates are mentioned in a survey article by M. D. Kopelman, 'The Korsakoff syndrome', *British Journal of Psychiatry*, 166 (1995), 154–73. German or French authors nominate others in turn.

[21] R. Lawson, 'On the symptomatology of alcoholic disorders', *Brain*, 1 (1878), 182–94.

[22] Lawson, 'Symptomatology', 183.

patient will deny ever having laid eyes on him before. Lawson sought the explanation in a malnutrition of the brain: the starved and shrivelled brain cells were no longer able to retain impressions. He had obtained good results with meat extract.[23] Lawson's article appeared in 1878, over ten years before Korsakoff's first publications on the subject. But if we compare the two, it is immediately clear that Korsakoff not only had a better hand, he also played it more skilfully. The condition which Lawson documented was described as one of several mental disorders which may arise from the excessive use of alcohol, while Korsakoff focused on that single disorder. Lawson's notes covered a scant two pages, and he provided only a few examples of typical memory loss. Korsakoff, on the other hand, presented elaborate case histories featuring patients who come alive for the reader, like characters in a novel. In examining the memory loss of each patient, he noted details such as what was spared 'in the unconscious sphere', aspects which Lawson did not notice or at least did not mention. Lawson's views on the subject were confined to that one article in a neurological journal, whereas Korsakoff embarked on a veritable campaign, in Russian, French and German. He targeted not only neurological and psychiatric journals, but also the widely read *Revue philosophique*. Unlike Lawson, Korsakoff interwove his hypotheses on cause and course with the existing theories on memory traces, such as those of Ribot. In other words, Korsakoff positioned his observations within a much broader geographical and disciplinary network, and kept the memory of his contribution alive by means of the association paths within that network.

The same could be said of the German neurologist Carl Wernicke. In 1881 (again well before Korsakoff) he described a disease which often accompanied chronic alcoholism and was characterized by three symptoms: acute confusion, visual problems (including double

---

[23] Meat does indeed contain relatively high amounts of vitamin B1.

vision and eye tremors), and an uncertain gait.[24] Known as the triad of Wernicke, these symptoms pointed in the direction of a disease he called 'encephalopathy' (which later came to be known as 'Wernicke's disease'). Some of the symptoms corresponded to those which Korsakoff had seen in his own patients, but in his publications he had not made the connection with the work of Wernicke. That would not happen until half a century later. In the acute phase of the illness, many Korsakoff patients have visual problems and experience difficulty walking, while Wernicke patients respond better to thiamine supplements than Korsakoff patients. In the 1980s, the theory that Wernicke's disease marks the crisis-like onset of what will ultimately develop into Korsakoff's syndrome, and that the two syndromes actually represent different stages of the same disease, led to the contraction 'Wernicke-Korsakoff syndrome'. This theory has since lost much of its appeal, and the current view is that the two syndromes can develop independently of one other. A patient may suffer from Korsakoff syndrome without having gone through the Wernicke stage, while the triad of Wernicke is not always an ominous portent of Korsakoff's. However, there does appear to be a genetically determined vulnerability to both diseases. There are a great many more chronic drinkers than there are Korsakoff or Wernicke patients and, according to the latest insights, this is due to the fact that in certain patients a thiamine shortage is quicker to result in damage to certain enzymes.[25]

Unconscious sphere of psychological life

Scattered throughout Korsakoff's case studies are numerous examples of a phenomenon which he appears to have found intriguing: no

---

[24] C. Wernicke, *Lehrbuch der Gehirnkrankheiten für Ärtze und Studierende* (Kassel, 1881).

[25] L. C. Heap *et al.*, 'Individual susceptibility to Wernicke-Korsakoff syndrome and alcoholism-induced cognitive deficit: impaired thiamine utilization found in alcoholics and alcohol abusers', *Psychiatric Genetics*, 12 (2002), 217–24.

matter how deep the memory loss was, the patient was often capable of registering an experience. The traces of that experience ended up in a layer of memory which was not accessible to his consciousness, but was nevertheless capable of influencing his mood, his associations and his reactions. For some time Korsakoff had been treating one of his patients with a 'Dr Spamer electric shock machine', by which a galvanic shock could be administered. When he entered the room, he asked the patient if he knew why he had come. The man said that he had no idea. Korsakoff asked him to look at the table, where he had deposited the closed box containing the device. With an uncomfortable glance at the box, the man ventured a guess that he had probably come to treat him by means of electricity. Korsakoff was certain that the man had never seen such a device prior to his illness. Apparently, there was such a thing as an 'unconscious sphere of psychological life'.

Korsakoff drew this conclusion on the basis of his observations during daily contacts with patients: the first time he came in they held up a hand in greeting. If he came in again five minutes later, they said that they hadn't seen anyone for hours, but no greeting was forthcoming. In 1907, the Geneva psychiatrist Édouard Claparède attempted to demonstrate empirically that what he called the 'unconscious memory' was still partially intact in Korsakoff patients.[26] But how can you test memory when the whole problem is that the reproduction function is defective? Claparède opted for the 'saving method', a technique introduced by Ebbinghaus in 1885. Instead of asking the patient to reproduce something directly from memory, he set out to establish how much less effort was required to learn something for the second, third or fourth time. Claparède's subject was a 47-year-old Korsakoff patient who was hospitalized in 1900. She displayed the

---

[26] É. Claparède, 'Expériences sur la mémoire dans un cas de psychose de Korsakoff', *Revue Médicale de la Suisse Romande*, 27 (1907), 301–3. Claparède's article was published in an English translation: S. Nicolas, 'Experiments on implicit memory in a Korsakoff patient by Claparède (1907)', *Cognitive Neuropsychology*, 13 (1996) 8, 1193–9.

classic symptoms: her previous knowledge was still present, she knew all the capitals of Europe by heart, but could not say what she had done that day or what year it was. One day, Claparède showed her a card containing ten arbitrary words, and asked her to read them. After reading them once, she was able to reproduce two words. Having read the list again, she could remember four. After going over the list five times, she could reproduce seven of them. When Claparède repeated the test the following day, she could remember seven words after reading the list twice, and a day later after only one reading. One month, two months, and ten months later, she was capable of reproducing seven words after one reading. All this time, the woman did not recognize Claparède, and could not remember ever taking part in a test involving words. And yet she had less and less difficulty 'learning' from the list. Equally striking was the fact that, while she was unable to repeat something that had been said to her, when Claparède forced her to make a guess, she often guessed right. One day, he had told her a story about a 64-year-old woman who was bitten by a snake while herding her sheep. The following day, when he asked her about the story, she couldn't remember anything about it. Claparède insisted, telling her that it was about a woman, and asking if she remembered how old the woman was. 'Wasn't she 64?', the patient said, quickly adding that she could just as well have said something else. For Claparède these results provided support for the dissociation theory formulated by Pierre Janet, a philosopher studying unconscious processes, who in his day was just as influential in the French-speaking world as Freud. While the patient was not capable of assimilating her memories in her consciousness, they did have some influence on her thinking and the way she experienced things.

These days, Korsakoff patients are popular subjects for experiments which focus on what since the 1980s has been known as 'implicit memory', the type of memory which is spared even in serious cases of memory loss, despite the fact that it is not directly accessible. What in Claparède's case was a passing observation became an experimental technique in the research focusing on implicit memory: forced guessing. The subjects are not capable of actively reproducing anything, but they do guess right more often than can be explained by pure chance. Nursing staff can make use of this secret power of learning. By housing subjects in fairly small communal units, it is possible to slowly introduce routines which promote the ability to manage on one's own. There are even some non-recurring experiences for which the anterograde amnesia which defines Korsakoff syndrome is not absolute. There are indications that events which give rise to strong emotions in patients, and which for that reason may activate other parts of the brain than emotionally neutral memories, are nevertheless stored. Researchers have established that seven months after the event, two out of three Korsakoff patients knew what had happened on 11 September 2001.[27]

If Sergei Korsakoff had reached the age of retirement, he would have experienced the isolation of vitamins and the recovery from polyneuritis in animals. But that was not to be. In the midst of a successful career, surging full-steam ahead as a physician, author and researcher, but with an insidious heart condition, Korsakoff died in 1900 at the age of 46.

---

[27] I. Candel, M. Jelicic, H. Merckelbach and A. Wester, 'Korsakoff patients' memories of September 11, 2001', *Journal of Nervous and Mental Disease*, 191 (2003) 4, 262–5.

SEVEN

Go to hell, idiot! Gilles de la Tourette syndrome

The year 1893 was an *annus horribilis* for Georges Gilles de la Tourette. On the night of 15 August, Jean-Martin Charcot died suddenly – the man who had been his master and patron at La Salpêtrière in Paris. The week before, Gilles de la Tourette had visited him in Neuilly, where he had a holiday home. Together they had gone over the proofs of *Traité clinique et thérapeutique de l'hystérie*, in which Gilles de la Tourette described the insights into the origin and treatment of hysteria which he had gained at La Salpêtrière.[1] The two men had been very close. That same year, Gilles de la Tourette lost his young son Jean to meningitis, while on 6 December he was involved in an incident that could easily have cost him his life.[2]

It was early evening when a woman dressed entirely in black rang the doorbell of his apartment. He was not at home at the time, and his manservant opened the door. She asked to speak to Gilles de la Tourette, and the servant let her in and asked her to wait. Shortly afterwards, when Gilles de la Tourette arrived home, she followed him into his surgery, pulled out a piece of paper bearing the names

---

[1] G. Gilles de la Tourette, *Traité clinique et thérapeutique de l'hystérie d'après l'enseigne-ment de la Salpêtrière*, 3 vols. (Paris, 1891–1895).

[2] Biographical information can be found in A. J. Lees, 'Georges Gilles de la Tourette: the man and his times', *Revue Neurologique*, 142 (1986), 808–16. See also P. Guilly, 'Gilles de la Tourette' in F. C. Rose and W. F. Bynum (eds.), *Historical Aspects of the Neurosciences* (New York, 1982), pp. 397–415.

Figure 7.1: Georges Gilles de la Tourette (1857–1904)

of the Salpêtrière physicians Luys and Charcot and told him that because of them she was ruined. She then demanded 50 francs. Gilles de la Tourette suggested to the woman, who was clearly disturbed, that it would be better if she were admitted, in his personal care. At this point the woman went into a rage, pulled out a pistol and fired three times. Having thus assured herself a place in the annals of neurology, she sat down again, announcing that she had finally obtained satisfaction – 'At least one of them has now paid for the others' – and calmly awaited her arrest.[3]

It was thanks to a quirk of fate that none of the bullets, including one in the neck, hit any vital organs, and Gilles de la Tourette survived the attack. A police inquiry established that the woman, the 30-year-old Rose Kamper, had previously been admitted to La Salpêtrière. At her trial, Kamper claimed that while under hypnosis she had been ordered to carry out this crime. At the time there was a controversy going on among French psychiatrists about whether there was indeed such a thing as 'criminal suggestion'. Charcot and Gilles de la Tourette had addressed this question by experimental means: their conclusion was that patients under hypnosis could not be induced to carry out criminal acts, and that their moral powers of

[3] Lees, 'Gilles de la Tourette', 813. The description of the attack is taken from this article.

judgement remained intact. The prime spokesman for this view was Gilles de la Tourette. In a newspaper interview just two days before the incident, he recounted that since 1887 he had been challenging his opponents to come up with a single instance in which someone committed a crime while under suggestion. Now it would seem that the single instance had appeared on his doorstep.

However, the preliminary investigation showed that hypnosis had played no role in the incident, and Rose Kamper's defence was rejected by the judges. However, she was declared of unsound mind and admitted to the closed ward of the mental hospital Sainte-Anne. There she embarked on what might be called a long and turbulent career in psychiatry. Several years later she again tried to kill someone, this time a nurse. In 1910, she managed to escape. When the police succeeded in locating her, she was working as a seamstress under her maiden name. By then, her mental state had markedly improved and it was not considered necessary to admit her. In extreme old age, however, she again began to suffer from paranoid delusions, and it was deemed safer to have her confined again. She spent her final years at Sainte-Anne, and died in 1955 at the age of 92.

Chaos of the choreas

But if truth be told, there had always been something 'not quite right' about Gilles de la Tourette himself. From childhood on, he had suffered from a lack of equilibrium, and in his later years, after spending most of his professional career ministering to psychiatric patients, he became so disordered that he himself had to be admitted. Georges Albert Edouard Brutus Gilles de la Tourette was born in 1857 in St Gervais-les-Trois-Clochers, a village in the west-central region of France. At secondary school he was described as hyperactive and troublesome, but also as extremely intelligent, the type of student who could easily have skipped a year. He began his medical studies

Figure 7.2: In 1893, Rose Kamper attempted to murder Gilles de la Tourette

at the university in Poitiers at the age of 16, and three years later he departed for Paris, where he passed his GP exams. As Wordsworth tells us, the child is father to the man: Gilles de la Tourette was not only creative and versatile, he was also impatient, easily distracted, and forever becoming embroiled in controversies and polemics. All his life, he was more inclined towards interruptions than quiet conversation, and altercations rather than a courteous exchange of views among colleagues. His voice was hoarse, shrill and loud, and was known to get on people's nerves. But Gilles de la Tourette (who himself said 'I'm as ugly as a louse, but I'm very intelligent') also made close friends in Paris, such as the physician and draughtsman Charles Richer, with whom he founded the celebrated journal *Nouvelle Iconographie de la Salpêtrière*.[4] Gilles de la Tourette also made a name for himself outside the field of neurology, as a theatre critic,

---

[4] Cited in Guilly, 'Gilles de la Tourette', p. 400.

for example.[5] In 1884, Charcot invited him to join his department at La Salpêtrière, and two years later he took his doctoral degree with a dissertation on movement disorders in diseases of the nervous system. In 1887, he married his cousin Marie Detrois. In that same year, Charcot asked him to become his scientific secretary, a position which he eagerly accepted. From then on, he took the minutes of the clinical lessons and patient demonstrations which played such an important role in the instruction at La Salpêtrière.

As a researcher and therapist, Gilles de la Tourette took on whatever came to hand. In the 1880s, that included an as yet undifferentiated practice of neurology and psychiatry, which encompassed diseases like Parkinson's and multiple sclerosis, alongside such disorders as delusions of grandeur and hysterical paralyses. The forms of treatment varied from surgery and electric shocks to hypnosis and cold showers. Gilles de la Tourette made his own contribution to this repertoire. In one of his lectures, Charcot spoke of successfully treating Parkinson patients by means of a shaking chair and a vibrating helmet devised by Gilles de la Tourette.[6] Charcot compared the helmet to the last which was commonly used by hat-makers, except that it was connected to an electromotor. Some 6,000 revolutions a minute were sufficient to make the head vibrate slightly. The gentle humming had a soporific effect, and after a ten-minute session around 6 o'clock in the evening, the patient was usually assured of a good night's rest. The therapeutic helmet was not only employed in cases of sleeplessness, but had also been known to nip a migraine headache in the bud. Gilles de la Tourette (who was taking the minutes) supplemented Charcot's lesson with the remark that fifteen sessions of a quarter of an hour on alternate days had been known to cure or alleviate the symptoms of neurasthenia, depression and impotence.

[5] H. Stevens, 'Gilles de la Tourette and his syndrome by serendipity', *American Journal of Psychiatry*, 128 (1971) 4, 489–92.

[6] G. Gilles de la Tourette, 'Considérations sur la médicine vibratoire: ses applications et technique', *Nouvelle Iconographie de la Salpêtrière*, 5 (1892), 265–75.

Figure 7.3: The 'vibrating helmet' which Gilles de la Tourette designed for the treatment of neurasthenia, insomnia and depression

While today, Gilles de la Tourette is remembered mainly for 'his' syndrome, his true passions were hysteria and hypnosis. He regarded the three-volume *Traité clinique et thérapeutique de l'hystérie* as his major accomplishment. It is a comprehensive account of hysteria down through the ages, including drawings based on medieval works of art (suggesting that the disorder has always been with us); overviews of organic complaints related to hysteria, such as epilepsy and migraines; a breakdown of the relationship between hysteria and such factors as gender, age, education and religion, and diseases like syphilis, diabetes, typhoid fever and arthritis. Alongside lengthy dissertations on triggering factors, including alcohol, mercury, tobacco and chloroform, the author presents the results of measurements such as the number of vibrations per second in hysterical tremors, and how they differ from the tremors accompanying Basedow's disease, as well as dozens of graphs showing the results of urine analyses before, during and after the hysterical attack, and much more. The monograph is based on many years of comparative and experimental research, precise statistical analyses flawlessly executed according to the methodological insights of the day. And yet in the collective memory of Gilles de la Tourette, 1,800 pages on hysteria are eclipsed by two, perhaps three articles on a subject which only briefly captured his imagination.

In 1884, Charcot asked him to bring some 'order to the chaos of choreas'.[7] The word chorea (literally 'dance') was a collective term for abrupt involuntary movements. Its best-known manifestation was 'Sydenham's chorea', a condition described in 1686 by Thomas Sydenham whereby the patient makes compulsive, dance-like movements. In 1881, before moving to Paris, Gilles de la Tourette had translated an article by the American neurologist George Beard about a curious movement disturbance.[8] While in Maine, Beard had come across a group of French lumberjacks at work and noticed how, when given an order, the men jumped up as if they had taken fright at something and compulsively repeated the order, to the accompaniment of spasmodic muscular movements. Gilles de la Tourette was intrigued by these 'jumping Frenchmen of Maine'. Two other publications he had seen contained accounts of phenomena which appeared to refer to the same disorder. In Malaysia, the tics were called '*latah*', while American naval officers stationed in Siberia had seen people making spasmodic movements, known as '*myriachit*', which were similar to those of the lumberjacks described by Beard. In 1885, Gilles de la Tourette published an article on a nervous disorder characterized by uncoordinated movements and accompanied by echolalia and coprolalia.[9] It consisted of nine case descriptions. The first concerned a patient he had not himself examined, and whom he had never even seen, as she died in 1884.

---

[7] Cited in Lees, 'Gilles de la Tourette', 810.

[8] G. M. Beard, 'Experiments with the "jumpers" or "jumping" Frenchmen of Maine', *Journal of Nervous and Mental Disease*, 7 (1880), 478–90.

[9] G. Gilles de la Tourette, 'Étude sur une affection nerveuse caractèrisée par de l'incoordination motrice accompagnée d'echolalie et de coprolalie (jumping, latah, myriachit)', *Archives de Neurologie*, 9 (1885), 19–42, 158–200. A large portion of the article appeared in an English translation: C. G. Goetz and H. L. Klawans, 'Gilles de la Tourette on Tourette syndrome' in A. J. Friedhoff and T. N. Chase (eds.), *Gilles de la Tourette Syndrome* (New York, 1982), pp. 1–16. The quotations are taken from this translation.

Marquise of Dampierre

The original account was then already 60 years old.[10] The author was Jean Marc Itard, a physician on the staff of the Institute for Deaf-Mutes in Paris. In 1825, he described the sorry symptoms of the marquise of Dampierre, then 26 years of age. As a girl of 7, she had developed tics which took on increasingly grotesque forms. Later, she began to utter strange cries, often curses and obscenities. This 'coprolalia' became permanent: until her death at the age of 85, she continued to greet her guests with a loud 'merde!' and 'fucking pig!' Gilles de la Tourette copied Itard's description verbatim. As a young girl, the marquise was much troubled by involuntary movements. While she was tracing the letters of the alphabet, her hand would suddenly shoot out. Punishment only made matters worse. When she reached puberty and the disturbance had still not disappeared, she was sent to a clinic in Switzerland. After a year of milk baths, she returned home, apparently cured. She married and for the next year and a half she was free of tics and grimaces. But then quite suddenly they returned, more intense than before. In his account, Itard notes with some surprise that the married state did not improve her condition. Among medical men it was generally thought that women's complaints had a tendency to disappear within conjugal relations. He suggested that perhaps the marquise ought to have had children: 'The patient, never having given birth to a child, has been deprived of the physical and emotional benefits ordinarily provided by the state of maternity.'[11]

[10] J. M. G. Itard, 'Mémoire sur quelques fonctions involontaires des appareils de la locomotion, de la préhension et de la voix', *Archives Générales de Médecine*, 8 (1825), 385–407. See, for Gilles de la Tourette's use of this case, H. I. Kushner, 'Medical fictions: the case of the cursing marquise and the (re)construction of Gilles de la Tourette's syndrome', *Bulletin of the History of Medicine*, 69 (1995), 224–54.

[11] Itard, 'Mémoire', 704. Cited from the translation by Goetz and Klawans, 'Gilles de la Tourette', p. 3.

The swearing and cursing led to embarrassing situations, for the marquise herself and for all those present. In the middle of a conversation, she would let fly words and cries which contrasted 'deplorably with her distinguished manners and background'.[12] Itard found the explanation provided by the marquise herself the most plausible: 'The more revolting these explosions are, the more tormented she becomes by the fear that she will say them again; and this obsession forces these words into her mind and to the tip of her tongue so that she can no longer control them.'[13]

Gilles de la Tourette had heard all these particulars from others, and perhaps for this reason he added: 'Professor Charcot saw this patient on several occasions and personally witnessed her movements and vocalizations. Until quite advanced in years she still manifested her incoordination and continued to say obscene words even in public places.'[14] The wording employed here borders on misrepresentation. Charcot had seen her once, and even then not in the medical sense of the word. On his way to the Salon, he was on the stairs when he suddenly heard an elderly lady call out 'sacré nom de Dieu', and it was then that he recognized the marquise. For Gilles de la Tourette, this was sufficient: Charcot had sanctioned his diagnosis with a retrospective confirmation.[15]

The irony of this particular case is that of all the patients described by Gilles de la Tourette, the marquise is the only one who displayed the complete range of symptoms which today lead to a diagnosis of Tourette syndrome. Each of the eight patients whom he personally observed had only some of the symptoms. There was SJ, who made grimaces and repeated words obsessively. When the arrival of Charcot was announced, he shouted 'Voilà Monsieur Charcot.

[12] Itard, 'Mémoire', 704. Cited from the translation by Goetz and Klawans, 'Gilles de la Tourette', p. 3.
[13] Itard, 'Mémoire', 704. Cited from the translation by Goetz and Klawans, 'Gilles de la Tourette', p. 3.
[14] Gilles de la Tourette, 'Étude', 711.   [15] *Ibid.* 708.

Monsieur Charcot. Monsieur Charcot!', while twisting his body into the strangest contortions. He was unable to suppress the swearwords, even in the presence of his mother, whom he was very fond of. On one occasion they had been forced to leave a restaurant when other guests complained about his obscene shouts. And then there was GD, aged 15, who barely escaped a whipping from other children who thought that his repeated shouts of 'bastard!' were aimed at them. Another boy had been through the German siege of Paris in 1870, during which a bomb exploded next to him, killing his friend; since then he was constantly plagued by nervous, convulsive movements. A girl of 15 from an impeccable family (although she did have an aunt who was 'bizarre, almost a lunatic') repeatedly called out 'Go to hell, idiot!', to the astonishment of her family: where on earth had she heard such curses and swearwords? When absolutely necessary, she was able to contain herself for a short period, but afterwards she sought out a quiet spot where she could let herself go. Other patients constantly blinked their eyes, jumped to their feet, stuck out their tongues, cried out or barked. None of them displayed all these phenomena, but according to Gilles de la Tourette, the syndrome formed a clear typology, one in which the accent was clearly on the strange tics.

Gilles de la Tourette was convinced that the condition was heredi-tary. One of the patients 'had a mother whose mental state became very peculiar during pregnancy', while others had grandparents who suffered from migraine headaches, an extremely nervous father, or a sister with similar tics, in addition to the girl with the strange aunt.[16] No fewer than five of the nine patients came from a family in which nervous diseases occurred. The tics only disappeared during sleep. And according to Gilles de la Tourette, that sleep was exceptionally deep and calm, no doubt because the tics took so much out of the sufferers during their waking hours. Some patients were able to

---

[16] Cited in the translation by Goetz and Klawans, 'Gilles de la Tourette', p. 4.

suppress the tics for short periods. Patient Ch 'was a government clerk who regularly visited clients in their offices. If the interviews were very brief, he could completely suppress his movements. But soon afterwards, the control which he had obtained at great mental cost evaporated, and the movements returned with greater violence than usual. His body was contorted, and he made strange tongue movements and jumped up and down in front of the house of the client whom he had just left. He was eventually obliged to give up his job.'

Equally noteworthy was the irrepressible tendency to imitate others, not only the words that had just been spoken, but also noises, movements and gestures. Gilles de la Tourette could make a patient clap his hands simply by suddenly clapping himself, or get him to take off his coat by doing so himself. In a courtyard at La Salpêtrière, he had witnessed how people took advantage of this urge to imitate others. One of the patients went up to S, raised his right arm and right leg, and started hopping around on his left leg. S imitated this action so enthusiastically that he came to fall. The nursing staff had to intervene in order to put an end to this dangerous 'game'. Other authors also noted the urge to imitate others. A naval officer recalled a steward who was the innocent victim of passengers who made grunting noises, suddenly clapped their hands, or threw their hat down on the deck.

The last symptom to appear is the coprolalia, which involves cursing, swearing and shouting obscenities. Gilles de la Tourette had no clue as to the origin of this habit. He wrote that it was not too difficult to understand how a boy of 19 might have obscene fantasies which he expressed in words, but he had no explanation for the fact that women, young girls and well-brought-up young men also shouted obscenities. Of his nine patients, five suffered from coprolalia. As in the case of echolalia, the obscenities appeared when the tics were at their most violent, and the bottled-up tension was at its height.

Figure 7.4: Georges Gilles de la Tourette, standing behind Jean-Martin Charcot

Gilles de la Tourette believed the disorder to be incurable, referring to it as 'a deplorable companion throughout life'.[17] This was a somewhat rash generalization, considering that the only thing that pointed in that direction was the case of the marquise. The eldest of his own patients was 24. The course would be progressive, with an unpredictable alternation of mild and extreme episodes. In its most violent form, the disease made the patient's life almost unbearable, interfering with schooling and work. Fortunately, however, there were also milder forms, while even in the most severe cases there were periods when the symptoms subsided and the patient was able to lead a more or less normal life: 'His friends and neighbours often adjust well to the involuntary obscenities; for instance, a lieutenant continued on active duty in spite of his prolific involuntary swearing.'[18]

Charcot was quite pleased with the research carried out by his pupil, and endorsed the neurological origin of the disorder. He had seen strange tics in his hysterical patients, but had succeeded in banishing them by means of hypnosis. This proved impossible

[17] *Ibid.* p. 12.   [18] *Ibid.* p. 13.

where the tics of Gilles de la Tourette's patients were concerned. Charcot proposed that 'la maladie des tics convulsifs' be called 'la maladie des tics de Gilles de la Tourette'. This was later changed to the 'syndrome of Gilles de la Tourette', in the Anglo-Saxon literature shortened to 'Tourette syndrome' (TS). Charcot was, of course, aware that Jean Marc Itard was the first person to describe this disorder. Why, then, was *he* not honoured with the eponym? It is perhaps an oversimplification to say that Itard was not a pupil of Charcot and, moreover, had been dead for some time. Hughlings Jackson was not one of Charcot's pupils either, and Parkinson had been dead for over half a century when Charcot bestowed the eponym upon him. In his policy on awards of this type, Charcot was clearly not led by that particular type of chauvinism. What he honoured in the work of Gilles de la Tourette must have been the attempt to distinguish a specific category of motor and verbal tics from other motor disturbances. And it goes without saying that in awarding the eponym, Charcot defined the boundaries of the disorder in keeping with his own insights.

Confidences of a tiqueur

At the end of his article, Gilles de la Tourette wrote: 'As for the underlying lesion, we have found no anatomic or pathologic cause. One can, by looking to psychology, try to interpret some of the symptoms, and we could recommend for those who wish to approach it from this vantage to refer to the interesting book by Monsieur Ribot, *Les maladies de la volonté*.'[19] At the time, Théodule Ribot, professor at the Collège de France, was the most prominent French advocate of the degeneration theory; his work on 'diseases of the will' appeared in 1883.[20] The concept of degeneration was introduced by Morel in the same year that Gilles de la Tourette was born.

---

[19] *Ibid.* pp. 14–15. [20] Th. Ribot, *Les maladies de la volonté* (Paris, 1883).

It manifested itself in a wide variety of symptoms, such as retarded mental powers, hysteria and epilepsy, but also in heightened impulsiveness and weakness of will. According to this theory, it is that weakness which plagues patients suffering from Gilles de la Tourette: their tics, shouts and curses are unleashed because the will is no longer functioning. Quite literally, they cannot help acting on impulse.

It was at this point that the syndrome of Gilles de la Tourette left the realm of neurology and entered the domain where it would remain until the 1970s: that of psychiatry and psychology. The event that triggered this departure was the publication in 1902 of a book entitled *Les tics et leur traitement*, by the physicians Meige and Feindel.[21] It opened with a curious document. The authors had already completed their study when one of them happened to come across a '*modeltiqueur*', whom they described as a 'living compendium of almost all known tics'.[22] This patient, a certain Mr O, recounted his life story in a series of lengthy and candid conversations, and Meige and Feindel decided to include the account of his life in their opening chapter under the title 'Les confidences d'un tiqueur'. It is a revealing document, not so much for the 'confidences' of O, but for the subtext, which reveals how a patient with tics interpreted his own story. In this self-portrait, he sketches the psychiatric regime to which such patients were condemned.

O was a 54-year-old businessman with a keen intellect and a strong constitution, who excelled in numerous sports. But, like his grandfather, brother and son, he suffered from violent tics. For Meige and Feindel, this was a clear case of hereditary taint: his grandfather and grandmother were first cousins, and there was a high incidence of asthma in the family, as well as a large number of stutterers. In the case of O, the tics began when he was 11 years old. He recalled that as a child he had a marked tendency towards imitation. Then, one day he saw an old man making grimaces: he started practising and finally

---

[21] H. Meige and E. Feindel, *Les tics et leur traitement* (Paris, 1902). [22] *Ibid.* p. 5.

he was able to give a perfect imitation. But what began as deliberate movements soon began to appear of themselves, even against his will. They became permanent and he later developed more and more tics. He had a continual urge to touch his lorgnette, which he was forever removing, closing or adjusting. He would sit for hours fiddling with his hat, to the benefit of his hat-maker, since he needed a new one every five or six weeks. During the French-German war he signed up for military service, and one day a new colonel came to inspect the troops. As the officer came closer, O found it impossible to stand to attention, with his head motionless and his gaze directed towards a spot fifteen paces away. 'And the longer the colonel stood there, inspecting me, the more grimaces I made. Things were clearly going the wrong way for me. When our own captain, who knew me, took my side, and declared that despite my involuntary grimaces, I was an excellent soldier, the colonel wouldn't hear of it. He sent me to the hospital and two weeks later, to my intense disappointment, I was declared unfit for military service due to "compulsive movements of the face".'[23] The tics only stayed away when he was concentrating, for example, just before his turn at billiards or when he was fishing and got a bite. Because his movements were hurried and brusque, he had a tendency to break things.

O also had a difficult time psychologically. He described himself as impatient and easily frustrated: nothing ever went fast enough for him. When he spoke, his words seemed to tumble over each other, writing was too slow for him, and in the end he resorted to dictation and was forever complaining that his secretary didn't write fast enough to suit him. Sometimes he was so frustrated that it was difficult not to lash out at others. It was a constant battle against his own impulses: 'There are two men in me: the tiqueur and the non-tiqueur. The former is the son of the latter, an unpleasant child and the cause of much concern to his father. He knows he should take

---

[23] *Ibid.* p. 7.

strong measures against him, but as a rule he is unable to do so, enslaved as he is by the whims of his offspring.'[24] O was the victim of a whole series of compulsive disorders. There were certain streets he felt compelled to take, while others were off limits. He suffered from arithmomania, an obsessive love of counting, and every time a carriage passed in the street, he felt compelled to count the ciphers in the carriage number. He was a hypochondriac, and believed that he was suffering from the most deadly diseases. Sometimes the idea of committing suicide occurred to him. He would stand at the side of the road, waiting for a carriage to approach and had to exercise enormous control to keep from dashing across the street just in front of the horse's nose. Thoughts of committing suicide are quite common among tiqueurs, according to Meige and Feindel, but fortunately the will is often too weak to actually carry out the deed.

Echolalia and coprolalia did not feature in O's list of symptoms, at least not openly. According to Meige and Feindel, he did display a covert form of coprolalia: the argot or thieves' slang in which he often expressed himself. He immediately apologized for using such language, but when the words formed in his mind, he could not help uttering them: the urge was simply stronger than he was. According to the authors, the tendency towards coprolalia is something that most people are to some extent familiar with. It is the vulgarity of certain expressions that makes them so appealing. Good manners usually prevent us from speaking them aloud. 'But among individuals whose will is out of balance, the suppression doesn't always come in time: the offending word is spoken before the inhibitory reflex has been activated.'[25] Lack of control and will power is a recurring element, not only in the commentary of Meige and Feindel, but also in O's own account. He is uncertain whether he has sufficient perseverance to conquer his tics: 'I am a tiqueur and I will always be a tiqueur.' His doctors add that in many respects O is still a

[24] *Ibid.* p. 11.   [25] *Ibid.* p. 26.

child, powerless in the face of the urges which arise within him. One feature which O has in common with all tiqueurs is his 'infantile mental state'.[26] Tell him to hold his tongue and he starts shouting, order him to sit still and he begins to wave his arms around. These patients never know where to draw the line, even when it comes to drinking and smoking. O responded to stomach pains like a 'nervous, ill-brought-up child'.[27] This created the breeding ground for infantility and weakness of will in which mental abnormalities flourish.

Writing on psychotherapy, the Dutch sociologist De Swaan coined the concept of 'protoprofessionalization', i.e., the tendency of patients or clients to formulate their symptoms or complaints in the jargon of the expert.[28] Imperceptibly they also adopt the psychiatric orientation of their practitioners. O's account is a touching example of this phenomenon. In his own perception, he is not the victim of a neurological or organic disorder, but rather a weak-willed individual. Everything that he recounts concerning his most intimate impulses and associations reflects the prevailing psychiatric view on the disastrous consequences of a degeneration of will power and control. O met his physicians more than half-way. Meige and Feindel in turn regarded their own interpretation as legitimized: if an intelligent patient, after an honest and impartial self-examination, acknowledges that he is weak-willed, then that conviction must lie at the very heart of the disorder. They expressed their satisfaction with the 'perfect agreement' between the insights of their model patient and the findings which they and other researchers in the field of tics had recorded.[29] There was equally heartfelt agreement between O and his physician on the moral reprehensibility of the individual suffering from this condition.

[26] *Ibid.* p. 25.   [27] *Ibid.* p. 29.
[28] A. de Swaan, 'Professionalisering en protoprofessionalisering' in A. de Swaan, R. van Gelderen and V. Kense (eds.), *Sociologie van de psychotherapie II: Het spreekuur als opgave* (Utrecht, 1979), pp. 17–24.
[29] Meige and Feindel, *Tics*, p. 45.

Leeches, showers and straitjackets

The historian of psychiatry, Howard Kushner, is the author of a history of Tourette syndrome.[30] It reads in places like a horror story. Itard, in his own account of the trials of the marquise of Dampierre (1825), writes that he was called in on a similar case, this time a young lady who was prey to strange, involuntary movements. He obtained good results with large quantities of chicken soup, a three-hour bath twice a day, and the placement of a dozen leeches on her vagina. The latter measure was presumably based on a suspicion that an unstable uterus might be the cause of her strange behaviour. The children whom Gilles de la Tourette saw had already been subjected to experiments with unusual remedies and forms of treatment. They had to endure lengthy showers, were sent to the country in an attempt to soothe their nerves, or were given a variety of tranquillizers – all to no avail. Not even an 'electrotherapeutic bath' (La Salpêtrière had facilities for various types of electrotherapy) had provided relief.

Gilles de la Tourette himself experimented with forced isolation and 'hydrotherapy', including ice-cold showers, but was forced to acknowledge that he had no effective therapy to offer. Doubtless it was with a sigh of resignation that he admitted that Beard, with his 'once a jumper, always a jumper' theory, was probably right.[31] Later generations of neurologists and psychiatrists contributed to the therapeutic arsenal such procedures as 'immobilization' (i.e., straitjackets), lobotomy and electroshocks. Tourette patients have been cut, shaken and struck, countless hours have been spent just talking to them, and every conceivable form of psychotherapy, from psychoanalysis to behavioural therapy, has been unleashed on the syndrome – but in vain.

---

[30] H. I. Kushner, A Cursing Brain? The Histories of Tourette Syndrome (Cambridge MA, 1999).
[31] Goetz and Klawans, 'Gilles de la Tourette', p. 10.

Figure 7.5: La Salpêtrière had a Laboratory for Electrotherapy where patients suffering from a wide variety of conditions were treated with static or galvanic electricity

Even today, Tourette syndrome remains a mystery. The disorder begins around the age of seven, usually with grimaces and blinking.[32] This is followed by motor tics and, in severe cases, by the parroting and coprolalia which can lead to social isolation, and are in themselves a source of considerable stress.[33] Many patients are hyperactive or suffer from obsessive-compulsive neuroses. The disease is chronic, but follows an irregular course, while fatigue and stress can aggravate the symptoms. Studies involving twins point in the direction of a

---

[32] An extremely extensive monograph is that of A. K. Shapiro, E. S. Shapiro, J. G. Young and T. E. Feinberg (eds.), *Gilles de la Tourette Syndrome* (2nd edn, New York, 1978). See also the survey article by M. M. Robertson, 'Tourette syndrome, associated conditions and the complexities of treatment', *Brain*, 123 (2000), 425–62.

[33] Coprolalia occurs in some 15 per cent of Tourette patients.

genetic susceptibility to Tourette. As in the Asperger syndrome, men are overrepresented by a factor of about four to one. Brain scans and EEGs seldom reveal abnormalities. In Gilles de la Tourette's day, the syndrome was quite rare, while today's estimates place the incidence at 30 to 50 cases per 1,000 children aged 13 or 14. Moreover, it is a diagnosis which is increasingly being made. The fact that this relatively high proportion of cases is not reflected in the street scene probably has to do with the alleviating effect of medication and the tendency of Tourette patients to avoid public places.

Possible explanations for the origin of Tourette syndrome have been forthcoming from virtually all the specializations within neurology and psychiatry. It could be due to a bacterial or viral infection which went unnoticed, or to an auto-immune reaction, i.e., the neurological damage is caused by the individual's own immune system. In other versions, Tourette is caused by forcing naturally left-handed children to become right-handed. Freud himself believed that Tourette had an organic cause, while his Hungarian pupil Sandor Ferenczi favoured a psychoanalytic explanation in which the patient's jerky movements were a symbolic expression of masturbation, resulting from the repression of erotic impulses.[34] A curious detail is the fact that Ferenczi based his study on the case history of O, although he had never had an opportunity to observe any of the patients he described. In his view, a better guarantee of absolute impartiality was hardly imaginable.

With intense effort, Tourette patients often succeed in temporarily suppressing their tics and shouts, and this has given credence to the view that the disorder is psychiatric rather than neurological in nature. The fact that the actual words used by the patient are often racist or insulting, suggesting a clear realization of the social context, has contributed to an interpretation in which the origin of the

---

[34] S. Ferenczi, 'Psycho-analytical observations on tics', International Journal of Psycho-Analysis, 2 (1921), 1–30.

syndrome lies in other than organic factors. Following the publication of the monograph by Meige and Feindel, the condition was to remain outside the domain of neurology for almost three-quarters of a century.

That development also marked the disappearance of the eponym Gilles de la Tourette from the medical literature. The combination of symptoms which had formed the syndrome were now categorized as 'psychogenic chorea', 'obsessive-compulsive neurosis', habit spasms, hyperkinesis, or even the old 'Sydenham's chorea', the condition which in 1885 Gilles de la Tourette had so painstakingly distinguished from 'tics convulsifs'. In the case histories dating from this period, a number of which are presented by Kushner, there is no shortage of misery. Therapists tell parents that their son has tics because he is suppressing the impulse to masturbate or, conversely, because he masturbates to excess. Mothers are told that their daughter developed tics because she was brought up in an overprotective environment, or, alternatively, because they have tolerated the excessive mobility of their child far too long: during the pre-school period sons and daughters were allowed to run to their heart's delight, and now it is too late to teach them self-control. The British neurologist Kinnier Wilson once proclaimed during a lecture that 'the association of fond parents and a spoilt child is too frequent an antecedent to the development of a tic in the latter to be a mere coincidence. Sometimes one glance at the mother or father of the youthful tiqueur suffices to explain it all.'[35] When parents were anxious and concerned, they were told that this was not the result of their child's condition but might very well be the cause. They were constantly under suspicion: as parents because they had passed on their own nervous, neurotic nature to their offspring, and as upbringers because each shout, each tic, each obscene word underlined their failure.

---

[35] Cited in Kushner, *Cursing Brain*, p. 75.

And then came haloperidol

In 1961, the French psychiatrist Jean Seignot published a report on a Tourette patient he had treated with the experimental drug haloperidol (later marketed under the name Haldol).[36] The man had an irresistible urge to bang his head against the sharp edges of doors and furniture. A daily dose of 0.6 milligrams reduced the number of incidents to several per day, while the coprolalia disappeared completely. These results, together with the hundreds of studies which followed, focused attention on the possibility that the condition was due to an organic defect after all. Today, it is assumed that the basal ganglia are involved, a collection of circuits deep in the brain which play a role in the control of movement. These circuits can become impaired due to an oversensitivity to the neurotransmitter dopamine. Haloperidol binds to the receptors of dopamine, thus inhibiting the transfer of the stimulus.[37] It has been suggested that in a sense Tourette syndrome is the reverse of Parkinson's disease: where Parkinson patients become slow and stiff due to a lack of dopamine, Tourette patients display an abrupt, involuntary motor locomotion, due to an oversensitivity to dopamine. The Parkinson patient wants to move, but is unable to, while the Tourette patient does not want to move, but is compelled to. The medication prescribed today targets the production, activity or breakdown of neurotransmitters. In many cases they alleviate the symptoms without curing the disorder. It is unclear how this oversensitivity originates.

The transition from psychiatry to neurology and from couch to chemist's shop did not take place without a struggle. For close to a decade, the authors of studies on the effectiveness of haloperidol continued to report that this medication suppressed the symptoms,

---

[36] J. N. Seignot, 'Un cas de maladie des tics de Gilles de la Tourette guéri par le R. 1625', *Annales Médico-Psychologiques*, 119 (1961), 578–9.

[37] A. K. Shapiro and E. S. Shapiro, 'Treatment of Gilles de la Tourette's syndrome with haloperidol', *British Journal of Psychiatry*, 114 (1968), 345–50.

but failed to eliminate the cause. They maintained that psychotherapy was the best solution, and that the most one could expect from
haloperidol was that it would have a calming effect on the patient,
making him amenable to therapy. Articles which argued in favour of
haloperidol *instead of* psychoanalysis were turned down by the professional journals. Typical of the glacier-like pace at which this
transition proceeded are the hybrid explanations put forward, such
as the notion that haloperidol checks aggression, including the
aggression of a child towards the father or mother. Thus, there
would be fewer ambivalent feelings for the child to suppress, while
the intrapsychological tension responsible for the tics would be tem-
pered. According to Kushner, what such explanations reflect above
all is the prevailing balance of power in psychiatry. Eventually, the
change in favour of a pharmacological treatment of Tourette syndrome was due to a grassroots movement of patients and their families, rather than to the authority of facts and the results of experiments
involving haloperidol.

In the 1970s, newspaper and magazine articles on Tourette
patients began to appear all across the United States. These pieces
were noticeably similar in content, invariably focusing on a child
who suffered from facial tics and later developed strange involuntary movements. The concerned parents consulted a physician, but
there was nothing he could do. Specialists (paediatricians, psychiatrists, and neurologists) had no idea what was going on. Often the
parents had already done the rounds of all the various health care
institutes: a long, discouraging and financially exhausting trek.
Then, in this desperate situation, when there were often problems
at school as well, or the parents' marriage was coming under
threat, the father or mother happened to read an article about a
certain physician in New York. It might have been in a periodical
picked up in the doctor's waiting room, in *Reader's Digest*, or a women's
magazine like *Good Housekeeping*. In any case, the message was that
this physician had treated children with exactly the same symptoms

as *their* child using a new medicine, and with considerable success. The medication was Haldol, the physician was Arthur K. Shapiro, and the source of all these articles was the Tourette Syndrome Association.[38]

In 1965, Shapiro, a psychiatrist at New York Hospital, was treating a 24-year-old woman suffering from tics, who also made barking and growling noises, and, later on, when she was more at ease, occasionally shouted 'cocksucker!'. From the beginning he was convinced that this behaviour could be traced to an organic disorder. Shapiro had her admitted and in the months that followed he treated her with no fewer than thirty-six different combinations of psychiatric drugs. Haloperidol ultimately proved to be the most effective. Together with his wife, Elaine Shapiro, a psychologist, he wrote an article in which he presented these results as a clear indication of some kind of organic disturbance. The article was supplemented by a critical commentary on the therapeutic impotence of psychoanalysis. This marked the start of the Shapiros' own long and fruitless trek past the editors and reviewers of American journals dominated by psychoanalysts. The article ultimately appeared in the *British Journal of Psychiatry*.[39] The Shapiros did not mince their words: the woman was suffering from the syndrome of Gilles de la Tourette. They concurred with the description of the symptoms which he formulated in 1885, and suggested, as he did, that the disorder was caused by an as yet unidentified neurological defect. It was at this point that the eponym began to shift back to its origin: neurology. The authors neglected to mention that Gilles de la Tourette regarded this organic defect, whatever its exact nature, as the result of degeneration. After all, they were not historians of psychiatry.

---

[38] For the history of the Tourette Syndrome Association and the role played by Shapiro, see 'The triumph of the organic narrative' in Kushner, *Cursing Brain*, pp. 165–93.

[39] Shapiro and Shapiro, 'Treatment of Gilles de la Tourette syndrome'.

Clearly, Arthur Shapiro could not count on the support of the psychiatric establishment. The Tourette Syndrome Association (TSA), founded in 1972 (at the instigation of Shapiro, among others), applied for a subsidy from the National Institutes of Health. It was rejected on the grounds that in the entire country there were no more than a hundred individuals suffering from Tourette syndrome.[40] However, support was forthcoming from the parents of Tourette patients, some of whom donated considerable sums, and from McNeill Laboratories, the manufacturer of Haldol. The company financed information films and reprints, as well as advertisements for the TSA. The vignette-like newspaper articles on children who ultimately received the correct diagnosis and treatment were part of a campaign set up by the TSA to prove that Tourette syndrome was dramatically underdiagnosed.[41] In 1982, ten years after its founding, the TSA was a patient association with 10,000 members, operating on a national level. Today, visitors to the website (www.tsa-usa.org) can click their way through information which radiates initiative and self-confidence. There are books written by Tourette patients (*How Tourette Syndrome Made Me the Teacher I Never Had*), interviews ('I have Tourette's but Tourette's doesn't have me'), reports on famous Tourette patients, such as Tim Howard, former keeper of the soccer team Manchester United, alongside information on scientific articles and symposia, as well as newsletters and educational programmes tailored to the needs of Tourette patients. The TSA now has thirty-five chapters in the United States, and over 300 support groups, as well as a worldwide network of sister organizations.

[40] Kushner, *Cursing Brain*, p. 179.
[41] According to a recent estimate of the National Institutes of Health, 100,000 Americans suffer from Tourette syndrome. Even this number is regarded by the TSA as an underestimate.

1,500 francs' worth of walking sticks

The disorder which the Tourette patient suffers from is of all time. Reports dating from antiquity refer to people plagued by strange involuntary movements, who also bark or curse uncontrollably. What is not of all time is the Tourette *patient*. Someone who suffered from the disease around 1900 saw himself, his behaviour, and his perception of that behaviour quite differently from a patient living in the Middle Ages or the late twentieth century. Even the word 'patient' is debatable, since in the Middle Ages someone suffering from this disease was not seen as 'ill' but rather as 'possessed'. Individuals who have access to counselling, medication and the support of fellow sufferers no doubt experience the condition quite differently from those who lived at the time of Gilles de la Tourette.

The disease is incurable, and in that sense it is still a 'deplorable companion throughout life'. But it is no longer the companion to which patients were condemned in the days before the advent of alleviating medication. In *The Man who Mistook his Wife for a Hat*, Oliver Sacks describes the case of a 24-year-old man named Ray.[42] He suffered from violent tics, which followed upon one another every few seconds. Although he finished secondary school, he was fired from a dozen different jobs. But he found a form of escape in music, performing as a jazz drummer on weekends. Moreover, his condition gave him an opportunity to improvise, coming up with the wildest, most fanciful extemporizations. In table tennis, he was a much-feared opponent, launching sudden 'frivolous shots', as he referred to them. Sacks suggested they try Haldol, and the first (minuscule) dose was injected. It worked immediately: the tics

---

[42] O. Sacks, *The Man who Mistook his Wife for a Hat* (London, 1985). See also O. Sacks, 'Tourette's syndrome and creativity: exploiting the ticcy witticisms and witty ticcicisms', *British Medical Journal*, 305 (1992), 1515–16.

disappeared for several hours at a time. Sacks prescribed a quarter of a milligram three times a day. But when Ray returned a week later, he had a black eye and a broken nose. It appeared that he had previously dashed in and out of a revolving door at breakneck speed. As a result of the medication, his timing was off. The tics had not disappeared, they were just executed much more slowly, even to the point where he 'froze' in the middle of a movement. Ray felt that he had become sluggish, apathetic and dull. His drumming also suffered: it was mediocre, lacking the tempo and passion it used to have. This made him decide to take Haldol during the week but not on the weekend. Such reservations are understandable: haloperidol can have unpleasant side-effects, which include a Parkinson-like stiffness, depression and apathy; there was even the occasional attempt at suicide. And in a small number of Tourette patients, the remedy had no effect at all, and the patient experienced only the side-effects.

In his later work, Oliver Sacks portrayed various other Tourette patients, including the surgeon Carl Bennett, who introduced him to three more surgeons, three internists, two neurologists, and a psychiatrist, all of whom suffered from Tourette.[43] There are certain similarities between the case histories of Ray and Bennett and the 'confidences of O', dating from 1902. They were all written by a physician reporting on his clinical observations, and interpreting the behaviour of the patient with the benefit of the medical insights available at the time. Sacks, as well as Meige and Feindel, interweave their observations with discussions on the origin of the disorder, its course and the therapeutic possibilities. They also allow the patients to speak. They take the reader inside the disease, showing him what it feels like when the tension builds up, the way the discharge comes, and the relief of the tic, the scream or the shout. The narrative perspective alternates between third person and first person: together,

[43] O. Sacks, *An Anthropologist on Mars* (New York, 1995).

the physician and the patient describe what it means to suffer from Tourette syndrome. One of the similarities between Ray, Carl Bennett and O is the fact that they all feel a certain responsibility for their disorder, although for different reasons. O believes that his behaviour is the result of a weak will and inadequate control over his impulses. If only he could train and strengthen his will, then he would be able to suppress his tics. Ray and Bennett know that their tics are caused by an organic disorder, but thanks to the availability of alleviating medication, it is possible to reduce their frequency. They decide for themselves whether and when to use that medication. Between 1902 and the present, Tourette syndrome has gone from a psychological defect to an organic condition. While this has done away with the sense of culpability, the feelings of guilt and self-reproach that brought such suffering to O, it has been replaced by a new kind of responsibility.

Still, there is a world of difference between the *subtext* of Sacks' case histories and those of his colleagues practising in the early twentieth century. Sacks does not search for asthma in the family, or stuttering cousins or bizarre aunts. All intimations of degeneration have evaporated. The same applies to the suspicion of a 'weak will'. Indeed, that very notion was dispelled during a recent experiment: flying in the face of theoretical expectations, when the task involved the suppression of reflexive, impulsive reactions, children with Tourette scored higher than children without Tourette.[44] Thus the new hypothesis is that, due to the need to control their reactions, they have developed stronger control mechanisms than their peers. But the most important difference is that, in the eyes of his physicians, O was an accumulation of handicaps, a veritable compendium of disorders. For Meige and Feindel, he was a

---

[44] S. C. Mueller, G. J. Jackson, R. Dalla, S. Datsopoulos and C. P. Hollis, 'Enhanced cognitive control in young people with Tourette's syndrome', *Current Biology*, 16 (2006) 6, 570–3.

successful businessman, adept at sport *in spite of* his disorder. For Sacks, the drive, the whims, and the pace of someone like Ray are part of his disorder: he excels at drumming and table tennis *thanks to* Tourette syndrome.

By the time *Les tics et leur traitement* appeared in 1902, a publication which transported the syndrome of Gilles de la Tourette out of the field of neurology and, for a long time, even hid the eponym itself from view, Gilles de la Tourette was no longer in a fit state to react to these developments. The articles which he wrote towards the turn of the century bore such eccentric titles as 'Hysterical manifestations following a fall from a height of 17 metres', 'A case of cerebral haemorrhage of hysterical origin', and even 'Hysterical nature of tetanus in pregnant women'.[45] In 1899, he wrote a piece in which he rescinded his former standpoint that the 'maladie des tics convulsifs' has a progressive course and ends in severe mental disturbances.[46] Not long afterwards, he himself fell prey to a mental disorder, the late consequence of a syphilis infection. Throughout 1900, Gilles de la Tourette's behaviour took on such bizarre forms that it differed only marginally from that of his patients. He was no longer able to continue in his function. In January 1901, he was sent on sick leave for an indefinite period. In order to shield him from the yellow press, his wife and children travelled with him to Switzerland. Jean-Baptiste Charcot, the son of his mentor and himself a physician, accompanied them. Following their arrival at the hotel in Luzern, Gilles de la Tourette continued to behave in a chaotic manner, stealing all the menus from the dining room, and purchasing 1,500 francs' worth of walking sticks. The situation rapidly became intolerable. During an intensely manic phase, Charcot told him that a famous patient in Lausanne required his

---

[45] Cited in Guilly, 'Gilles de la Tourette', p. 410.
[46] G. Gilles de la Tourette, 'La maladie des tics convulsifs', *La Semaine Médicale*, 19 (1899), 153–6.

assistance. On 28 May 1901, Gilles de la Tourette walked into the Cery Clinic on the way to his consultation. This was followed by a compulsory admission to a closed ward. His condition gradually deteriorated and towards the end he sank into a psychosis. Georges Gilles de la Tourette died in 1904, at the age of 46.

EIGHT

A labyrinth of tangles: Alzheimer's disease

In the photographs taken of her in 1902, Auguste Deter looks older than her 52 years. Her husband has brought her to the psychiatric clinic in Frankfurt am Main, because he is no longer able to care for her at home. Auguste is confused and restless. She suffers from paranoia and is convinced that her husband is carrying on with the woman next door. At times she doesn't even recognize him as her husband. The family doctor notes in his referral that her memory is seriously affected, and that she suffers from insomnia. His diagnosis is 'paralysis of the brain'. On 26 November 1901, the day after her admission, Alois Alzheimer has a conversation with his new patient.[1] The first sentence in the dossier reads: 'Sitting up in bed, expression distraught'. He asks her what her name is. 'Auguste'. Last name? 'Auguste'. What is your husband's name? 'I think it's Auguste'. Are you married? 'To Auguste'. When Alzheimer asks her how long she has been there, she says 'three weeks'. He shows her various objects: a pencil, a pen, a key, a cigar. She is able to identify them, but shortly

---

[1] K. Maurer and U. Maurer, *Alzheimer. Das Leben eines Arztes und die Karriere einer Krankheit* (Munich, 1998). The opening chapter contains extensive quotations from the notes which Alzheimer made in the dossier.

Figure 8.1: Auguste Deter (52), the 'first Alzheimer's patient'

afterwards when Alzheimer asks her to name the objects without showing them to her, she has forgotten everything. When the noon meal (cauliflower and pork) is served, he asks her what she is eating. 'Spinach'. He asks her to write down 'Mrs Auguste Deter', but after 'Mrs' she's forgotten what she was supposed to write. Two days later, Alzheimer notes on her chart: 'Constantly distraught, anxious', and a day later 'distraught, resists everything'. He asks her where she thinks she is now, when she was born, what her name is. She is unable to answer any of the questions. Auguste would ultimately spend almost five years in the clinic. Towards the end she lay in bed, dazed and incontinent, her legs drawn up, in a condition which Alzheimer described as 'total feeble-mindedness'.

In 1995, Auguste Deter's file was rediscovered in the archives of the Frankfurt clinic, where it had been filed under the wrong year. Two years later, five photographs were also found.[2] The desperation which had made such an impression on Alzheimer is written all over her face. Auguste died in the spring of 1906. In the sections which

[2] On the dossier and the photos: K. Maurer, S. Volk and H. Gerbaldo, 'Auguste D. and Alzheimer's disease', *The Lancet*, 349 (1997), 1546–9.

Figure 8.2: Alois Alzheimer (1864–1915)

Alzheimer took from her brain he found the tissue abnormalities characteristic of what is today known as Alzheimer's disease.

Alzheimer, neuropathologist

Alois Alzheimer (baptised Aloysius) was born in 1864 as the son of a notary in the town of Marktbreit, near Würzburg, Germany.[3] After finishing secondary school, he decided to study medicine. He had already opted for Würzburg, as it was close to home and his half-brother Karl was already at the university there. But his father was more ambitious than Alois himself (indeed, his entire life he would be surrounded by people with more ambition than he had), and he sent his son to Berlin, then the Mecca of medicine. This was the institute where, in 1882, Robert Koch had discovered the tuberculosis bacillus and then, in 1883, the year that Alzheimer began his studies, the pathogen responsible for cholera. But, after one semester, Alois

---

[3] J.-E. Meyer, 'Alois Alzheimer (1864–1915)' in K. Kolle (ed.), *Grosse Nervenärzte* (Stuttgart, 1959), vol. II, pp. 30–8. For a biography which combines Alzheimer's life with information on Alzheimer's disease, see M. Jürgs, *Alzheimer. Spurensuche im Niemandsland* (Munich, 1999).

packed his bags and headed for Würzburg. The extracurricular activities offered by the Corps Franconia left little time for study, and during a sabre duel, he incurred a scar that ran from his left eye to his chin. It was not until the 1884–1885 winter semester that Alzheimer began to take his medical studies seriously. He was drawn to forensic psychiatry and microscopic tissue study and from then on there was no stopping him. In 1887, he completed a dissertation devoted to the glands that produce ear wax. Alzheimer was an excellent draughtsman and, as in his later work, he used stunning drawings of tissue sections to illustrate his dissertation. The following year he took the last of his medical exams. He was then 23 years old and ready for the next step in his career.

In late 1888, he applied for the position of assistant physician at the Asylum for Lunatics and Epileptics in Frankfurt. He already had some psychiatric experience, having recently returned from a five-month journey as private physician to a mentally ill woman. He also made mention of the lectures and laboratory sessions in microscopic pathology which he had attended. The director of the institution, Emil Sioli, sent him a telegram to inform him that the job was his. The salary was 1,200 marks a year, including room and board. Alzheimer found in Sioli a kindred spirit. Both men endorsed the principle of non-restraint. Like Korsakoff, who that same year (1888) took over as head of a psychiatric clinic in Moscow, they strived to introduce a type of nursing devoid of any form of coercion, such as isolation cells and straitjackets. The premises lent themselves to this striving. The institution was set amid spacious parks and gardens, and the various pavilions reflected the psychiatric classifications then in use: calm lunatics, agitated lunatics, the feeble-minded and epileptics. Sioli also saw to it that the dissection lab cum mortuary (a cramped and malodorous hall in the centre of the building) was replaced by a free-standing, well-lit dissection laboratory.

During the day, Alzheimer made the rounds of the various wards, and yet he saw himself primarily as a neuropathologist. Indeed, he rendered his greatest service to his patients after their death: in the evenings he would sit down at his microscope to examine the nerve tissue collected during post mortem examinations. A few months after Alzheimer joined the staff, a second promising neuropathologist arrived in Frankfurt: Franz Nissl. His departure from Munich, where he worked in the laboratory of Bernhard von Gudden, was prompted by a drama that took place in the summer of 1886.[4]

Von Gudden, together with three prominent psychiatrists, had been asked to draw up a declaration of insanity for Ludwig II of Bavaria. The king suffered from a persecution complex combined with delusions of grandeur, and the plan was to temporarily depose him, so that he could be treated. Von Gudden had Berg Castle on Lake Starnberg made ready, and late in the afternoon of 13 June, Von Gudden and his patient took a stroll through the adjacent park, followed at a distance by two male nurses. They saw Ludwig whisper something in Von Gudden's ear, after which the physician motioned to them to retreat. Several hours later the bodies of the king and the doctor were found floating in Lake Starnberg. The circumstances surrounding the deaths have never been fully clarified. The most probable scenario is that Ludwig, who the day before had just barely been prevented from committing suicide, ran into the lake, followed by Von Gudden. Traces found in the mud of the lake floor seemed to indicate that at some distance from the shore, Von Gudden had succeeded in grabbing the king by his collar, after which a struggle ensued. It is conceivable that Ludwig (41 years old, muscular and weighing in at 120 kilos) held the 62-year-old physician under water and then drowned himself. The bodies were found close together.

The tragedy had a devastating effect on Nissl's personal life. As a medical student, he had won a competition organized by Von Gudden which focused on pathological changes in brain cells. His

[4] E. Grünthal, 'Bernhard von Gudden' in Kolle (ed.), Grosse Nervenärzte, vol. I, pp. 126–34.

Figure 8.3: Von Gudden's microtome. The brain to be sliced was lowered into the cylinder (a). Using the setscrew (c), the anatomist could slide the brain upwards, micrometre by micrometre, in the direction of the knife, which was drawn across the surface (b). To ensure that the specimen did not adhere to the knife, the procedure was carried out under water, and the membrane floating in the water was scooped up in a saucer. Von Gudden reported that he had taken some 810 specimens from a monkey's brain measuring 4.5 cm in diameter, which would mean that they were only around 0.055 mm thick. It is clear from the design of the microtome that the Biedermeier style (1815–1848) had even found its way into anatomical laboratories, albeit somewhat belatedly

entry described a method of impregnating nerve cells with magenta red in order to make their structure visible. Later he would use methylene blue to that same end, a technique which is still known as the Nissl stain. Immediately after graduation, Von Gudden took him on as assistant physician. Von Gudden had himself given his name to a neurological innovation. Because the brain is made up of very soft tissue, it is extremely difficult to slice it into sections. In 1875, Von Gudden designed a device called a microtome, which made it possible to cut sections over the full length of the brain.[5]

The sudden death of Von Gudden knocked Nissl totally off-balance. His research stagnated and his health began to suffer, and after a stay in a spa, he decided to apply for the position of second physician

[5] B. von Gudden, 'Über ein neues Microtom', *Archiv für Psychiatrie*, 5 (1875), 229–31.

in the Asylum for Lunatics and Epileptics in Frankfurt. He and Alzheimer became good friends and respected colleagues, working together for many years. In 1894, Nissl was a witness at Alzheimer's wedding. The circumstances of this marriage were no less tumultuous than those surrounding Nissl's arrival in Frankfurt.

The Heidelberg physician, Wilhelm Erb, had a patient suffering from syphilis, a certain Otto Geisenheimer. He was originally from Frankfurt, but at the age of 20 he had gone to New York, where he made a fortune in the gem trade. When he was 38, he returned to Frankfurt intent on finding a wife, and in 1883 he married Cecilia Wallerstein (23), likewise from a well-to-do Jewish family. Geisenheimer was suffering from what was then called 'softening of the brain'. In 1892, Erb accompanied the Geisenheimers on a scientific expedition through North Africa, serving as their personal physician. They had just arrived in Algeria when Geisenheimer's condition worsened. Erb sent a telegram to Alzheimer, who had specialized in the study of syphilis and had experience as a private physician, requesting him to come as quickly as possible and to accompany the couple home. Despite excellent care, Geisenheimer died shortly after the group reached Nice. It may have been on the trip home, or perhaps somewhat later, but Alois and Cecilia fell in love and were married in April 1894. The marriage made Alzheimer financially independent.

In Frankfurt, the couple lived well. Every day, Cecilia went into town by coach, to buy the artwork and antiques which gradually filled their home. Eight maids saw to the housekeeping, and there were frequent dinners and receptions. Cecilia, who had lived in New York for a time and travelled extensively with Geisenheimer, brought with her a sophistication to which Alois was not born, but which fitted him like a glove. As Kraepelin later recalled, 'Alzheimer appreciated comfort and smoked a great deal'.[6] This is reflected in photographs: there are few if any pictures of Alzheimer *without* a cigar, and in his

---

[6] Quoted in Jürgs, *Alzheimer*, p. 95.

mid-thirties he already had an embonpoint which betrayed a talent for living the good life. Two daughters and a son were born to the couple in quick succession.

In February 1901, the death of Cecilia brought to an end what Nissl described as 'an extremely happy marriage'.[7] At 36, Alzheimer was now a widower with three young children. His sister Elisabeth, eight years his junior, moved in with him and helped to raise the children. Alzheimer's conversations with Auguste took place during what must have been the most miserable year in his life.

A trail of cigarette butts

In the autumn of 1903, Alzheimer moved to Munich, together with his children and Elisabeth. Emil Kraepelin, director of the Royal Psychiatric Clinic, had asked him to head the Anatomical Laboratory. It was not possible to offer him a salary, but then Alzheimer had no need of one. On the third floor there was a large, well-lit room fully equipped for pathological research. Underneath the windows were rows of microscopes on long tables and a *camera lucida*, which was used to draw microscopic sections. The laboratory had a microtome as well as cameras to photograph sections, at the time a new technique. There were two telephones on the wall for phoning in results. The laboratory was visited by students and guest researchers from all over the world: indeed, the visitors' list reads like a compendium of eponyms. There was Friedrich Heinrich Levy, who later moved to the United States and changed his name to Frederic Lewy. He is remembered for the Lewy bodies which he discovered in 1912 in the brains of Parkinson patients, and which consist of protein deposits.[8] Two other guest researchers were

---

[7] F. Nissl, 'Zum Andenken A. Alzheimers', *Allgemeine Zeitschrift für Psychiatrie*, 73 (1917), 96–107 (107).

[8] B. Holdorff, 'Friedrich Heinrich Lewy (1885–1950) – Initiator der Erforschung der Parkinson-Krankheit' in G. Nissen and F. Badura (eds.), *Schriftenreihe der Deutschen Gesellschaft für Geschichte der Nervenheilkunde* (Würzburg, 2001), pp. 67–79.

Hans-Gerhard Creutzfeldt and Alfons Jakob, who independently of one another described the deadly virus disease which bears their name. Every morning and every afternoon, Alzheimer did the rounds of twenty workplaces, invariably with a cigar. He pulled up a stool, took as long as necessary to explain what was to be seen, and then moved on, leaving behind a trail of cigar stubs. Not only did he work for nothing, he also bore the cost of employing draughtsmen and photographers, and financed the purchase of the necessary equipment.

Alzheimer himself set up a research programme focusing on the possible relationship between abnormalities of the nervous system and such conditions as epilepsy, schizophrenia, Huntington's chorea and multiple sclerosis. But his speciality was 'progressive paralysis', also known as 'dementia paralytica', a syndrome which in the larger cities accounted for 30 to 40 per cent of admissions to psychiatric hospitals. As is now known, and was then suspected, progressive paralysis is caused by a syphilis infection. It affected two to three times as many men as women, more soldiers than clergymen, and bachelors more often than married men. From 1888, just after his arrival in Frankfurt, until his departure in 1903, Alzheimer studied no fewer than 320 cases.[9] As he had done with Auguste, he held long talks with his patients, during which he casually introduced short exercises designed to test memory, concentration and powers of abstraction. After the death of a patient, he carried out a post mortem examination of the brain and spinal cord. Progressive paralysis, popularly known as 'softening of the brain', is the result of severe but diffuse damage to the nervous system. It manifests itself in a wide variety of symptoms. Alzheimer: 'Memory and judgement, emotion and will are the first to be affected. The patient becomes increasingly cut off from the outside world, since he finds it more and

[9] A. Alzheimer, *Histologische Studien zur Differentialdiagnose der progressiven Paralyse* (Jena, 1904).

more difficult to process the impressions which reach him from his surroundings, and to relate the few things which do register with him to his own personality. Soon he also loses all self-awareness and judgement.'[10] What Alzheimer wrote about the final stage could also have been written about a patient in the early stages of dementia: 'His powers of observation become blunted, his old memories and experiences no longer resonate, his interests intermingle and ultimately fade away. Nothing remains of his earlier personality.'[11] In the end, the patient is overcome by agitation, delusions, memory loss and paralysis. Alzheimer submitted this account as *Habilitationschrift*, earning him the coveted 'venia legendi', which qualified him to teach at the university. It was awarded in the summer of 1904, a few months after Gilles de la Tourette died in a Swiss asylum from the effects of syphilis.

On Christmas Day 1904, Alzheimer surprised his children by announcing that they were all going to Wessling am See, where they had spent their summer vacation that year. They were astonished: Now? In the middle of winter? Hans Alzheimer would later recount how his father and the rest of the family boarded the steam train to Wessling, how the children tramped through the snow that covered the frozen lake, and finally arrived at a large door set in a wall. Father tried the door handle: locked. Then he reached into his pocket and pulled out a huge key: 'Shall we see if this fits?'.[12] The children stared open-mouthed as the door swung open with a grating sound, revealing a staircase covered in moss. At the top of the stairs, in the dazzling winter light, they saw what their father had bought: an enormous white villa, complete with gardens, outbuildings and a boathouse. The Alzheimer family would spend many weekends and vacations there, often together with aunts and uncles and their offspring, who were given a warm welcome. To this day, the house is still in the family.

[10] Cited in Maurer and Maurer, *Alzheimer*, p. 152.   [11] *Ibid.*   [12] *Ibid.* p. 156.

Plaques and tangles

In April 1906, Alzheimer received a telephone call from Frankfurt: Auguste Deter was dead. He asked the caller to send not only her brain, but also her medical dossier. It consisted of some thirty pages. Re-reading his own notes, Alzheimer reconstructed a course which even today is characteristic of patients with this disease. At home, her memory began to fail and she wandered restlessly around the house, hiding things and then forgetting where. As for cooking a meal, she no longer knew where to begin. After her admission, she became even more disoriented. She thought she was living in Kassel (where she was born), and that Alzheimer was a guest in her house ('My husband will be home soon!'), and she had no idea what year it was or how long she had been in the institution. She told him she had a daughter of 52 but a little later mentioned that she herself was 56, without noticing the inconsequence. It is clear from the verbatim accounts of these interviews that many automatisms remain intact for some time. Auguste could recite the months of the year without a hitch, except that she was unable to name the eleventh month. When asked 'how much is nine times seven?', she answered '63', but when the question was 'If you buy six eggs at seven pfennig apiece, how much do you have to pay?', the answer was 'Poached'. Often she felt around her as if she were blind, running her hands over the faces of her fellow patients. Towards evening she would become quite anxious and restless, wandering through the wards with her bedclothes draped around her. Sometimes there was no other solution but an isolation cell, despite the non-restraint policy. No doubt Alzheimer realized early on how important the case of Auguste was. In addition to the extensive documentation and the photos, the dossier contained correspondence recording Sioli's opposition to plans to transfer her to another institution. Before his departure, Alzheimer made him promise to follow developments closely. He didn't want to run the risk of her being buried before he received word of her death. A few sketchy notes documented her final days: 'Evening of April 6: is very groggy; whimpers from time to time, perspiring heavily. April 7: very groggy all day, temperature 41 in the afternoon, in the evening 40. April 8: died at quarter to five in the morning. Cause of death: blood poisoning as a result of bedsores.'

In his letter to Sioli, in which he thanked him for sending the brain and the dossier, Alzheimer mentioned that he intended to give a lecture on Auguste's case in Tübingen in November 1906, at a regional meeting of psychiatrists and neurologists. He did indeed give the lecture, but it proved to be a great disappointment.

According to the text of the lecture, which appeared in the *Allgemeine Zeitschrift für Psychiatrie* in 1907, Alzheimer first presented the clinical picture as he himself had recorded it in Frankfurt:[13]

> In the institution her whole manner betrays total despair. She is completely disoriented in both time and place. From time to time she makes a remark about not understanding what is going on or not being able to remember something. Sometimes she greets the doctor as if he is a guest and apologizes for not having finished her work, and the next time she screams at him, accusing him of wanting to cut her with a knife, or indignantly orders him to leave in terms that suggest she fears for her virtue. From time to time she is completely delirious, she lugs parts of her bedclothes around with her, calls for her husband and her daughter, and appears to suffer from auditory hallucinations. Often she has frightful screaming fits that go on for hours at a time.[14]

The autopsy revealed that large portions of the cerebral cortex had atrophied. Alzheimer displayed slides of various sections, pointing out the irregularities he had found in the nerve tissue: strange tangles and albumin deposits. He had also done drawings of several of those tangles. In Alzheimer's view, these abnormalities did not fit any of the known categories of disease. Everything pointed in the direction of a previously unknown condition, and he expressed the hope

---

[13] A. Alzheimer, 'Über eine eigenartige Erkrankung der Hirnrinde', *Allgemeine Zeitschrift für Psychiatrie*, 64 (1907), 146–8.

[14] Alzheimer, 'Erkrankung', 146.

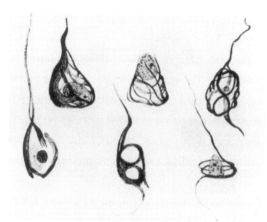

Figure 8.4: Alzheimer's drawing of the 'tangles' which he had found in the brain of Auguste D

that continuing neuropathological research would help to define the boundaries of the disease.

Thus it was in Tübingen that an audience consisting of his peers got their first glimpse of the malformations referred to as 'tangles' and 'plaques', which to this day point to a diagnosis of Alzheimer's disease. But this historic moment passed unnoticed. When Alzheimer finished speaking, the chairman opened the floor for discussion. No one in the audience felt the urge to speak, nor had the chairman prepared any questions. Alzheimer sat down again. The next speaker was then introduced, whose subject was 'the analysis of psychotraumatic symptoms'. For the remainder of the afternoon those present (including Carl Gustav Jung, who had come all the way from Zurich) engaged in a heated debate on the scientific value of psychoanalysis. The following day, the local newspaper published a detailed account of the impassioned arguments which had been voiced for and against Freud. A single line was devoted to a 'remarkable and grave pathological process which, over a period of four and a half years, led to a sharp decline in the number of nerve cells'.[15]

---

[15] Cited in Maurer and Maurer, *Alzheimer*, p. 211.

'We sit here so happy together'

What, then, was the state of affairs in 1907? There was a clinical description based on a single female patient, a neuropathological analysis of her brain, and one publication in a scientific journal. Alzheimer was aware that this was a slender basis on which to identify a new disease. One of his guest researchers, the Italian Gaetano Perusini, was asked to search for similar cases. He found three patients, all of whom had died shortly after admission and whose remains were available for neuropathological examination. One of them, a basket-maker who spent his days pacing back and forth in his room, anxious and disoriented, and immediately forgot everything, was even younger than Auguste – only 45 years old. The other two were 63 and 65 respectively. Perusini also reanalysed the case of Auguste, and in 1908 he presented a detailed account of his findings.[16] On the basis of Auguste's dossier, he sketched the details which, in a thousand unhappy variations, are today regarded as characteristic of the contact with Alzheimer patients: '27 November 1901. When the doctor comes over to her bed, she says (with a worried expression), "You don't have a very good opinion of me, do you?" "Why?" "I don't know. We've never been in debt or anything like that. It's just that I'm confused. Don't be angry with me."'[17] The brains of all four patients were subjected to a detailed pathological examination. The energetic Italian researcher studied sections taken from all parts of the brain, from the frontal lobe to the cerebellum and from the top to the brainstem, using twenty different colouring methods. In each case, he found the plaques and tangles which Alzheimer had described.

[16] This account would not appear until 1909: G. Perusini, 'Über klinisch und histologisch eigenartige psychische Erkrankungen des späteren Lebensalters', in F. Nissl and A. Alzheimer (eds.), *Histologische und histopathologische Arbeiten*, 3 (1909), 297–351.

[17] Perusini, 'Klinisch', p. 297.

Meanwhile, Alzheimer himself continued his research. In November 1907, a patient was admitted to his clinic with the same clinical symptoms displayed by Auguste. He followed the man, a 56-year-old day labourer named Johann Feigl, until his death.[18] In this patient, too, a number of automatisms initially remained intact: he managed to get half-way through the 'Our Father'. He could button his coat and, at Alzheimer's request, he was able to strike a match and light up a cigar. But less than six months later, when the same request was made, he rubbed the cigar helplessly against a matchbox. Alzheimer's notes read: '5 May 1908: Other patients have taught him to sing. When asked to, he will launch into the folk song "*Wir sitzen so fröhlich beisammen*" ("We sit here so happy together"). He needs constant prompting for the words, but usually manages to get the melody right.' '12 June 1908. Out in the garden he walks very quickly, stopping for no one. If he is not interrupted, he does the same lap over and over, bathed in sweat; all the while he holds the long panels of his coat wrapped around his hand, clutching them tightly. In bed, he does the same thing with the blanket.' '14 December 1908. He urinates and defecates wherever he happens to be. He no longer speaks and is constantly fussing with his bedclothes or his coat. When prompted by others, he still sings *Wir sitzen so frohlich beisammen*.' '3 October 1910. Dies of pneumonia.'[19] Alzheimer carried out the post mortem himself. The convolutions of the frontal lobe and the temporal lobes were considerably narrowed: 'The grooves were wide open.'[20] The dissection book contains (in Alzheimer's handwriting) the diagnosis of the unfortunate day labourer: '*Alzheimer'sche Krankheit*'. It was to Kraepelin that he owed the eponym. He regarded it as a questionable honour.

---

[18] The details of Feigl's illness appear in A. Alzheimer, 'Über eigenartige Krankheitsfälle des späteren Alters', *Zeitschrift für die gesamte Neurologie und Psychiatrie*, 4 (1911), 356–84.

[19] Alzheimer, 'Krankheitsfälle', 360–1.   [20] *Ibid.* 360–2.

The Linnaeus of psychiatry

As far as his academic career was concerned, Alzheimer went through life in a state of sovereign nonchalance. Having published his dissertation at the age of 23, he seemed to be on his way, and yet he didn't get around to writing his *Habilitationsschrift* until after he turned 40. That was a good ten years too late. He does not appear to have been interested in prestigious positions outside the university, and this betrayed a somewhat laconic philosophy of life. He could afford to be nonchalant, given his financial independence, but it was also an attitude which was inherent in his character. This is reflected in the unusually generous praise which he bestowed on others in his articles, even when he could have claimed the honour for himself: praise for Perusini, who had carried out such solid pathological research, for Nissl, who had developed such brilliant colouring methods, for Bonfiglio who in 1908 had described a comparable case, for Fischer who in 1907 discovered deviant hearths in the cerebral cortex, and for Redlich who (as Alzheimer later learned) had discovered plaques in the brain of senile patients as far back as 1898. The moment tributes appeared to be heading his way, he immediately deflected them in the direction of colleagues, assistants and predecessors. The fact that he was able to do the work he did, at the scientific heart of neurology, and that his research received the visibility it deserved, was not to the credit of Alzheimer himself. It was thanks to the man who was the driving force behind a great many German careers.

Mention a trait which is typical of Alzheimer, and Kraepelin represents the opposite.[21] To begin with, Emil Kraepelin, eight years older than Alzheimer, resolved while he was still a student that he would receive a professorship by the time he turned 30, and he did. Alzheimer did not become a professor until he was 48. Kraepelin did

---

[21] Kurt Kolle is the author of a splendid biographical portrait: 'Emil Kraepelin (1856–1926)' in Kolle (ed.), *Grosse Nervenärtze*, vol. I, pp. 175–86.

not marry money; on the contrary, in 1883, at the age of 27, he wrote a psychiatric handbook in the hope that the proceeds would allow him to marry the girl he had been engaged to since he was 15. Every few years he revised his handbook, which expanded with each new edition, until it encompassed four hefty volumes. In 1926, three days before his death, he dictated the foreword to the ninth edition. It contained the latest categorization of psychiatric disorders which he had drawn up and which had earned him the eponym 'the Kraepelin classification' and the nickname 'the Linnaeus of psychiatry'. A lesser-known eponym was 'Kraepelin sekt', an insipid lemonade which the dour teetotaller introduced after he was appointed director of the clinic, together with a total ban on alcohol. Their enjoyment of stimulants was just one more area in which Kraepelin and Alzheimer had different tastes. But perhaps the greatest contrast was the fact that, in the republic of letters, Alzheimer felt himself surrounded by colleagues, Kraepelin by rivals. From the Royal Psychiatric Clinic in Munich, Kraepelin kept a keen eye out for openings, not because he had ambitions to fill them himself, but in order to ensure the appointment of kindred spirits. That demanded influence, wielded from a position on the editorial board of journals and the executive committee of neuropsychiatric societies. He had no affinity with Alzheimer's favourite activity, looking down a microscope. While he had attracted promising pathologists and put them to work in a superbly equipped laboratory, he himself was never seen anywhere near a microscope. Once in a great while he would make an appearance on the third floor. 'He strode through the vast halls', one of his assistants later recalled, 'taking everything in with great interest. Before he left the lab, everyone looked at him in expectation. "Well, well, well. I see that the anatomical mills grind slowly!" said the man whose word was law in German psychiatry.'[22]

---

[22] Cited in Maurer and Maurer, *Alzheimer*, p. 167.

While Alzheimer felt perfectly at home in the microworld of brain tissue, Kraepelin delighted in traversing the wider world of conferences, guest lectures and study tours. This meant that someone had to be appointed to serve as deputy director in his absence. In Kraepelin's view, there was no more suitable candidate than Alzheimer. The man himself disagreed. He hated anything that took him away from his work, and for some time he resisted Kraepelin's repeated urgings. When he finally allowed himself to be persuaded, he agreed only on condition that immediate steps would be taken to find a deputy for the deputy. Not surprisingly, for the first few years that search proved fruitless. According to his biographers, in 1908 alone Alzheimer had to substitute for Kraepelin for almost five months.

In the early spring of that year, Kraepelin left for Switzerland, where he remained for six weeks, preparing the eighth edition of his handbook. He was also in the process of revising the section on 'senile dementia'.[23] Toward the end of that section, he recorded the fact that Alzheimer had discovered a characteristic group of cases which displayed marked cell changes. First, he presented an overview of the major symptoms, together with Alzheimer's neuropathological findings. This was followed by the attribution of the eponym, albeit formulated with a certain reserve:

> At present, the clinical significance of Alzheimer's disease is still unclear. While on the basis of anatomical findings, one would be inclined to believe that what we see here is an exceptionally severe form of senile dementia, that finding is in a sense contradicted by the fact that the disease often begins around the age of 50. In such cases, one might be more inclined to lean towards a diagnosis of 'senium praecox', while in fact it is probably only a curious clinical picture which presents more or less independently of age.[24]

---

[23] E. Kraepelin, 'Das Seniele Irresein' in *Psychiatrie, ein Lehrbuch für Studierende und Ärzte* (8th edn, Leipzig, 1910), vol. II, pp. 594–630.

[24] Kraepelin, 'Seniele', pp. 625–6.

Here, Kraepelin concurred with the argument put forward by Alzheimer in Tübingen in 1906. In a clinical and neurological sense, the symptoms resemble senile dementia, also known as *Altersblödsinn* or *Greisenblödsinn*, but Auguste was only around 50 when she fell ill. Perhaps there was such a thing as '*pre*-senile dementia'. But, if so, was this a *different* disease from senile dementia, or an atypically early onset of the same disease?

Alzheimer revisited this issue in 1911. By then, he had at his disposal Perusini's three new cases, the Feigl case, and another patient who did not begin to display the clinical signs of senile dementia 'until he was in his late sixties'.[25] The ages of the patients now ranged from 45 (Perusini's basket-maker), 51 (Auguste), 56 (Feigl), 63 and 65 (Perusini), to the 'late sixties' (Alzheimer). 'Thus,' Alzheimer concluded, 'there appears to be no valid reason to regard these cases as caused by an exceptional course of the disease. They are senile psychoses, atypical forms of senile dementia.'[26] The irony of the case is that Alzheimer's disease is now universally regarded as an age-related disease, while in 1906 Alzheimer himself believed that he had discovered a new disease because his patient was relatively young. Today, many people are surprised to hear that someone in his early fifties, or even younger, can fall prey to Alzheimer's disease.

What prompted Kraepelin to bestow an eponym the clinical significance of which was 'still unclear'? This question has given rise to a number of speculations.[27] Did he seize the first opportunity that presented itself to reward his faithful deputy? Was he trying to emphasize the productivity of his Munich laboratory? Did he hope to beat his Prague colleague Arnold Pick to the mark, whose associate Oskar Fischer authored publications on neuropathological

[25] Alzheimer, 'Krankheitsfälle', 383.   [26] *Ibid.* 384.
[27] M. M. Weber, 'Aloys Alzheimer, a coworker of Emil Kraepelin' in *Journal of Psychiatric Research*, 31 (1997) 6, 635–43.

abnormalities in senile dementia in the same year as Alzheimer?[28] We will never know exactly what Kraepelin's motives were, since he did not discuss the subject. As the pope of German psychiatry, he was simply in a position to bestow this kind of honorary prize and he took advantage of that fact. By the time the eighth edition of his handbook appeared in the summer of 1910, Alzheimer's name had been firmly attached to the disease.

War and nerves

In 1912, Alzheimer was called to assume a post in Breslau, as professor and director of the psychiatric clinic at Friedrich-Wilhelm University. He would be taking over the chair which for close to twenty years had been occupied by Carl Wernicke, the man who gave his name to Wernicke's aphasia and Wernicke's disease (later in part incorporated into the Korsakoff syndrome). The appointment was a source of 'great satisfaction' to Alzheimer, Kraepelin later wrote, 'since although he was fully aware of his inner worth, he suffered from the fact that his position was not commensurate with his importance'.[29] We do not know whether this is what led Alzheimer to accept the new position: there is something decidedly Kraepelinian about the presumed motive. And in the same breath, Kraepelin noted that Alzheimer's departure meant that 'the high point of his scientific career lay behind him'.[30] This may have been a reference to the administrative tasks which awaited him in Breslau, or the transition from Munich to a provincial town; or perhaps he was aggrieved because Alzheimer was leaving his laboratory. We know that he had previously sabotaged

---

[28] O. Fischer, 'Miliare Nekrosen mit drusigen Wucherungen der Neurofibrillen, eine regelmässige Veränderung der Hirnrinde bei seniler Demenz', *Monatschrift für Psychiatrie und Neurologie*, 22 (1907), 361–72.

[29] E. Kraepelin, 'Lebensschicksale deutscher Forscher (Alzheimer, Brodmann, Nissl)', *Münchener Medizinische Wochenschrift*, 67 (1920), 75–8 (76).

[30] Kraepelin, 'Lebensschicksale', 76.

applications by both Nissl and Alzheimer, because he wanted them to remain in his own laboratory. Be that as it may, his prediction came true. From the start, things went badly for Alzheimer. He fell ill on the train trip from Munich to Breslau (angina, complicated by a kidney infection) and upon arrival he had to be admitted to a sanatorium. Recovery was slow in coming, and when Kraepelin and Nissl first saw him again, at a conference in Breslau the following year, they were shocked by his condition. Kraepelin: 'Although outwardly calm, he seemed despondent, and contemplated the future with apprehension.'[31] Nissl persuaded him to go to Wiesbaden to take the waters, but this failed to bring about the desired improvement.

In 1914, the First World War brought new cares and concerns. His son Hans volunteered for service at the front (which was a source of pride to his father) and was sent to Flanders. Alzheimer himself had to take over for doctors called up for military service. At this time, he appears to have been caught up in the fiercely Prussian-nationalistic atmosphere which prevailed in Breslau. In a lecture on 'Krieg und Nerven', he predicted that the war would result in a great many nervous afflictions, but that in the end this might have a fortifying effect, ultimately producing a 'more energetic, courageous, and intrepid generation. With nerves of steel, the German people will undertake to address the exigencies of peace. In so doing, they will also conquer many of the phenomena which proliferated during the long period of peace, and which some over-anxious citizens now regard as proof of the spiritual degeneration of our people.'[32] Up until then, Alzheimer's observation of nerves had been limited to those he examined under a microscope. Now, having escaped from the narrow confines of the objective prism, he spouts opinions which introduce readers

---

[31] E. Kraepelin, *Lebenserinnerungen* (Berlin, 1983), p. 172.
[32] A. Alzheimer, *Krieg und Nerven* (Breslau, 1915). Cited in Maurer and Maurer, *Alzheimer*, p. 257.

to a conceptual world which had become so common within the psychiatry of the day that it is not surprising that Alzheimer – even Alzheimer – endorsed them. In that same speech, he referred to a malady known as 'benefit neurosis'. This is a disturbance whereby:

> a minor injury such as a glancing pistol shot, or a fall from a horse or wagon, results in a series of subjective symptoms for which no cause can be found, and which are disproportionate to the minor nature of the injury. The phenomenon is regularly seen in peacetime as well, among those suffering from a work-related injury, or passengers involved in a train accident. It is referred to as traumatic hysteria, and occasionally as benefit neurosis, since the public may rightly believe that the prospect of receiving benefits is the psychological factor which perpetuates the symptoms.[33]

This early reference to what we know as 'secondary gain' soon gave rise to a now familiar – but in the Germany of 1915 ominous – attitude attributed to people with a congenital susceptibility to this disturbance, namely the 'so-called degenerates, psychopaths or mentally deficient. Often these are the children of the mentally disturbed, epileptics, criminals or alcoholics.'[34] In other articles, however, Alzheimer took a more moderate view of the concept of degeneration: the designation 'so-called' was there for a reason. But his summary of the classic elements in the category of degeneration suggests that he was part of a long tradition. And he would not be the last.

The speech on 'Krieg und Nerven' marked the end of Alzheimer's scientific work. In December 1915, while Hans was in Breslau on Christmas leave, Alzheimer's condition rapidly deteriorated. The lining of the heart became inflamed and Alzheimer breathed his last. He was 51 years of age. Nissl attended the funeral. 'The ceremony proceeded as quietly and simply as his life had ebbed away. He had requested that there be no funeral orations. On 23 December we

---

[33] Maurer and Maurer, *Alzheimer*, p. 256. [34] *Ibid.*

accompanied our unforgettable friend to his final resting place. In keeping with his wishes, he was buried in the Frankfurt cemetery, alongside his wife, who had preceded him many years before, and with whom he was so briefly united in a very happy marriage.'[35]

Alzheimer's diseases

After reading the third or fourth 'In Memoriam', something begins to jar. *Whatever happened to Alzheimer's disease?* In most of the necrologies there is no mention at all of his articles on Auguste and Feigl, and even the *Zum Andenken* of his faithful friend Nissl does not refer to the eponym. Looking back, a strange reversal seems to have taken place in the posthumous reputation of Alzheimer. In his own day, he was honoured mainly as an expert on the consequences of syphilis infections. That expertise was of vital importance for psychiatric institutions deluged by patients with symptoms of progressive paralysis. Alzheimer's disease, by contrast, was actually quite rare in an age when no more than five people in a hundred reached the age of 65. Auguste, Johann Feigl, and Perusini's three patients were simply lost among the masses of patients suffering the late consequences of syphilis. In any case, the fact that of the entire neuropathological oeuvre published by Alzheimer, precisely the two articles dealing with 'pre-senile dementia' have been highlighted is a reflection of the rapid increase in the number of Alzheimer patients in our day. Alzheimer died as an expert on syphilis and was resurrected as the discoverer of Alzheimer's disease.

But perhaps there was another reason why in 1915 he was not remembered as the man who discovered Alzheimer's disease. Many contemporaries shared the reservations which Alzheimer himself had: was it actually a separate disease, a clearly defined entity? In the brain of Auguste he had found two sorts of deviant cells: tangles

---

[35] Nissl, 'Zum Andenken', 107.

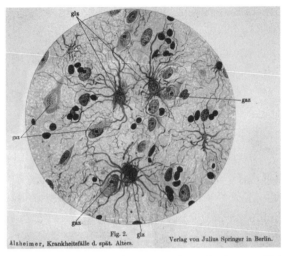

Figure 8.5: Photomicrography of a section from the brain of Johann Feigl

and plaques. The clinical picture of Feigl was an exact match to that of Auguste, but Alzheimer had discovered no tangles in his brain. That finding would be confirmed by later research. The brain of Johann Feigl, in the form of 150 preparations, is still in the archives of the Institute for Neuropathology in Munich. In 1992, when they were rediscovered, those sections were re-examined.[36] Techniques not available in Alzheimer's day confirmed the absence of tangles. Like true neuroarcheologists, the researchers then left a portion of the material untouched, awaiting new techniques or new insights into the genetic background of Alzheimer's disease.[37] In 1997, it was discovered that those same archives housed the brain of Auguste: the

[36] M. B. Graeber *et al.*, 'Rediscovery of the case described by Alois Alzheimer in 1911: historical, histological and molecular genetic analysis', *Neurogenetics*, 1 (1997), 73–80.

[37] H.-J. Möller and M. B. Graeber, 'The case described by Alois Alzheimer in 1911: historical and conceptual perspectives based on the clinical record and neuro-histological sections', *European Archive of Psychiatry and Clinical Neuroscience*, 248 (1998), 111–22.

270 colourful sections, each one-tenth of a millimetre thick, had survived two world wars.[38]

After the death of Feigl, Alzheimer recorded a diagnosis of 'Alzheimer'sche Krankheit'. But once he had examined the brain of this patient under his beloved Zeiss microscope, doubts must have arisen. It would appear that Alzheimer's disease was not the same thing as 'tangles plus plaques'. But without tangles, was he looking at a different disease or a variant of the same disease? Alzheimer himself made no pronouncement on this issue, but later generations of neurologists opted for the latter conclusion: Johann F was suffering from the 'plaques-only' variant of Alzheimer's disease.[39]

And then there is Gaetano Perusini. When in the spring of 1908, Kraepelin attributed the eponym, he did not have at his disposal the findings of Perusini, whose account was not completed until December of that year. He recorded the details of three new cases, as well as a histopathological study which was much more detailed than that of Alzheimer. Not too long ago, Italian physicians suggested that the name be changed to 'Alzheimer-Perusini disease'.[40] That manoeuvre was doomed to failure: once an eponym has gained acceptance, it is cast in stone. But it would have been a fitting tribute to a pathologist whose promising career ended at the age of 36, when he was killed in the First World War, ten days before the death of Alzheimer.

Alzheimer and Perusini were pathologists, and in all their writings, there is not a single word about treatment or therapy. Kraepelin, director of an institute, did address the subject, but his recommendations are limited to a single brief and somewhat bland paragraph: give due attention to personal hygiene; combat insomnia with baths; treat

[38] M. B. Graeber et al., 'Histopathology and APOE genotype of the first Alzheimer disease patient, Auguste D.', Neurogenetics, 1 (1998), 223–8.
[39] Möller and Graeber, 'Case', III.
[40] G. Macchi, C. Brahe and M. Pomponi, 'Alois Alzheimer and Gaetano Perusini: should man divide what fate united?', European Journal of Neurology, 4 (1997), 210–13.

'delirious states of agitation' by adding sedatives to the diet; and allay anxiety by administering small quantities of opium.[41] We do not know whether Alzheimer was optimistic or pessimistic about the likelihood of finding a cure for 'his' disease. At that juncture in history, many physicians would have found it difficult not to be optimistic, when pathogens responsible for various dreaded epidemic diseases were regularly being discovered: gangrene (1881), tuberculosis (1882), cholera (1883), rabies (1885), diphtheria (1890), tetanus (1892), dysentery (1898). There had been revolutionary developments in Alzheimer's specialism as well. In 1905, one year after the appearance of his own research into 'progressive paralysis', two German zoologists discovered the cause of syphilis, and a year later Wassermann developed the test which made it possible to establish the presence of a syphilis infection in a living being. In 1910, Ehrlich launched the remedy 'Salvarsan', putting an end to the dangerous mercury cures which had been employed up until then. Thus, within twenty years it had become possible to treat, cure or prevent a whole series of diseases. However, these were all infectious diseases, and up to then there was no indication that Alzheimer's disease fell into that category.

But if Alzheimer was indeed optimistic about the possibility of finding a remedy, he must have been just about the last person on the planet to hold that view. Ageing occurs in those parts of the world where there is money to be made from disease, and despite enormous investments in pharmaceutical research, the medication that can cure or prevent Alzheimer's is still beyond the horizon. Remedies capable of slowing the course of the disease have minor (barely measurable) effects, while the side-effects which accompany them often place a greater burden on the sufferer and his loved ones than the confusion and forgetfulness. A great deal of expertise has been accumulated with respect to the biochemical course of the catastrophe, the composition

---

[41] Kraepelin, 'Seniele', p. 630.

of the plaques, the formation of the tangles, the nature of the genes on chromosomes 1, 14, 19 and 21 (which appear to play a specific role in the susceptibility to the disease), the sections of the brain which are initially and most severely affected, and the order in which the clinical symptoms present themselves. And yet all this knowledge has not created a single opening in the direction of treatment. In the history of Alzheimer's research, a whole list of risk factors pertaining to nutrition, environmental influences and lifestyle have been put forward and subsequently refuted or retracted. And even when taken together, they are as nothing in comparison with that single risk factor over which we have so little control: ageing. Given the long trajectory of aspirant medicines during the test phase, any medication scheduled to become available in the next three or four years would have to have been discovered several years ago. It is unlikely that one fine day someone will take a key out of his pocket and, murmuring under his breath 'Shall we see if this fits?', take the first step leading to the eradication of Alzheimer's disease. Where this malady is concerned, what Kraepelin announced to the waiting pathologists as he left Alzheimer's lab – about the slow grinding of the anatomical mills – has proved to be a sombre but accurate prediction.

When in 1906 Alzheimer referred to 'future research', he was hoping that it would one day be possible to classify the disease more accurately by means of histopathological research. That has not proved to be the case. A hundred years later, the borders of 'Alzheimer's disease' are more ragged than ever. Since the mid-1990s, many researchers have preferred the term 'Alzheimer's diseases', a category which encompasses a spectrum of variants, types and subtypes.[42] One mysterious detail is the fact that tangles and plaques are sometimes found in the brains of people who did not display the clinical picture of Alzheimer's. The border with a form of dementia caused by the above-mentioned Lewy bodies is likewise

---

[42] A. D. Roses, 'The Alzheimer diseases', *Current Opinion in Biology*, 6 (1996), 644–50.

unclear. In one out of four Alzheimer patients, the brain contains Lewy bodies, and in the case of the plaques-only variant, that proportion is much higher. Often the symptoms bear such a close resemblance to those of both Alzheimer's disease (confusion and memory loss) and Parkinson's (rigidity, tremor, shuffling gait) that it has been suggested that Lewy bodies dementia should be classified as a variant of one of these two diseases. One out of three Parkinson patients ultimately develops Alzheimer's, while the Alzheimer's diseases are themselves part of a spectrum of dementias. Although Alzheimer's accounts for about three-quarters of all cases of dementia, the condition can also develop as a result of damage to the blood vessels in the brain (multi-infarct or vascular dementia).

If a committee of today's neurologists, geneticists and molecular biologists were asked to suggest a name for what we know today as 'Alzheimer's disease', they would not have opted for this particular eponym. The clinical significance of Alzheimer's disease, which in 1908 was characterized by Kraepelin as 'still unclear', is today no less than a medical arena. To some extent, the conflicts and controversies arise because the borderlines in one discipline are totally natural and practical (in terms of neuropathological findings, say), while in another discipline they appear quite artificial. It might be more correct to say that the Alzheimer diseases exist in the same way that Scorpio and the other signs of the zodiac exist: no one would deny the existence of the various stars which make up the signs of the zodiac, but it is also undeniable that they could just as well have been arranged in different constellations.

Since Alzheimer's day, the life expectancy of human beings has doubled, while the percentage of elderly people has tripled. There has also been a rapid increase in the number of patients with Alzheimer's disease. And not only will there be more Alzheimer's patients in the future, they will also suffer from the disease longer. In the Western world, there is a generation emerging which consists of people who have carefully monitored their nutrition and lifestyle, and are therefore in relatively good health as they approach old age. Many of these fit and healthy bodies will be the abode of a confused mind for a longer and longer period. Sooner or later, the patient with early symptoms of Alzheimer will visit his GP or a memory psychologist, who will patiently ask the questions that Alzheimer asked. What is your name? What day is it today? How old are you, what are the names of your children, what year is it? Can you tell me what time it is? The knowledge – still intact – that these are things that a normal individual ought to know gives rise to shame, frustration and an embarrassing series of excuses. The patient knows that he is being subjected to the simplest exam that he has ever had to take, and that he will be unable to pass. Between the first visit to the family doctor and the death of the patient lies a period of some five years.

In the past, people suffering from the symptoms of Alzheimer's disease were said to be 'in their second childhood'. That comparison is far too romantic: the harsh reality has nothing whatsoever to do with that care-free period in our lives and the expectations normally associated with childhood – not for the patient, and not for those around him. In the course of the disease, many skills disappear in reverse order, beginning with the higher processes such as judgement, memory and concentration, and later on the motor skills. Ultimately that regression of functions also applies to reflexes. Newborn babies spread their toes upwards when you touch the soles of their feet, the Babinski reflex. After about six months, that reflex disappears and babies spread their toes downwards when touched, in the direction of the stimulus. In the very last stages of Alzheimer's, the Babinski reflex returns, together with other reflexes characteristic of newborn babies, such as sucking and grasping. It is the last stop on the return voyage. Like Auguste, the patient will curl up into the foetal position and die. Even today, the most common causes of death among Alzheimer patients are the same as for Auguste and Feigl: bedsores and pneumonia.

In the asylum in Frankfurt, Auguste dragged her bedclothes around with her, and in Munich Feigl did the rounds of the garden, at top speed and bathed in perspiration, gripping the tails of his coat. Today the architecture of most nursing homes is designed around that restlessness. Modern Augustes and Feigls are mercifully steered into an Escher-like labyrinth of tangles with no beginning and no end. Though they have long since lost their way, they will not go astray.

NINE

The Mercator of neurology: Brodmann's areas

When a seventeenth-century merchant vessel sailed home from the East Indies and moored in Amsterdam harbour, no living soul was allowed to leave the ship before a sealed chest had been taken from on board. That chest was transferred, under armed guard, to the headquarters of the VOC or Dutch East India Company. Not until its contents had been verified was the ship released and the crew allowed to disembark.

The contents of the trunk consisted of the logbook, the navigational readings and, most important of all, the charts.

Charts are many things at once: power, knowledge, capital. Since they can lend to one's own actions a decisive advantage, they are not always shared with others and have often been defended by force of arms. The prosperity of the great sea-faring nations of the sixteenth and seventeenth centuries was closely bound up with their insight into the strategic importance of charts. The high level of cartography in countries like Portugal, Italy, Spain and Holland was both condition and effect. Cartographers like Joan Blaeu and Gerard Mercator in Holland and Amerigo Vespucci in Florence actualized and perfected their atlases thanks to a commercial and military expansion to which they had contributed with their charts.

The prestige of cartography is also apparent beyond the field of geography. Science can make use of images, words and numbers; cartography is all three at once. Each chart is a visual document, the legend is the written word which tells you what you are seeing, and the scale represents the numerical relation to reality. Secretly, all the sciences would really rather be cartography, which is why so many sciences have atlases.

Brain maps

With the exception of geography, there is no science which has been so susceptible to the rhetorical appeal of cartography as the science of medicine.[1] The anatomical atlas has a tradition that goes back almost as far as the geographical atlas. In 1543, in Basel, Switzerland, *De humani corporis fabrica* by Andreas Vesalius saw the light of day. It contained 300 woodcuts by Jan Stephan van Calcar.[2] The drawings were not maps, any more than *De fabrica* was an atlas (the term 'atlas' for a collection of maps was only introduced in 1585 by Mercator). But we can already point to certain elements in the drawings which were borrowed from geographical maps. In a portrayal of the top of the brain, letters have been inserted: A and B indicate the right and left brain halves, and C the convolutions; the flaps P, which are folded forward, represent the hard cerebral membrane, while O indicates portions of the arachnoid. Vesalius has pulled the two halves of the brain slightly apart, revealing the corpus callosum L. The letters make it possible to render the topography of the various structures in detail. In the legend, Vesalius provides clarification, explaining to the reader what can be seen at each location. Thanks to the 'realistic' drawing

---

[1] L. Cartwright, *Screening the Body: Tracing Medicine's Visual Culture* (Minneapolis, 1995).

[2] A. Vesalius, *De humani corporis fabrica* (Basel, 1543).

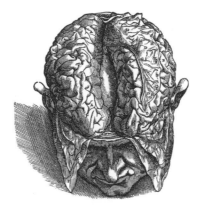

Figure 9.1: This illustration of the brain in *De fabrica* by Andreas Vesalius is the second in a series of instructional drawings for purposes of dissection. In the *dedicatio* of a previous print publication, Vesalius explains that these drawings are an exact representation of what there is to see: 'Not a single line of the drawn illustrations is unnatural; the plates faithfully represent the organs of the body as they will be shown to the students in Padua.' The implicit metaphor is that of the eye-witness: it was the task of Van Calcar to record what someone present at the dissection could see. But in order to steer the observation process, Vesalius made use of cartographical conventions

technique, with hatching, depth and the inclusion of the parts of the head which are still intact, Vesalius has also provided a decisive answer to the question of the relative size of the different parts of the brain, i.e. he has respected the scale of the representation.

Less than ten years after the publication of *De fabrica*, Bartolomeo Eustachius, personal physician to the Pope, commissioned a magnificent series of copper engravings of the human anatomy. After his death they were found in his estate, unpublished, and it was not until 1714 that they appeared in print as *Tabulae anatomicae*.[3] By means of scale divisions in the margin of the prints, like those seen on maps, Eustachius ensured that the proportions were accurately quantified. In the legend, the scales provided the coordinates.

---

[3] B. Eustachius, *Tabulae anatomicae* (Rome, 1714).

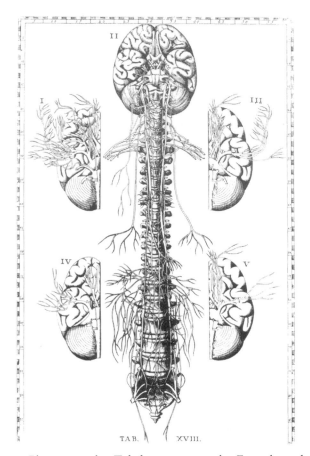

Figure 9.2: Plate 18 in the *Tabulae anatomicae* by Eustachius shows the sympathetic nervous system. The nerves, which originate on the underside of the brain and the spinal cord, branch out in a double strand along the spinal column. The surrounding space has been reserved for enlargements of the cerebellum and the brainstem

Maps played a crucial role in the great nineteenth-century debates on the localization of functions. In 1810, together with his colleague Spurzheim (1776–1832), Gall published a treatise on the brain in which he included many of his findings based on post mortems.[4]

---

[4] F. J. Gall and J. C. Spurzheim, *Anatomie et physiologie du système nerveux* (Paris, 1810–1819).

This *Anatomie et physiologie du système nerveux* was accompanied by an *Atlas*, with maps of the brain and the skull. Gall observed that, in a sense, it was unfortunate that inside the skull the brain is spherical in shape, since its actual structure is flat. One of his followers, the Dutch clergyman Stuart, wrote in his *Memories of the Lessons of Frans Joseph Gall* that the Viennese anatomist had proved that 'the brain is actually a flat layer of ash-grey medulla over which the nerves are spread out, and which is only folded into coils, while all those coils, after the removal of the thin cerebral membrane and the cobwebby tissue, by its very weight falls apart and presents itself as a thin, very soft cake, ash-grey on top and grey underneath'.[5] Without the supporting structure of the cerebral membrane, you could simply spread the brain out in front of you. The subsequent cartographic process would not be difficult: the brain could be copied onto the map without any projective manoeuvres such as waxing latitudes. In reality, however, the brain is more like a crumpled card carelessly stuffed into the brainpan, so that the draughtsman must martial his entire arsenal of cartographic techniques in order to ensure that both hemispheres are reliably portrayed in the flat plane.

The same problem presented itself when it came to drawing the locations of the faculties on the skull. The perspectivistic distortion increased from the centre of the map, but was tolerated. The decreasing size of the sections on the edge made it impossible to write the names of the 'organs of the mind' in the appropriate spaces. Although map-makers were able to engrave extremely small letters – well into the nineteenth century they were required to demonstrate their professional skill by engraving the 'Our Father' on a surface no bigger than a 10-cent coin – it was more practical to number the spaces and provide a legend, and this became common practice.

[5] M. Stuart, *Herinneringen uit de lessen van Frans Joseph Gall, Med. Doctor te Weenen, over de Hersenen, als onderscheiden en bepaalde werktuigen van den geest* (Amsterdam, 1806), p. xi.

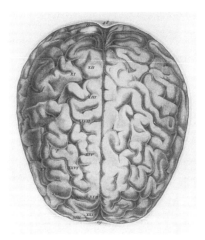

Figure 9.3: Brain map from the *Atlas* by Gall and Spurzheim, seen from above. Roman numerals indicate the 'brain organs'. Most of these are in the frontal lobe (here the bottom of the drawing). The numbers are on one side only: according to Gall, all faculties were represented double

For the brain maps, Gall and Spurzheim opted for the same solution. Intact brains are portrayed three-dimensionally from above, from the side, and from below. Shadow is used to create depth, but that is the depth of the surface (the cerebral cortex) rather than the interior of the brain. To map deeper structures, Gall and Spurzheim had another means at their disposal, one which, moreover, solved the problem of reducing the image to two dimensions: the cross-section. Many of the maps in the *Atlas* are sectional charts. The vertical plane, from the forehead to the back of the head, made it possible to portray not only the origin of the brain in the brainstem and the cerebellum, but also the faculties located in the convolutions of the cortex. The numbered 'skull elevations' were clarified in the legends. On maps with cross-sections, Gall and Spurzheim also used shadow to accentuate the convolutions with their roundings and depths, like mountain massifs on a geographical map. There were also the usual mixed charts, as in a real atlas.

But alongside comprehensiveness, precision and objectivity, the maps suggest something else as well. As a rule, what is to be charted consists of unknown areas, calling up images of explorers and voyages of discovery. Gall never claimed that status for himself, but his followers had fewer qualms when it came to appropriating the heroism inherent in the metaphor. Doornik wrote that the skull had become the map, 'on which, as in a real atlas, areas and places are delineated where Man is described, as in a small world. On a human skull one travels around, as on a globe, to search for and discover the places where our perceptions, desires, and mental powers are housed.'[6] His assessment of Gall's significance neatly fitted the metaphor of the explorer: 'Columbus discovered a new world *outside* us, and Gall discovered a new world *inside* us.'[7]

After the downfall of phrenology, the influence of the cartographical metaphor within neurology was sustained and even enhanced. The work of Broca and Wernicke during the 1860s and 1870s demanded new maps in order to record the relationship between the understanding of language, the motor system involved in speech, and the representation of the meaning of words. The introduction of experimental techniques such as extirpation and the electric stimulation of the cerebral cortex led to a wave of discoveries, each of which had to be drawn in. Alterations in the mapping of the brain required fundamental revisions of the brain atlases.

The portrayal of the brain in a drawing, complete with legends, scale and coordinates – in a word, the projection onto a map – turned neurologists into cartographers, surveyors and atlas-makers. In this way, they shared in the prestige of cartography. Maps ordered space in the same way that timepieces ordered time. They both quantified and visualised relationships; and they were a prerequisite for navigation and orientation.

Neurology (indeed, medical science as a whole) would be lost without atlases. An atlas which is known even outside the world of

---

[6] J. E. Doornik, *Voorlezingen over F. J. Gall's herssen-schedelleer in Felix Meritis and Doctrina et Amicitia, Winter 1805–1806* (Amsterdam, 1806), p. 4.

[7] Doornik, *Voorlezingen*, p. 4.

science is the *Visible Human*, a digitalized anatomical atlas of cross-sections. There is both a *Visible Man* and a *Visible Woman*. The material for the *Visible Man* was provided by a prisoner on death row for murder, who had bequeathed his body to science. After the execution, the bequest was dipped into gelatin, frozen, and then sliced into two thousand sections. These were photographed and digitalized, after which the sections were transformed into three-dimensional representations of organs and joints. Like the *Visible Woman*, for which a 59-year-old woman from Maryland donated her body, the *Visible Man* is partially accessible via the Internet.[8]

In the four and a half centuries between Vesalius and the *Visible Human*, the body has been charted and projected onto paper thousands of times. The chronology of the anatomical charts reflects the changes in the techniques of illustration: woodcuts in the days of Vesalius, copperplates in the sixteenth and seventeenth centuries, followed by the emergence of the wood engraving around 1830, and in 1873 the first photographic atlas, the *Iconographie photographique des centres nerveux* by Jules Luys. Before long, photography was itself offering a variety of specialized procedures like microscopic imaging and x-ray photography, while in our day there are such advanced techniques as magnetic resonance imaging and PET scans. But regardless of how the images are produced, they all find their way into the old, familiar anatomical atlas, testifying to the intriguing persistence of cartography as a metaphor.[9]

The *atlas maior* of neurology

What Blaeu and Mercator were to geography, Korbinian Brodmann was to neurology. While first editions of his *Vergleichende*

---

[8] For the *Visible Man* and the *Visible Woman*, see www.nlm.nih.gov/research/visible
[9] In the parlance of imaging techniques, the cartography metaphor has more or less merged with photographic metaphors, so that you occasionally hear someone say that maps have a certain 'resolution'.

Figure 9.4: This portrait of Korbinian Brodmann was printed by Oskar Vogt to accompany his necrology in 1919. It is one half of a double portrait with his wife, which means that it dates from around 1917

Lokalisationslehre der Grosshirnrinde (*Comparative Localization Studies in the Brain Cortex*), which appeared in 1909, may not fetch the prices which people are prepared to pay for the maps of Blaeu, they are extremely sought-after. Brodmann's topography has defined navigation on the surface of the brain. His division of the human brain into forty-seven areas is still largely adhered to: neurologists refer to 'Brodmann's areas', customarily abbreviated to references such as 'BA 44' (Brodmann Area 44). His explorations took place in a *terra incognita* quite close to home: a world that would be discovered by cutting brain tissue open and sliding it under a microscope.

Korbinian Brodmann was born in 1868 in the village of Liggersdorf, not far from Konstanz.[10] His father was a farmer. After finishing secondary school, he entered medical school in Munich, and later

---

[10] At www.korbinian-brodmann.de there is a biographical sketch of Brodmann, supplemented with photos, illustrations of maps, and a brief memorandum that Brodmann wrote on his life and his career. See also the 'In Memoriam' written by Oskar Vogt: O. Vogt, 'Korbinian Brodmann', *Journal für Psychologie und Neurologie*, 24 (1919), i–x.

continued his studies in Würzburg and Berlin. He graduated from the university in Freiburg im Breisgau in 1895. These peregrinations set the tone for the future. Brodmann's nomadic career, consisting of a seemingly endless series of temporary positions and interruptions due to circumstances beyond his control, was not of his own choosing. After completing his medical finals, he left for Munich to work in a children's clinic, but he contracted diphtheria and went to convalesce in the Fichtel Mountains in Bavaria. It was there that he met the neurologist Oskar Vogt, who had a practice in a neurological clinic in Alexanderbad. He offered Brodmann a position as assistant and convinced him to go into psychiatry and neurology. However, Brodmann felt that he lacked the necessary background to make a real contribution to clinical neurology, and enrolled in new courses of studies in Berlin and Leipzig which focused on psychiatry and the anatomy of the brain. He obtained his doctorate in Leipzig in 1898, with a dissertation on the atrophy of nerve tissue.

Of his ten or so appointments in the course of almost twenty years, which took him to clinics, sanatoriums, psychiatric institutions and laboratories throughout Germany, it was above all his stay in Frankfurt am Main which was instrumental in preparing him for the neurotopographical work with which his name is associated. Starting in 1900, Brodmann worked for a year and a half in the city's Asylum for Lunatics and Epileptics, where he became acquainted with Alzheimer's neuropathological research. It was in that same autumn of 1901, as Brodmann was preparing to move on again, that Alzheimer recorded his first findings on Auguste D. Franz Nissl had left several years before, but while in Alzheimer's laboratory he had introduced various staining techniques. In the hands of Nissl and Alzheimer, the 'Nissl stain' was used to study the pathology of nerve cells, as in dementia or sclerosis. It was also an indispensable tool for researchers involved in topographical anatomy.

In 1899, Vogt had founded the Neurologische Zentralstation, a private neurological clinic, and in 1901 he invited Brodmann to come to Berlin. Vogt had a major project in mind for him: a topography of the entire cerebral cortex. Brodmann was able to work on this project continuously from 1901 to 1909. Interim reports appeared in neurological journals in the form of seven *Mitteilungen* (reports). In 1909, the firm of Barth in Leipzig published the synthesis of some ten years of patient and painstaking mapping: the *atlas maior* of the cortex or, to give it its full name, *Vergleichende Lokalisationslehre der Grosshirnrinde in ihren Prinzipien dargestellt auf Grund des Zellenbaues.*[11]

Brodmann's topography

Brodmann's topography was a 'comparative' localization theory, which means that he was attempting to record the topography of the human brain alongside that of mammals in general. While he devoted a separate section to the human brain, Brodmann was convinced that its topography had a great deal in common with that of apes, kangaroos, marmots and hedgehogs. This will be apparent to any reader leafing through Brodmann's atlas, with its numerous maps pertaining to a wide variety of animals. Some of them, such as cats, dogs, rabbits and rats, were not difficult to find, but Brodmann also studied the brains of the orang-utan, Capuchin monkey, lion, brown bear, tiger, seal and elephant. The *Lokalisationslehre* reads like roll call at the zoo. Small wonder that in his foreword, the author expresses his special gratitude to two zoologists at the Zoo in Berlin. They saw to it that, once deceased, a large portion of their menagerie found its way to Vogt's Neurologische Zentralstation. There, Brodmann removed the brain, which was then cut into sections, mounted, stained, placed under a microscope, photographed and described. Regardless of whether they had crawled, crept,

---

[11] K. Brodmann, *Vergleichende Lokalisationslehre der Grosshirnrinde in ihren Prinzipien dargestellt auf Grund des Zellenbaues* (Leipzig, 1909). In 1994, an English translation of the *Lokalisationslehre* by L. J. Garey appeared: *Brodmann's 'Localisation in the Cerebral Cortex'* (London, 1994).

Figure 9.5: The double-bladed microtome which Brodmann used to cut brain sections. While there is something almost endearing about the small Biedermeier-style microtome used by Von Gudden in 1872, those employed by Vogt and Brodmann have an industrial air about them: they are the instruments of a discipline that means business

jumped, flown or swum while alive, whether they had roared, barked or trumpeted, the brains of all these animals ended up mute and motionless, captured between two tiny glass plates in a drawer in Brodmann's archives.

Between the moment when the brain of the animal (a guenon, say) became available, and the moment its brain map was published as figure 90 in the *Lokalisationslehre*, lay a series of technical interventions. After the actual slicing of the sections (still a ticklish procedure), they were photographed. Given the weak lighting in the microscope, the sections had to be almost transparent, no thicker than 10 microns (0.01 mm). In those early years, Brodmann and Vogt experimented with various microtomes and preparation techniques designed to bring that ideal within reach.[12] Brodmann made use of two microtomes. One of them, for the coarse work, was 'eine Art Guillotine' which cut sections several millimetres thick. These were placed in a paraffin bath, and once the paraffin was absorbed and

---

[12] K. Brodmann, 'Zwei neue Apparate zur Paraffinserientechnik', *Journal für Psychologie und Neurologie*, 2 (1903), 206–10.

the section had gained the necessary firmness, the 'double-bladed microtome' was capable of producing sections of between 5 and 10 microns.

Both machines were built by the *Feinmechaniker* Becker in Göttingen, according to the instructions of Vogt's laboratory. The double-bladed microtome was a highly sophisticated piece of apparatus: the blade was stabilized on both sides, so that it could not be displaced by the section and, thanks to an ingenious cardan construction, the tissue could be sliced in any desired plane. Moreover, the thickness could be adjusted and read off with a high degree of accuracy. Vogt later designed a 'pantomicrotome' which sold for 1,300 German marks and produced larger sections. However, the knife continued to present problems: the sharper it was, the more prone it was to damage, and if the tempering of the blade was even slightly irregular, an electric current was created which promoted rust formation. This was ascertained, Vogt wrote, in the Krupp laboratory in Essen.[13] It would later become clear that these were not the only connections between Vogt and Krupp.

There are many different ways in which brain tissue can be charted, each of which produces its own maps. Many of the maps in existence around 1900 were based on tracing the trajectories of fibres and nerves. But Brodmann's mapping was based on 'cytoarchitecture': the structure, shape and position of cells. The method was that of microscopic research, and microscopic research alone: injury studies such as those of Broca and Wernicke, or the extirpation experiments carried out by Flourens, were mentioned by Brodmann only in order to make it clear that there was no place for them in his localization theory. The physiological characteristics of cells or cell groups, such as their reaction to electrical stimulation, were likewise irrelevant. In Brodmann's view, designating portions

---

[13] O. Vogt, 'Das Pantomikrotom des Neurobiologischen Laboratoriums', *Journal für Psychologie und Neurologie*, 6 (1905), 121–5.

of the cerebral cortex as sensory or motor projection areas, or as association areas, would border on the irresponsible. He always placed such terms in quotation marks: it was far too early for a reliable function localization. Moreover, Brodmann wrote, there were considerable discrepancies between the various authors as regards the exact borders of those projection areas. Only when the cytoarchitecture had been mapped would it be possible to draw up an exact correspondence between areas and functions.

In passages such as these, the reader senses Brodmann's almost physical abhorrence of contradictory results, differences in terminology, changing conventions, and variations in the techniques used to slice, mount and stain the sections, in short, everything which neurology had as yet been unable to standardize. It is clear from the first two tables just how great Brodmann's aversion was. We see an enumeration of the layers which, according to different authors, make up the cerebral cortex. In Man, the number of layers varies from five to nine, in other animals from three to ten: an intolerable variation. The naming likewise differs from one researcher to the next. Not only does one and the same layer bear different names, there are also cases where different layers share the same name. In the *Lokalisationslehre*, Brodmann presented research results designed to make it unambiguously clear that there were *six* layers, in Man and in all other mammals. And he gave those layers Latin names, which referred to the cell types they were made up of. It was clear that Brodmann wanted to be more than just a voice in the choir, he wanted to be the conductor.

Wherever possible, Brodmann strove for standardization. The sections were of a standard thickness, were subjected to a standard preparation (fixed in formalin, followed by a paraffin bath), and treated with a standard stain (Nissl stain). All the sections were cut perpendicular to the surface. The microscope was set to a standard enlargement. The illustration of the sections, in the form of 'photomicrographs', was standard. Brodmann explained that it was only against this uniform background that quantitative comparisons of such qualities as cell density and cell size were possible. In this way, he discovered, among other things, that the thickness of the six cell layers varies with the body weight of the various animals, and is independent of the order to which they belong. Thus, as regards thickness, the cell layers of a cat bear a closer resemblance to those of a rabbit than to those of a large feline such as a lion.

In the second section of his book, Brodmann presents the topographical maps of the cortex, based on the counts and measurements in the six layers. In maritime terms, Brodmann was 'hugging the coast': his maps pertain to the surface, which in Man is nowhere thicker than three millimetres. The structures deeper within the brain play no role at all. Before presenting the maps, he commented on the complications and limitations of cartography. His brain maps were schematic representations in which certain distortions were unavoidable. How do you draw regions and areas whose borders lie hidden in the depths of grooves? How can you represent more or less spherical areas on the flat surface of a map? How do you draw clear borders in areas of the brain with a diffuse transition? These were all familiar cartographical problems. Distortions were inherent in maps, Brodmann wrote, but the relative position of the areas in relation to one another was respected and, when all was said and done, a map was itself no more than a crutch for purposes of orientation.

Brodmann had already finished the maps of Man and the hedgehog, and quite a few animals in between: various apes, the fruit bat, the honey bear and the Siberian chipmunk. These brains were sampled across the main orders of mammals, in itself an extremely time-consuming process. Even when map-making was confined to the surface of the brain, it required hundreds of sections, each of which had to be prepared and analysed. Throughout the history of neurology, Brodmann's two maps of the human brain, the side view of the left hemisphere (above) and the interior of the right hemisphere (below), are among the illustrations most often reproduced.

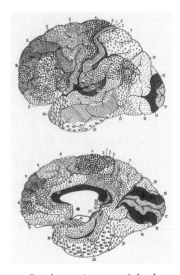

Figure 9.6: Brodmann's map of the human brain

The numbers refer to the 'areae', which would come to be known as Brodmann's areas. Although Brodmann numbered through, up to and including 47, he did not assign an area to each number. For the time being the numbers 12 through 16 were left open, since area 11 might later have to be subdivided. On a detailed map he gave another area the number 52, which helped to disseminate the mistaken belief that Brodmann had divided the cortex into 52 areas. He discussed the cell structure of each area, the nature of its borders, its shape and position, and its relationship to other areas. Some of those which had already been identified on the basis of injury studies or physiological characteristics were also found to form a unit on the basis of their cytoarchitecture, such as Broca's area, which corresponded to Brodmann's area 44, or Wernicke's area (BA 22). In part, Brodmann made use of his own topography in describing the position of the areas ('area 19 lies like a ring around area 18'), as well as traditional designations such as the position with respect to the Sylvian groove.

The atlas also contains maps of the apes and lower animal species. Their brains display the same global fields, but the number of areas steadily decreases. The equivalents of the areas 36, 37 and 44 and several others present in Man are lacking in monkeys. Brodmann included detailed maps of human brains, in order to demonstrate how they differ from the topography in apes.

Later on, he discussed in greater detail the construction of the human brain and how it differed from that of apes. While the overall structure was comparable, the surface of the cortex in Man was many times larger, due to the extent and depth of the folding. That of Man measured some 200,000 square millimetres, or a surface area of about 40 by 50 cm, compared with no more than 50,000 square millimetres for an orang-utan.

The ape sulcus

Brodmann also carried out comparative research into the differences between the brains of people of 'different ethnic origins', to borrow a contemporary expression. He himself used the term 'foreign races'.[14] When a colleague from Jena made him a present of three brains of Javanese origin, Brodmann had an opportunity to confirm or deny the existence of a so-called 'Affenspalte' or 'ape sulcus' in the human brain. The English anthropologist Elliot Smith had examined a large number of Egyptian and Sudanese brains, 70 per cent of which displayed a fissure in the occipital lobe at the back of the head, something which until then had only been seen in anthropoids. Brodmann had noted this finding with some degree of scepticism, but after examining his three Javanese brains, he had no choice but to conclude that they, too, had the ape sulcus.[15] Moreover, another area in the Javanese brains was closer in size to the corresponding

---

[14] Cited from Brodmann, *Localisation*, p. 227.

[15] In *Lokalisationslehre*, Brodmann published only the conclusions of his research; the complete account appeared in one of the *Mitteilungen*: K. Brodmann, 'Beiträge zur histologischen Lokalisation der Grosshirnrinde. Fünfte Mitteilung', *Journal für Psychologie und Neurologie*, 6 (1906), 275–400 (295–309).

area in orang-utan brains than to that in 'European brains'. By presenting detailed maps of the occipital lobe of one of the Javanese brains and the occipital lobe of a five-year-old male orang-utan, Brodmann provided visual proof of the ape sulcus which the two had in common. In addition, he took no fewer than 2,100 sections from the very tip of the occipital lobe of the orang-utan, and portrayed every one-hundredth section as a hand-drawn diagram. These eighteen diagrams likewise demonstrated that the orang-utan brain was closer to the Javanese than to the European brain. Later, Brodmann also had at his disposal a number of Hottentot brains: these likewise bore a greater resemblance to the brains of anthropoids than to those of Europeans.

This part of Brodmann's work is a revealing excerpt from the history of neurology. There are all manner of methodological objections which could be made to his research. For one thing, there is the question of how representative the three Javanese brains were. There is no information available on age, disease or cause of death. Nor do we know what condition the brains were in after the long journey from Java to Berlin. Had they been embalmed, preserved in formalin? Brodmann's study was not performed 'blind', since he always knew exactly which brain the sections came from, a procedure which left room for prejudice. But the main issue here is the fact that the *entire* atlas was compiled in the same way, and that no such objections have been raised against the rest of his results. All one can say is that Brodmann's research, executed according to the then current rules of the art, did not refute the prevailing prejudice that all races except the white race have lagged somewhat behind on the road from anthropoid to human, but rather lent it scientific status. As he counted, measured, weighed, observed and compared, making use of the most advanced instruments available, Brodmann practised neurology at the highest level, and his facts conformed unerringly to what European scientists and their public already held to be true.

The visual argument

The publication of the *Lokalisationslehre* gave rise to detailed discussions. This was due in part to the tone of the book. In his introduction, Brodmann discussed the views of his predecessors in such a way that the reader could easily get the impression that until his arrival in the realm of brain science, the field had been plagued by total anarchy: in terminology, methodology, topography and theory. Brodmann magnified the conflicting results of those who had gone before, rounding off the discussion with a rhetorical question such as 'What are the real facts?'.[16] Despite the respect which the new atlas commanded, the tone gave rise to considerable annoyance. The Amsterdam neurologist Ariëns Kappers, in his extensive and appreciative review, suggested that in the following edition Brodmann might make more of an effort to see the good in the research of others.[17]

In his *Lokalisationslehre*, Brodmann appealed to the persuasive power of visual arguments. Broadly speaking, the 150 '*Abbildungen*' in the book fall into two categories: drawn maps and 'photomicrographs'. In the same year that Brodmann arrived in Berlin, Vogt had also taken on a photographer, Wilhelm Riedel, who developed a process which made it possible to take relatively sharp photos of the sections. The vast majority of the illustrations in the *Lokalisationslehre* consist of such photomicrographs. In the margin alongside the photos Brodmann has noted which cell layers or cell types could be distinguished. No matter what differences of opinion might arise with respect to the number of layers, cell density, or size, Brodmann wrote, they could all be settled by inspecting the sections: 'I believe that my illustrations, even when examined rapidly,

---

[16] Brodmann, *Localisation*, p. 63.
[17] C. U. Ariëns Kappers, 'Besprechung', *Zeitschrift für Psychologie und Physiologie der Sinnesorgane*, 58 (1911), 277–94 (294).

can give an unequivocal answer to the questions that have been posed.'[18] And indeed, this is one of the most striking aspects of the atlas: the arrangement of the areas was based on the count and measurement of the cells, while the photomicrographs were the representation of *what* had been counted and measured. The quantitative comparison on which the entire topographical project was based is visible in only a few places, as a collection of figures. Here again, Brodmann shows himself to be a true map-maker, with a clear preference for the visual.

No other cytoarchitectural maps have achieved the same broad acceptance accorded those of Brodmann. The French historian of science Bruno Latour coined the phrase 'proof race'.[19] The designation is quite apt here, given that what is needed to produce evidence inevitably forces rivals to resort to increasingly strong measures. The cost, in terms of time, money and equipment, can reach such proportions that the opponent is ultimately forced to acknowledge the hopelessness of his position. Just imagine the plight of a researcher who came along after Brodmann and was determined to present an alternative cartography of the cortex. How would he go about gathering his evidence? To begin with, he would have to have at his disposal a decade of undisturbed observation, a well-equipped laboratory, a passion for work bordering on the manic which effectively precludes anything but a celibate life, as well as an excellent relationship with the local zoo. He would also need a devotion to precision, planning and standardization and, for good measure, a polemical attitude and a passion for 'getting it right' which together provide the necessary motivation for such a long-term project. This was in effect the remarkable constellation of factors which hovered over Berlin between 1901 and 1910 and subsequently broke up and disappeared into thin air.

---

[18] Brodmann, *Localisation*, p. 63.
[19] B. Latour, 'Drawing things together' in M. Lynch and S. Woolgar (eds.), *Representation in Scientific Practice* (Cambridge MA, 1990), pp. 19–68, 35.

Another factor of importance was Brodmann's excellent sense of scale. The Vogts, husband and wife, published a brain map based on fibre architecture which distinguished almost four times as many areas as Brodmann had done, but ultimately proved overly detailed. The division into some fifty areas was considerably more convenient. Of course, this does not mean that no more brain maps were forthcoming. Brodmann's cartographical selection left sufficient room for other topographical projects. He himself did not chart anything that lay deeper than a few millimetres, and this lent his maps a quality reminiscent of the sixteenth-century maps of newly discovered continents, with their detailed drawings of coastlines and the large empty plains further inland. Many of the atlases which appeared after Brodmann were derived from vertical or horizontal cross-sections of the entire brain. Moreover, they were more heterogeneous, containing maps of the larger structures, bundles of nerves and maps of the vascular system or the structure of the cerebellum.

There was another limiting factor inherent in Brodmann's working method. The random cutting up of individual brains into hundreds of sections, the analysis of the cell structure and the process of transforming the counts into a topography, a process which was repeated with a large number of mammals (the *Lokalisationslehre* included over sixty), meant that the brains examined were indeed *individual* brains. All told, Brodmann probably examined only a handful of different human brains under his microscope. Seeing that the size of certain areas of the brain can vary by a factor of eight or nine, many neurologists later opted for a topography based on the *average* brain size. Moreover, Brodmann's decision to confine himself to healthy adult brains meant that there was ample opportunity for others to chart brain development from the embryonic phase, through maturation, to the decline, or to map the neuropathology which lies at the root of diseases such as Alzheimer's and Parkinson's.

He could only look down his microscope

A century after the publication of the *Lokalisationslehre*, 'Brodmann's areas' are still in use as topographical coordinates, even in the dozens of atlases based on totally different cartographic departure points. In many cases, it was possible to project structure and function onto one another, so that Brodmann's areas 1, 2 and 3 now form the somatosensory cortex, 17 and 18 the primary visual cortex, and 41 and 42 the auditive cortex. The advent of imaging techniques in brain research gave neurological cartography a new impulse. In her dissertation, the science researcher A. Beaulieu shows how brain maps, like the atlases of Blaeu long ago, not only reflect the results of research but also give direction to new research, thus representing a strategic interest within the world of researchers.[20] She also notes that brain cartography is now a form of high tech: a far cry from the quiet tasks of slicing and counting performed in the laboratory of Oskar Vogt. An atlas which has been in common use since the 1990s is the 'Talairach', compiled by the Paris neurosurgeons Talairach and Tournoux.[21] Like Brodmann, they charted a single hemisphere (in this case, that of a woman over 60 years of age) and placed the photographic sections in a Cartesian space with three axes. This made it possible for users to indicate brain locations in coordinates that refer to a three-dimensional grid, after which Brodmann's areas are simply projected onto the surface of this brain.

A cartographic project has recently been launched which resembles that of Brodmann.[22] The initiator is Karl Zilles, a fellow countryman of Brodmann who is associated with the Cécile and Oskar Vogt Institute for Brain Research at the University of Düsseldorf. When

---

[20] A. Beaulieu, *The Space Inside the Skull* (Amsterdam, diss., 2000).

[21] J. Talairach and P. Tournoux, *Co-planar Stereotaxic Atlas of the Human Brain* (Stuttgart, 1988).

[22] K. Zilles and N. Palomero-Gallagher, 'Cyto-, myelo-, and receptor architectonics of the human parietal cortex', *NeuroImage*, 14 (2001), S8–S20.

Figure 9.7: Brodmann at work in the neurophotographic laboratory of the Neurobiological Institute in Berlin

completed, the atlas will be based on the averages of fifteen brains. Each brain is encased in a paraffin block and then sliced into between 5,000 and 8,000 sections, 20 microns thick. Each section is stored on a glass plate; every fifteenth section is stained in order to make the cells visible, and every sixtieth section is actually analysed. This is done by means of a scanner. A computer then calculates the cell density and determines where the borders lie on the basis of statistically significant differences. According to Zilles in an interview in *Nature*, 'there is 1.2 mm between each section analysed, which at the moment is sufficient'.[23] If in future there should be a need for more detailed maps, the stored sections can then be analysed.

Like Brodmann before him, Zilles sings the praises of his atlas, which makes use of 'objective techniques'. For Zilles, the essence of that objectivity lies in the automatic registration of cell density, and the use of a computer to define the borders of areas, using a statistical program. It is a form of mechanical objectivity designed to distance cartography as far as possible from human intervention.

[23] A. Abbot, 'Neuroscience: a new atlas of the brain', *Nature*, 424 (2003), 249–50.

During the interview, Zilles made a casual remark about the work of his illustrious predecessor, employing a term which would have set Korbinian Brodmann's teeth on edge: 'Brodmann's judgement about what constituted cortical areas was, by necessity, subjective – he could only look down his microscope and report.'[24]

In one of the few photos of Brodmann at work, that is exactly what he is doing: seated at a table opposite the window, so that the light falls on the section, he peers intently down a microscope. The contrast with the two photos which accompany the interview with Zilles in *Nature* is striking. In one, we see the microtome that will automatically slice the sections, which will later, likewise automatically, be counted and mapped by the computer. The other shows the researcher himself, smiling as he poses alongside several enlarged sections which are mounted on the wall, by way of art. The transition to 'mechanical objectivity' has also produced a new iconography of the scientist.

Krupp steel

No doubt the year 2009 will see the commemoration of how nearly ten years of peering down a microscope and reporting the results produced a cartography which is still part of the neurologist's daily instrumentarium. The maxim *vita brevis, ars longa* was eminently applicable to Brodmann, for the story of his life after the atlas is exceedingly short. In 1910, Kraepelin suggested that he consider submitting his study on the pro-simian cortex to the Medical Faculty as habilitation treatise. He was bitterly disappointed when it was rejected as '*ungeeignet*' (unsuitable). In the previous ten years he had built up a solid reputation in anatomical topography and, as Vogt later wrote in his necrology, by arrogantly rejecting one of his best studies, the Berlin Medical Faculty had shouldered a 'guilt which

---

[24] Abbot, 'Neuroscience', 249.

could not be redeemed'.[25] However, the irony of the situation is that that rejection was the result of Vogt's own machinations.

At crucial moments, Brodmann's career was bound up with that of Vogt, and not always to Brodmann's advantage. Oskar Vogt, two years his junior, had studied medicine in Jena.[26] Having grown up in straitened circumstances, Vogt always kept a sharp eye out for anything calculated to enhance his social position and, if necessary, he was prepared to create the desired conditions. In 1896, he accepted the lowly position of Kurarzt at the Alexanderbad in Bavaria, in the hope of rubbing shoulders with the rich clientele taking the waters there. His plan was eminently successful, for one of his patients was the sister-in-law of steel magnate Friedrich Albert Krupp. Soon he was ministering to Krupp's wife Margarethe and finally to the magnate himself. All three benefited from Vogt's therapy, which consisted largely of hypnotism. The charming Vogt soon became the trusted confidant of the Krupp family, and in 1898 he accompanied them on a cruise around the Mediterranean. It was during this voyage that he succeeded in persuading Friedrich Albert to help finance a laboratory devoted to brain research, which, initially at least, would circumvent the academic bureaucracy. In 1899, Vogt, by then married to the French neurologist Cécile Mugnier, founded his Neurologische Zentralstation in Berlin.

The fact that on Magdeburger Strasse a well-equipped neurological institute was functioning caused considerable ill-feeling at the Medical Faculty of Friedrich-Wilhelm University. Vogt and Krupp felt that the Zentralstation should ultimately be incorporated into the university, and to that end, Vogt submitted a research programme. It was rejected almost by return of mail. However, Krupp had influential friends, including Kaiser Wilhelm II, and in 1902

[25] Vogt, 'Korbinian Brodmann', viii.
[26] I. Klatzo, Cécile and Oskar Vogt: the Visionaries of Modern Neuroscience (Vienna/New York, 2002).

the university authorities felt compelled to allow the Zentralstation to be administratively incorporated into the university's Physiological Institute, where it was known as the 'Neurobiological Laboratory'. A year earlier, Brodmann had joined the staff as a neurotopographer.

In November 1902, the survival of the laboratory was hanging by a thread. An Italian gossip magazine had published stories about Krupp's homosexual involvement with young Italian men at his holiday villa on Capri. On 15 November, the German socialist party voiced similar accusations in its own publication. On 22 November, Vogt was called to the bedside of Krupp, who was dying. He signed the death certificate, entering 'acute heart failure' as the cause of death. When Wilhelm II publicly accused the socialists of causing Krupp's death, and speculation was rife about a possible suicide, Vogt found himself in a difficult position. The scandal died down, however, and in 1906, Krupp's successor at the helm of the steel empire honoured all his predecessor's commitments, including those made to the Neurobiological Laboratory. But relations with the university were never anything but tense. The fact that Brodmann's neurotopographical study, carried out in Vogt's laboratory, was rejected point-blank by the Medical Faculty came as a surprise to no one – except perhaps the author.

Brodmann drew his own conclusions. Resuming his nomadic existence, he accepted a position as physician in the anatomical laboratory of the clinic for mental patients associated with the university in Tübingen. It was there that he finally gained his *habilitation* qualification, and in 1913 he was appointed extraordinary professor. War broke out soon afterwards, and this marked the end of his research. Brodmann registered as a volunteer, and served on the mental ward of a military hospital in Tübingen. It was not until 1916 that he obtained an appointment in Halle an der Saale which guaranteed him financial security. Here he met Margarete Franke, who became his wife in 1917.

In the meantime Kraepelin, director of the Royal Psychiatric Clinic in Munich, was looking for new staff members for his Anatomical Laboratory. There were openings, following the departure of Alzheimer and Lewy. He had Brodmann in mind for head of the department of histotopography. In the spring of 1918, Brodmann moved house yet again for career reasons, but this time in the company of his wife and newborn daughter Ilse. At long last, things were going his way. He had a happy marriage and a family. He had been approached for a position at the most prestigious institution in his field, where he would have at his disposal the most advanced instruments then available, heading a group of talented guest researchers.

That happy state lasted less than five months. In early August, an infection contracted during a dissection flared up again. The subsequent blood poisoning had a rapid and fatal course. Brodmann died on 22 August 1918, aged 49. A few months later his wife also died, after a brief illness. Ilse was raised by her grandparents. When in 1993, two American neurologists launched a discussion in *Neurology* about Brodmann's 'missing numbers', one of the requests for a reprint came from Ilse Brodmann.[27]

---

[27] D. G. Gorman and J. Unützer, 'Brodmann's "missing" numbers', *Neurology*, 43 (1993), 226–7. The request was addressed to M. Fix, 'Brodmann's numbers', *Neurology*, 44 (1994), 1984–5 (1985).

TEN

The headquarters of madness:
Clérambault syndrome

It could be the opening of a film. Paris, 4 December 1920. A woman in her early 50s, who appears somewhat agitated, gets off an underground train and addresses two gendarmes. She says that she's being followed and that other passengers were ridiculing her. She demands protection. The gendarmes have no idea what is going on. The woman becomes more and more upset, frustrated by their refusal to take action. In the end, she is so angry that she gives them a box on the ears. Then she is taken into custody.

In the following scene, she is taken to the Infirmerie Spéciale, a psychiatric crisis centre on Île de la Cité. The woman is sitting opposite a perfectly groomed man. The interview does not last long. He records her name (Léa-Anna B, 53 years of age) and jots down a few characteristics of her delusion. She believes that the king of England is in love with her, and that strangers are trying to rob her of her money. He refers her to the psychiatric institution Sainte-Anne. The certificate of admission is no more than ten lines long. The signature is: Dr de Clérambault.

Several weeks later, Clérambault and his colleague Brousseau discuss her case during a session of the Société Clinique de Médecine Mentale.[1]

---

[1] G. de Clérambault and A. Brousseau, 'Coexistence de deux délires: Persécution et Érotomanie (présentation de malade)' in G. de Clérambault, *L'Érotomanie* (Paris, 2002), pp. 42–64.

Figure 10.1: In the Infirmerie, Clérambault questions a woman taken into custody

Léa-Anna's delusions go back a long way. She was once a saleswoman in a dress shop, but soon became the mistress of a rich, highly placed lover. The relationship lasted eighteen years. When he died in 1907, it did not take her long to find a new lover, who owned a castle. He bought a house for her, and asked her to come and live there with him. But the days were long in the French countryside, and she became lonely. After four years, the relationship ended, according to Clérambault because her delusions were already developing. In 1917, she became convinced that the American general who commanded a nearby army camp (this was during the First World War) was in love with her. Now, in 1920, she was convinced that George V of England was her admirer. He had been making advances to her since 1918, via secret messages. She said that this was the problem, in her eyes the only problem: she initially failed to notice his advances.

The English king tried to make his intentions clear to her through special officers who suddenly appeared in Léa-Anna's surroundings. They were disguised as sailors or tourists, and she didn't realize until it was too late that they had been sent by George V. Looking back, she recalled the knowing glances, the cryptic remarks, and the secret signs which were intended for her, but which at the time she had failed to understand. It did not become clear to her until one day, while travelling by train, she met an officer from the retinue of General

Liautey, who revealed to her in guarded terms that he was an emissary of George V. All those other incidents suddenly fell into place, like that knock on the door of her hotel room late one evening. It must have been the king, hoping for a rendezvous.

But this resulted in a delicate situation. Because she had failed to respond to his advances, George V must have concluded that she was rejecting him. Nothing was further from the truth! She felt a great love for him. What she had to do now was to explain to him in person that she returned his love. Léa-Anna set off for London, in the hope of finding an opportunity to speak to the king. For days she wandered around in the vicinity of Buckingham Palace. There was the occasional sign from the king – a curtain moved behind one of the windows of the vast palace, letting her know that he could see her – but there was never any direct contact between them. After the latest vain attempt, and expenditures totalling thousands of francs, she returned to Paris, angry and frustrated. It was on an underground train platform that the incident took place which led to her admission.

Erotomania

Clérambault explains to his colleagues that his patient is suffering from a disorder which he calls 'erotomanic syndrome' or 'erotomania'. Léa-Anna B displayed most of the classic characteristics, beginning with delusions of grandeur. The 'love object' is always a highly placed person who is rich or has a great deal of prestige. According to the patient, the advances came from the 'love object'; in other words, he initiated the contact, and she responded. He communicates by means of signals which only she understands, and his position is such that it is impossible for him openly to declare his love. Everything that she experiences is interpreted in the light of the delusion that the man desires her and is trying to make contact. The only aspect in which Léa-Anna deviated from the characteristic course of the disorder was the gradual beginning: the delusion almost always begins directly after a meeting, a true *coup de foudre*.

After this introduction, Léa-Anna is brought in. Clérambault has told her that she is to appear before a committee of important men, whose reputation even extends to England, and she must seize this opportunity to plead her cause. During the demonstration, he pretends that he actually is in a position to arrange a meeting with the king, but says he is not sure that it would be a good idea. Will she be able to control herself when she comes face to face with her admirer?

> 'I'll keep my hands like this, behind my back, so you can stand behind me and restrain me.'
> 'I'm also afraid that you'll immediately throw your arms around his neck.'
> 'But you can hold me back.'
> 'Yes, but what will the princesses say about all this?'
> 'They probably won't even be there.'
> 'Didn't you tell me they were very interested in all this?'
> 'That is something between him and me.'[2]

At Clérambault's suggestion, Léa-Anna retires to write a letter to the king. After a quarter of an hour, she hands him the letter in all confidence. It is written in good faith. She opens her heart, assuring the king of her deepest affection. She tells him that she hopes he will arrange for her to come to England. It is signed: 'L. Anna B … à l'hôpital Ste-Anne. Paris, le 20 décembre 1920.' As Clérambault tells his colleagues, such a ruse invariably works in the case of patients with this disorder.

From 1920 on, Clérambault authored over a dozen articles on what is now known as 'Clérambault syndrome'.[3] The patients were invariably women, employed in modest positions such as factory worker, domestic servant or seamstress, while the 'infatuated' men were officers,

---

[2] Clérambault, *Érotomanie*, pp. 54–5.
[3] The collected works of Clérambault were published by the Presses Universitaires de France as *Œuvre psychiatrique* (Paris, 1942). The studies focusing on erotomania also appeared as separate publications. See note 1.

priests, doctors or judges. In the primary variant, known as 'érotomanie pure', the only symptom pointing to a disorder is the conviction that one has an admirer. In 'érotomanie associée', the secondary variant, the condition is part of an extended delusionary system. The 50-year-old Clémentine D, who formerly worked in a dress shop and was presented to the Société in July 1921, was a case of 'érotomanie associée'. Clémentine believed not only that a priest was in love with her and had rented an expensive apartment for her, but also that the neighbours were trying to gain control of her by means of electromagnetic machines.[4] Whether it took the form of the primary or the secondary variant, the disorder invariably followed a fixed course. It begins with a personal contact, however fleeting and one-sided – perhaps the patient had heard his sermon or attended his surgery. In the initial stages, she is optimistic about her chances, and seeks contact by means of visits, letters and small gifts. When the man rejects her efforts, she gradually becomes discouraged and ultimately turns spiteful. In some cases, she tries to take revenge on the man himself or the people around him. It does not seem to bother her that the man is already married, which is often the case. The marriage is irrelevant in her eyes, since he is in love with her and no one else. Many of these patients ended up in the Infirmerie, after being picked up by the police for aggression directed against the wife. Clérambault was convinced that the condition was incurable. Henriëtte H, who was interviewed at the Infirmerie in May 1923, fell in love with a young priest at the age of 17. Some thirty-seven (!) years later, after various arrests for disturbance of the peace, she worked as a domestic servant, but only in households with a telephone, so that she could continue her pursuit by phone.[5]

---

[4] G. de Clérambault, Érotomanie pure, 'Érotomanie associée. Présentation de malade' in G. de Clérambault, *Érotomanie*, pp. 79–118.

[5] G. de Clérambault, 'Érotomanie pure persistant depuis trente-sept années' in Clérambault, *Érotomanie*, pp. 176–87.

The headquarters of madness

The full family name was Gatian de Clérambault.[6] Of the six first names which Clérambault was given at his birth in 1872, he wisely used only the first: Gaëtan. At the age of 13 he went to Paris to study at the Collège Stanislas. The young Clérambault was regarded as 'un peu turbulent', but he completed secondary school and went on to study law. His university courses were combined with intensive drawing studies at the École nationale des Beaux-Arts. After graduation he was called up for military service. He served with the artillery, through the intervention of friends of his parents, since he was 3 centimetres under the not unreasonable minimum height of 1 metre 60 cms.

Clérambault developed a lifestyle which tended towards the martial. He was an excellent horseman and practiced jiu-jitsu, which had only recently been introduced into France. Later, during the First World War, he was detached to positions at the front at his own request, and on two occasions was seriously wounded. He was known for his quick temper. During a session of the Société, Clérambault mistakenly thought that the speaker had stolen his ideas and flew into a rage. Although duelling had been banned in France since the days of Louis XIV and had never been part of the academic discourse, that is precisely what Clérambault demanded – a duel.[7] Colleagues were forced to intervene.

After fulfilling his military service, he decided to study medicine and obtained his doctorate in 1899. His dissertation was devoted to the growth responsible for the condition known as 'cauliflower ear'.

---

[6] Two biographies have been devoted to Clérambault. That of Elisabeth Renard is somewhat hagiographic: *Le Docteur Gaëtan de Clérambault, sa vie et son œuvre (1872–1934)* (Paris, 1942). It was republished in 1992 with an introduction by the psychiatrist Serge Tisseron. A more factual and critical work is the biography by Alain Rubens, *Le maître des insensés. Gaëtan Gatian de Clérambault (1872–1934)* (Paris, 1998). One of Clérambault's associates published a biographical retrospective: G. Heuyer, 'G. G. de Clérambault', *l'Encéphale*, 39 (1950), 413–39.

[7] Renard, *Clérambault*, p. 62.

Figure 10. 2: Gaëtan Gatian de Clérambault (1872–1934)

By that time he had lost his heart to psychiatry and in 1898, together with Capgras, he joined the staff of a conglomerate of psychiatric institutions known as 'asiles de la Seine', as assistant physician.

In 1905, Clérambault had various options. He could go into private practice, work in a hospital, or embark on an academic career. But he took a different decision, opting for the Infirmerie. Its official name was Infirmerie Spéciale du Dépôt, 3 Quai de l'Horloge, founded in 1872 in order to ensure that mentally disturbed individuals were not simply locked up. This policy ran counter to what had been common practice in the early decades of the nineteenth century. When Clérambault joined the Infirmerie, there were eleven cells for men and seven for women, three of which were padded. During the almost thirty years that Clérambault was associated with the Infirmerie, he witnessed an endless procession of disordered minds: each year the fate of some two to three thousand souls had to be decided. As a rule, this meant choosing between a jail cell and the asylum. What all these people had in common was the fact that they had been picked up from the streets by the police. They were absinthe drinkers, ether-sniffers, morphinists and opium smokers, people who had attempted suicide or had an epileptic seizure, alongside arsonists, exhibitionists, fetishists, muggers, the demented elderly, and retarded people adrift in society. Following a brief interview, Clérambault drew up a certificate, one of an estimated 13,000 such documents which he wrote in the course of his career. They are psychiatric 'mug shots' containing, in addition to the personalia, a description of the symptoms, the reason for the detention, the present state of the individual, and a tentative diagnosis, all recorded in terse telegram style. The options open to the staff of the Infirmerie were to release the person in question, or refer him or her to a hospital. In the majority of cases the next step was admission to the Sainte-Anne.

For most Parisians who ended up in the Infirmerie, the humane principles upon which the institution was founded quickly faded into the background. The institution was housed in a forbidding black neo-Gothic building, and the interior was a slum. The cells were filthy and the treatment at the hands of the personnel downright gross. But what gave rise to the most resistance was the omnipotence of the chief physician. He decided between freedom and compulsory admission but, at his own discretion, he could also order the patient to be detained for observation in the Dépôt, for a period of three, six or perhaps nine days. The press was unanimously hostile to the Infirmerie. There were regular articles on people who had been released and immediately repeated their offence or, conversely, individuals who were incarcerated for an indeterminate period. Occasionally, someone from more exalted social circles ended up in the Infirmerie, usually as a result of drunkenness or brawling. He found himself among petty thieves, knife fighters and strumpets, temporarily deprived of his rights and locked up in a filthy cell, waiting for psychiatrists to decide his fate. Of course, the same thing could also happen to someone from the lower classes, but the difference was that once they were released, the more privileged detainees went straight to the press, which resulted in periodical campaigns against the regime in the Infirmerie.

One of Clérambault's predecessors referred to the institution as 'the headquarters of madness'. But it was also the headquarters of French forensic psychiatry. Ultimately, from every corner of the huge and hectic capital, came all the perpetrators of a delict in which mental illness may have played a role, ending up in that same room in the Infirmerie. And after the interrogation, they all fanned out across the city's hospitals, institutions and prisons. Clérambault never had to look elsewhere for his study material: it filed past his desk on a daily basis and, thanks to the funnel function of the Infirmerie, in a concentration which was never reached in the institutions. Almost all the case studies recorded by Clérambault feature men and women who once sat opposite him. The manner in which he allowed his psychiatric work to be fed by the individuals whom the gendarmerie delivered to him is illustrated by the articles which he wrote on four women who appeared before him between 1902 and 1906.[8] There was a common factor in the background to their crime which was probably only visible from his privileged observation post on the Quai de l'Horloge, and even then only to someone who, even before he began his questioning, must have had his own suspicions about their true motives.

Hysterical, frigid, perverse, degenerate

The four women in question, all in their 40s, were arrested for the theft of silk. All four were repeat offenders, and one of them had been sentenced dozens of times, always for stealing silk. Why silk? The questioning of the first woman, the 40-year-old VB, detained in the women's prison Fresnes, lasted five days. She was transferred to the Infirmerie for the interviews. After repeated urging, her testimony punctuated by crying spells, the woman explained that she used the silk to masturbate. She hadn't even told her lawyer, for fear he would make it known during the sitting. The other women stole silk for the same reason. The desire for silk was so strong that it was irresistible.

[8] 'Passion érotique des étoffes chez la femme' in Œuvre psychiatrique, pp. 682–715, 715–20.

They walked into a dress shop, grabbed an article made of silk (a length of material, a girl's dress or a corsage) and dashed into a fitting room or an elevator, where they rubbed the material against their private parts. There were a number of noteworthy similarities between the four cases. It was essential to the titillation that the silk had been obtained by theft. One woman was a seamstress who had as much silk available as she could possibly want, but could only masturbate with silk when the experience was preceded by the excitement of the theft. Masturbation took place while the women were still experiencing the 'high' of the theft. Some of them took the time to search out a quiet corner of the store, but one of them had masturbated in the middle of the store. After achieving orgasm, the women lost all interest in the silk: they simply dropped it or tossed it behind a door. Two of them stole the silk while under the influence of ether. One drank ether and then rum, to mask the odour of the ether, and then white wine to get rid of the smell of the rum. The ether had a liberating effect: the women became lively, exuberant and aggressive, and when the impulse to steal silk arose, it could not be stifled.

All four women had once been married, but now lived without a man. None of them had derived any pleasure from marital sex. From the beginning VB was revolted by her husband's grunts and grimaces. She would wait until he had gone off to work in the morning and then masturbate. The preference for masturbation was shared by the other three. Even when they were not masturbating, they enjoyed handling the silk, letting it glide through their fingers. Two of them still took pleasure in dressing dolls, preferably in silk.

What struck Clérambault was the specific preference for silk. None of the women took the slightest interest in other materials, such as fur, velvet, flannel or satin. According to them, there was something erotic about the touch of silk, and even more in the sound it made. They all experienced the rustle and crinkle of stiff raw silk as titillating: 'elle crie'. The 46-year-old F, taken into custody in October 1902, gave an open-hearted account, here abridged:

Feeling silk is better than looking at silk, but crumpling silk is even
better; it's arousing, you can feel the wetness coming, no other sexual
sensation can compare with it. But it's even better when it's silk I've
stolen. Stealing silk is delicious. I could never get the same sensation
from buying it. I'm powerless to resist the temptation. When I get hold
of the material, I crumple it up and after that I experience a pleasure
that takes my breath away. It's as if I'm drunk, I tremble … not from
fear, but from excitement. As soon as I have the material in my hand,
I spread my legs, so I can touch myself. That's how people see me.
When the pleasure is over, I'm exhausted, my breathing is accelerated,
my arms and legs are quite stiff. Stealing silk is my delight. My children
have tried in vain to cure me by buying yards and yards of silk for me. If
someone made me a present of the length of silk I was just about to
steal, it would give me no enjoyment at all. In fact, it would totally ruin
my enjoyment.[9]

Just as F, unknowingly, spoke for the other three women, in his
analysis Clérambault spoke for French psychiatry. His diagnosis was
a diatribe. To begin with, all four women were 'hysterical'. On this
point, Clérambault did not mince his words. He placed them firmly in
the domain of the mentally deficient, with a nervous system susceptible
to overexcitation, specifically through the sense of touch. Furthermore,
all four of them were 'frigid'. This label indicated that they were not
capable of normal (i.e., heterosexual) titillation. For Clérambault, the
frequent masturbation served to underscore their frigidity. Two of
them occasionally fantasized about a woman during masturbation,
and this, together with the preference for masturbation, was sufficient
reason to declare them 'perverse'. Nor could there be any doubt about
a fourth label: 'degenerate'. This judgement was reinforced by the
women's background. VB had a grandmother who died a lunatic, as
did an aunt who had also masturbated. Her father and brother, both
dead, were 'très nerveux'. A nephew of 18 was likewise a masturbateur.
When Clérambault summoned B's ex-husband for an interrogation,
one look was enough: the man was living proof of the 'mutual

9 *Ibid.* p. 694.

attraction of degenerates'.[10] The other women had a similarly tainted family history.

His argumentation was solid, conclusive and eminently circular. For the most part, hysteria, frigidity, perversion and degeneration were defined in each other's terms. Masturbation pointed to frigidity and perversion and those two aberrations were together an indication of degeneration. Although Clérambault probably regarded the women as psychiatric patients, since he consistently referred to them as *malade*, he could find no mitigating circumstances in their illness, nor are there any indications that he attempted to prevent them from ending up in prison. On the contrary: one gets the impression that he regarded them as both ill *and* perverted, as well as hopelessly disturbed, with an abnormality which was rooted in a fatal and inescapable genetic derailment. When VB was sentenced to twenty-six months for theft, he recorded the verdict without further comment. The fact that some of the women were desperately afraid of being deported to a penal colony prompted him to issue a steely warning to his colleagues to be extra on their guard for malingerers. He also noted that these women were 'amoral'. The fact that they spoke so candidly about the most intimate details of their sex life only served to confirm this.

Is it possible that in some way the passion for silk resonated with Clérambault himself? In 1910, the year that he wrote about the silk thieves for the second time, he developed a passion for oriental robes and veils during a stay in Tunisia. In the First World War, he had volunteered for a tour of duty in Morocco, then a French protectorate, and he fell in love with the country. He became fluent in Arabic and returned there after the war to photograph Moroccan robes. The collection which gradually took shape was extensive (some 4,000 print clichés in all) and of a monomaniacal one-sidedness: no landscapes, no cities, almost no recognizable human figures, only an endless procession of veiled men, women and children. These secret

---

[10] *Ibid.* p. 690.

Figure 10.3: Clérambault took some 4,000 photographs of the robes commonly worn around the Mediterranean Sea Basin. Almost all the figures portrayed are veiled

photos were never exhibited in Clérambault's lifetime, nor did he ever refer to them during the series of lectures on the draping of fabric which he gave at the École des Beaux-Arts during the 1920s.[11] After his death, another collection was discovered by friends who were clearing his house. It seems that Clérambault was himself enamoured of unusual fabrics: there were lengths and lengths of fur, silk, velvet, satin, taffeta, tarlatan and cotton. They also found the mannequins on which he draped the fabrics. No doubt Clérambault also took pleasure in the sensation of fabric gliding through his fingers.

A parade of women

While in the nineteenth century the Napoleonic stature of Charcot would have been sufficient grounds for the bestowal of eponyms such

[11] In the spring of 1990, part of this collection was exhibited in the Centre Pompidou: Gaëtan Gatian de Clérambault, psychiatre et photographe, Paris 1990.

as Parkinson's disease, Jackson's epilepsy and Gilles de la Tourette syndrome, the decision to rechristen 'erotomania' Clérambault syndrome was taken by a medical committee, at a psychiatric conference convened in Paris in 1935. Clérambault was without doubt the most productive author to have turned his attention to this disease, but he was not the first. Somewhat earlier, Kraepelin had described the case of a woman at a theatre performance who believed that the king (in this case the German monarch) had bowed in her direction upon entering the theatre. That delusion had taken on such proportions that she ended up believing that all sorts of details in clothing and conversation were proof that the king was in love with her. Kraepelin suspected that the delusion was actually a kind of psychological compensation for the disappointments in her life.

The term 'erotomania' already had a long history when Clérambault embarked on his case studies.[12] From antiquity until the middle of the eighteenth century, erotomania was used to denote a disease which is rooted in an intense but unrequited love. Later, the meaning shifted to what is currently known as nymphomania or satyrism: an excessive sexual drive. In the half-century before Clérambault, erotomania gradually went from a somatic to a mental condition. It became the delusion rooted in unrequited love, and ultimately the delusion that it is the other person who is in love. The literature on erotomania retained its casuistic nature after the publications by Clérambault. All the case studies again form a parade, initially consisting mainly of women. Most of them are lonely, often unemployed. Their delusion focuses on men in high positions or celebrities from the world of politics, sport or the arts. Physicians, clergymen and teachers have likewise been the object of the delusion. Since the 1980s, the number of male Clérambault patients recorded in the literature has increased. The German psychiatrist Brüne collected 246 case histories,

---

[12] G. E. Berrios and N. Kennedy, 'Erotomania: a conceptual history', *History of Psychiatry*, 13 (2002), 381–400.

published between 1900 and 2000.[13] He focused on the characteristics
of Clérambault patients, broken down by gender. The patients seldom have a high social status, and the vast majority are unmarried.
These two characteristics are almost the only ones shared by male and
female Clérambault patients. Women are overrepresented by a ratio
of 70 to 30 per cent. Only about 4 per cent of the women get into
trouble with the law as a result of their disorder, compared with over
half the men. In the women's group, the 'love object' is older in three-
quarters of cases, while among the men the reverse is true. The sexual
appeal of the 'love object' almost always plays a role among men,
while this holds true for only about half of the women.

Theories about the cause of Clérambault syndrome cover the entire
psychiatric spectrum, from psychoanalysis to brain damage. The delusion is thought to be a defence mechanism against a distressing sense
of being unloved. The fantasy that someone is in love with you can
assuage the loneliness and depression. Cases have also been described
in which neurological damage may play a role, although to date no
clear association with organic disorders has been established.[14] A
recent perspective is that of evolutionary psychology. The above
mentioned study by Brüne suggests that Clérambault syndrome is a
pathological extension of the evolutionary mating strategies which
men and women employ: women look for a partner whose status and
wealth make him an attractive candidate to father their children, while
men are more inclined to look for a young, sexually attractive partner.[15]
Here, it must be said that Brüne's data may not actually be representative. Due to their behaviour, male Clérambault patients may be under-
represented: they are more likely to end up in a criminal trajectory, thus
remaining outside the field of vision of psychiatrists. In the last ten or

[13] M. Brüne, 'De Clérambault's syndrome (erotomania) in an evolutionary perspective', *Evolution and Human Behavior*, 22 (2001), 409–15.
[14] S. F. Signer and J. L. Cummings, 'De Clérambault's syndrome in organic affective
disorder', *British Journal of Psychiatry*, 151 (1987), 404–7.
[15] Brüne, 'De Clérambault's syndrome', 410.

fifteen years, much of the literature related to Clérambault syndrome has been incorporated into the literature on stalking.

DSM-IV code 197.1

In the psychiatric classification system *DSM-IV* (1994), erotomania appears under code 197.1: 'delusional disorder, erotomanic subtype'.[16] The accompanying *Casebook*, a collection of over 200 case histories, provides an impression of each disorder. Under the heading 'Dear Doctor', we find the profile of a female patient with Clérambault syndrome.[17] 'Myrna Field', a 55-year-old waitress in a hospital canteen, suddenly became convinced that one of the doctors was head over heels in love with her. This idea was fabricated on the basis of hints, innuendos and knowing looks, but never openly expressed – according to Myrna, because he was still married. Every time he came into the canteen, she became frightfully nervous. Two years later, the situation had become untenable, and she had to quit her job. Her own marriage was unhappy, asexual and childless, and she had never told her husband about her 'love affair'. It appears from the subsequent discussion that her psychiatrist prescribed an anti-psychotic remedy, which did go some way towards alleviating her symptoms. A subsequent depression was treated with anti-depressants, but three years later, she still believed that the doctor was in love with her.

In the literature on Clérambault syndrome there are several lists of inclusion and exclusion criteria in circulation. In 1985, two medical psychologists, Ellis and Mellsop, drew up a list of the diagnostic criteria employed by Clérambault:[18]

---

[16] American Psychiatric Association, *Diagnostic and Statistical Manual of Mental Disorders* (4th edn, Washington, 1994).

[17] R. L. Spitzer *et al.* (eds.), *DSM-IV Casebook* (Washington, 1994).

[18] P. Ellis and G. Mellsop, 'De Clérambault's syndrome: a nosological entity?', *British Journal of Psychiatry*, 146 (1985), 90–3.

(1) entertains the delusionary belief that one is in an amorous relationship with someone;

(2) that person has a high social status;

(3) was the first to fall in love;

(4) made the initial advances;

(5) the onset was sudden;

(6) the object of the delusion is unchanging;

(7) the patient has an explanation for the dismissive or hostile
reactions of the object;

(8) the course is chronic;

(9) there are no hallucinations.

They then examined fifty-three cases from the recent literature to see
how many of them met the above criteria. Conclusion: only two or at
most three cases. Often there were attendant psychiatric conditions,
such as paranoid schizophrenia or a manic-depressive disorder; in
other cases, the delusion had begun gradually, or the object later
changed. A 'pure' Clérambault patient proved to be rare, so rare that
Ellis and Mellsop began to have doubts about whether 'Clérambault
syndrome' actually existed, and whether it should be retained as a
psychiatric diagnosis.

More recently, researchers asked colleagues in their district to report
any patients with erotomanic symptoms.[19] Following interviews and a
study of the dossiers, fifteen cases were studied in order to determine
the extent to which the Clérambault criteria (Ellis and Mellsop's list)
were applicable to them. The eleven women and four men were on
average in their mid-40s. Only three were married, the others were
single (eight), divorced (three) or widowed (one). Six of them had
never had a sexual relationship. Twelve patients were unemployed or
disabled. In thirteen cases the object had a higher social status. In six

---

[19] N. Kennedy, M. McDonough, B. Kelly and G. E. Berrios, 'Erotomania revisited:
clinical course and treatment', *Comprehensive Psychiatry*, 43 (2002) 1, 1–6.

cases they were celebrities, such as an opera singer or (by now a classic) a member of the royal family.

The results of the research warrant a more detailed study, since they shed light on the boundaries of Clérambault syndrome. For example, only one criterion, the delusion that one has an admirer, is met by all fifteen cases. All the other criteria on the list drawn up by Ellis and Mellsop apply only to some of the cases. Not all the objects had a higher social status, and according to the patients, not all of them had made the initial advances. In four of the fifteen cases, there was no fixed object. Other criteria, such as the sudden onset (nine cases), the absence of hallucinations (eight cases), and the chronic course (seven cases), proved unreliable as a criterion for the diagnosis of Clérambault syndrome. In one patient, a man of 52, only half the criteria were met.

This suggests that the profile of Clérambault syndrome is too ragged to be useful as a psychiatric diagnosis. But this conclusion may be somewhat hasty. Although there were only two cases that met all the criteria on the list drawn up by Ellis and Mellsop, *as a group* these fifteen cases do unmistakably represent the prototypical Clérambault patient: woman, unmarried or divorced, unhappy, unemployed and suffering from the delusion that she has a high-placed admirer. These results make it possible to draw certain conclusions on how the syndrome is seen in psychiatric diagnostic practice. The delusion that someone is in love with you is apparently a necessary but also a *sufficient* symptom to be diagnosed as a Clérambault patient. In principle, all other symptoms, convictions or characteristics can be lacking. The one man of 52 was perhaps an atypical case, but that does not mean that he was *not* a Clérambault patient. In the course of the diagnostic process, psychiatrists establish where Clérambault syndrome begins and where it ends: for the beginning, the delusion of being in love is sufficient and – with the aid of the other criteria and without too much consultation – they have succeeded in constructing a prototype in which we have no trouble identifying Léa-Anna B and Clérambault's other patients.

A physician's memories of a cataract operation

Clérambault himself searched in vain for an organic origin of the syndrome. For a time he even thought that there might be a tie-in with certain eye reflexes, but due to health problems he was unable to develop this hypothesis. Even as a child, Clérambault had suffered from eye problems, and in his mid-50s his eyesight deteriorated so rapidly that within a few years he was, in his own words, 'half blind'. He decided on an operation. He has described the operation and its aftermath in great detail, an account which is now a precious monument in the annals of ophthalmology: *Souvenirs d'un médecin opéré de la cataracte.*[20]

When he was approaching 55, Clérambault wrote, his eyesight was so poor that he could only read for brief periods at a time, for fear of being plagued by headaches and dizziness. In the years that followed, he began to see strange shapes, especially at night. Each pinpoint of light appeared in five- or six-fold, and together these 'false lights' formed geometrical patterns connected by luminous threads. A lamp might take on the form of a phosphorescent starfish. This multiplication gave the nocturnal lights of the city a strange beauty, and the boulevards and quays had an almost magical quality, as if the sky itself was strewn with a luminous powder. All those lights, detached from façades and street-lamps, turned his field of vision into a starstudded firmament. In the same way, extra letters multiplied around the printed word, so that he found it almost impossible to read. A magnifying glass provided temporary solace, and later a pair of opera glasses, but eventually he had to have everything read to him: the newspaper, scientific articles, dossiers, etc. The situation became untenable. Walking down the street, he found it difficult to judge

---

[20] The account appeared posthumously in Clérambault's *Œuvre psychiatrique*, and later in book form: G. de Clérambault, *Souvenirs d'un médecin opéré de la cataracte* (Paris, 1992). The quotations are taken from the latter publication.

distance, especially when there were car head-lamps to deal with. While waiting to cross the street, Clérambault wrote, he kept an eye out for some stalwart soul with a sensible look about him, and crossed over when he did. At home there were falls, and collisions with chairs and tables. When he put down smaller articles, such as his pen, they immediately disappeared from sight, so that he had to feel his way across the desk blotter until he found them again. It was almost impossible to locate a specific sheet in a pile of papers. Moreover, Clérambault discovered, to his surprise, that his thought processes were becoming laborious. Even in our daydreams and reflections, he explained, we rely on the outside world, for distraction or as a means of picking up the thread of our musings. When you are half blind, you are constantly at the mercy of the resolute march of your own thoughts. Although a physician himself, he did not discover what the problem was until much later. When he saw in the mirror the crystals in his right eye, and friends told him that his iris had turned silver, he realized that he was developing cataracts.

Clérambault had heard about a new technique whereby cataracts could be removed while they were still developing. The method was devised by the Spanish ophthalmologist Ignacio Barraquer.[21] To this day, the 'Barraquer operation' is a well-known eponym in the world of ophthalmology. A crucial step in the process is the removal of the crystals by means of a suction cup. Barraquer had come up with the idea while sitting at the bedside of his father (his predecessor as professor of ophthalmology). He noticed how one of the leeches in a jar next to the bed lifted up pebbles by placing its cup-shaped protuberance on a pebble and creating a vacuum. He invented a device which made it possible to adjust the suction cup to a high

---

[21] A. K. Greene, 'Ignacio Barraquer (1884–1965) and the Barraquer family of ophthalmologists', *Canadian Journal of Ophthalmology*, 36 (2001), 5–6.

degree of accuracy.[22] In Paris, Clérambault visited a patient who had already undergone the operation and was willing to show him what his pupils looked like: they proved to be perfectly round, while his vision was totally restored. After this visit he resolved to leave for Barcelona as soon as possible.

The overnight train journey feels like the beginning of his liberation. The lights along the way give him an opportunity to observe the strange optical deformations, hopefully for the last time. The operation takes place the day after his arrival, and all goes well. After the procedure he has to remain in bed for five days, in absolute rest since the slightest movement could cause the minute stitches to tear. Only at the end of that period can the bandages be removed. Barraquer comes by twice a day. His visits last longer and longer. The eye doctor and the psychiatrist clearly enjoy each other's company, which is not surprising, given that they both take an interest in technology, teach at an art school, and pursue wide-ranging studies outside of their own field. Barraquer chats about the animals in the small zoo he set up at the clinic. On the fifth day the bandages are temporarily removed: Barraquer holds up five fingers, and Clérambault is allowed to look at Barraquer's wristwatch through a magnifying glass. After that, the bandages are replaced. What he saw in those brief moments makes him jubilant: colours and contours! And there is no doubt that the eye will recover.

But the following night things go wrong. In his sleep he turns onto the side where the eye was operated on. The pressure causes the stitches to give way and the eye fills with blood. Clérambault feels a piercing pain. 'At eight o'clock Barraquer declares that there are no

---

[22] The Barraquer dynasty is still practising at the forefront of ophthalmology: the son of Barraquer, José-Ignacio Barraquer, founded a now world-famous eye clinic in Bogotá, Colombia, and in 1949 was the first to develop a technique whereby a laser ray is used to scrape away an infinitely thin layer of the cornea, so that the refraction changes and the patient no longer needs glasses. The sons are also active in the clinic – the fourth generation of eye doctors.

worse patients than doctors, that he regrets having permitted me to have so many visitors, that the overexertion caused by all that talk gave rise to a terrible dream, or irritated my stitches, so that I inadvertently rubbed my eye.'[23] Barraquer quickly stitches the eye again, and warns Clérambault that it is still extremely vulnerable. He recalls that one of his patients, a naval officer, was overjoyed that he could see again and tensed the muscles in his face so strenuously that the stitches snapped, and the eye was ultimately lost. Another patient, a wealthy American, was embraced by his joyful daughter on the sixth day: the brim of her hat grazed the eye, which was likewise lost.

Fortunately, Clérambault is spared such disasters. The eye recovers, as does the other eye after the second operation several days later. Once back in Paris, Clérambault does discover a few small abnormalities. For example, he consistently underestimates distances, so that when he goes to pick something up, he has to remember to reach 10 centimetres further than his eyes tell him to. And street kerbs are always just that little bit further away than he estimates. With his right eye he sees figures that resemble a treble clef. All the colours seem to be bathed in a blue wash, something which Barraquer had predicted. It is as if his field of vision is stretched over a sphere, so that even straight lines and angles display a curvature. When reading, he is forced to hold the text unnaturally close to his eyes. But to his great relief, he can at least read and write again. He concludes cheerfully: 'Our eyes remain available to any colleague who desires to examine them.'[24] However, no one is able to take him up on the offer, since the account is not published until after his death.

'I am a finished man'

On one occasion in 1919, a friend recalled fifteen years later, the conversation turned to suicide. Clérambault maintained that a person

---

[23] Clérambault, *Souvenirs*, p. 39.   [24] *Ibid.* p. 49.

doesn't have to be mad to take his own life. 'I live for my work and I love art. Imagine what would happen if I went blind! Suppose my life has become worthless, and I commit suicide, does that mean I'm mad?'[25] It was true that Clérambault's life resembled an art project. He was a dedicated painter, and collected art and exotic garments. He remained a bachelor and when he entertained, he wore a caftan and served tea brewed from mint leaves he grew himself. He was in the habit of receiving his friends individually, and each of them may well have had the impression that he was his one and only friend.

In his early 60s, Clérambault began to worry about his scientific legacy. He had always kept careful notes and published extensively, but his writing usually took the form of brief accounts, commentaries and case histories. The *leçons de Vendredi*, the lectures in forensic psychiatry which he gave every Friday as chief physician of the Infirmerie, were likewise disseminated to all and sundry. Now the time had come for a synthesis of his insights. He started editing his notes, with the help of a secretary. The work proceeded slowly, and one day he shoved the papers aside and said despondently, 'I am a finished man!'[26] In the course of 1934, he was besieged by one complaint after the other. For months at a time, he was confined to his bed by arthritis. To the end, he did his best to continue his visits to the Infirmerie, but only a recumbent position provided relief from the pain. Ill and depressed, he then learned that Dr Brousseau, co-author of his first publication on erotomania and one of his closest friends, had accepted an appointment in the provinces and would be leaving Paris. After the operation in Barcelona, he was unable to estimate depth, an inestimable loss for a painter and aesthete who took great pleasure in capturing the gentle folds of fabric. He noticed that the light which had been returned to his eyes was slowly ebbing away, this time for good.

---

[25] Renard, *Clérambault*, p. 74. [26] *Ibid.* p. 77.

It could be the end of a film.[27] On Friday afternoon, 16 November, Clérambault arrives at the Infirmerie for his clinical lesson. It is the first lesson of the new season and someone has forgotten to hang up the notice at the medical faculty. The hall is almost empty. The following morning he writes a hasty, incoherent letter to Brousseau, followed by an equally incoherent testament, written in a shaky hand and full of deletions. He rambles on about a painting which he did not come by honestly and which now weighs on his conscience.[28] He bequeaths his photographic collection to various ethnographic museums. 'More than anyone else', he writes, 'I have been punished by losing the results of all my labours. The documents which I have collected over the last forty years will be scattered. Important truths I have uncovered will sink back into oblivion.'[29] He asks forgiveness of the memory of his father and mother, his friends and, above all, his fellow psychiatrists, 'so easily and so often maligned and yet so morally upstanding'.[30] Then he takes his duty weapon from 1914–18, and goes into the garden, telling his housekeeper not to be alarmed if she hears shots. He fires several times and then storms up the stairs, places a chair against the edge of the bed, sits down opposite the linen cupboard mirror, and puts the muzzle of the revolver in his mouth.

[27] The film *Le cri de la soie* (1996), directed by Yvon Marciano, is loosely based on the life of Clérambault.

[28] Later it emerged that Clérambault had actually purchased the painting in a second-hand shop.

[29] Rubens, *Maître*, p. 281.   [30] *Ibid.*

ELEVEN

A cup of tea for the *doppelgänger*:
Capgras syndrome

On a June day in 1918, Madame M walked into a Paris police station to report that a gang of bandits had kidnapped several children and were holding them prisoner in the cellar of her house. She could hear them whimpering and calling for their mother. And all over Paris there were people being held underground. She asked for two gendarmes to go with her to free the prisoners. But instead, Madame M was taken to the Infirmerie Spéciale, an emergency shelter for the mentally disturbed. Two days later she was admitted to the mental hospital Sainte-Anne, and in the spring of 1919 she was transferred to another large psychiatric hospital in Paris, Maison-Blanche. There she was given into the care of Joseph Capgras.

The fact that we know so much more about the case of M than about the thousands of other people with similar delusions in a large city like Paris, whether inside or outside the asylums, is due to a single bizarre detail in her account. She told Capgras that her husband and her daughter had disappeared and had been replaced by *doppelgängers*. M called them '*sosies*', people who are the spitting image of someone else. This designation was recorded in the case study of M which Capgras and his assistant Reboul-Lachaux drew up in 1923: M displayed the symptoms of the 'illusion des sosies'.[1] This phenomenon, the delusion that individuals in your immediate surroundings (your husband or wife, parents or children) have been replaced by *doppelgängers*, is known today as 'Capgras syndrome'.

Mathilde de Rio-Branco

At the time of the case study, Madame M was 53 years old. She was a seamstress by trade. Of the five children she bore, four died young, and she was convinced that they had been poisoned or kidnapped. Her remaining daughter was now 20 years old. M's husband owned a large dairy company. He told Capgras that after the death of their twins in 1906, his wife had fallen prey to delusions of grandeur. Over the years those delusions had centred on two themes, which Capgras charted on the basis of conversations and the many letters which M wrote. One delusion was that her father had confessed to her on his deathbed that he was not her real father, but that he had stolen her from a wealthy family when she was 15 months old. Her birth mother was Mademoiselle de Rio-Branco, a direct descendent of Henri IV. M insisted upon being addressed as Mathilde de Rio-Branco. She was heir to an immense fortune: mines in Argentina, the whole of Rio de Janeiro, seventy-five houses in France. But all these possessions had been stolen from her (and this was the second delusion) by her enemies, who would stop at nothing to deceive and swindle her. They did away with people, tried to poison her and stole documents, in an effort to get their hands on her fortune. Even her marriage papers were forged, so that her apartment was now occupied by a *doppelgänger*.

[1] J. Capgras and J. Reboul-Lachaux, 'L'illusion des "sosies" dans un délire systématisé chronique', *Bulletin de la Société de Médecine Mentale*, 11 (1923), 6–16. This article appears in an English translation in H. D. Ellis, J. Whitley and J.-P. Luauté, 'Delusional misidentification: the three original papers on the Capgras, Frégoli and intermetamorphosis delusions', *History of Psychiatry*, 5 (1994), 117–46.

Kidnappings, disappearances, stolen identities – all crimes dating from far back in her past. One of her children was kidnapped while staying with a nanny, and the child that had taken her place died of poisoning: 'There I was, at the funeral of a child that wasn't mine.'[2] The delusion involving *doppelgängers* began during a crisis in 1914. One day, M no longer recognized her daughter. She became convinced that someone had kidnapped her and left another girl in her place. Not long afterwards, the new girl was herself replaced, and in this way an endless procession of *doppelgängers* took the place of her daughter. They were recognizable by tiny stitches in the face, which remained after their thoughts had been removed. Her husband had also disappeared and been replaced by *doppelgängers*. She had already filed for divorce.

The delusions of M were bizarre but systematic. The events taking place in Paris between 1914 and 1918 were incorporated into her stories in a totally natural manner. According to her, the cellars all over the city were a trap: those who took refuge there were never heard from again. The German fighter planes shot blanks in order to force more and more people into the metro corridors and the catacombs. Houses were destroyed, not as a result of bombings, but deliberately, so that children would lose their way. There were large underground operating rooms where people were mutilated, and when they were released, people said that was the way they had returned from the war.

In Maison-Blanche, too, M saw all around her *doppelgängers* of nurses, fellow patients, visitors, doctors and housemen. She warned her doctors: 'You know you have a *doppelgänger* who countermands all your orders, in order to discredit you.'[3] She had her own *doppelgängers*, who succeeded in luring her visitors away or stealing the articles she had ordered. Every day more *doppelgängers* and *doppelgängers* of *doppelgängers* appeared. She went on and on about

---

[2] Capgras and Reboul-Lachaux, 'Illusion', 122.   [3] *Ibid.* 125.

gangs and societies of *doppelgängers*, the way other people talk about a police force or a society of freemasons.

Madame M was a calm patient. She refused politely but firmly to work. The only times she became irritated was when she was addressed as Madame M instead of Mademoiselle de Rio-Branco. She spent her days writing long letters to the Public Prosecutor, the Senate or the Ministry of War. Except for her delusions, she displayed not a single abnormality: her intellect was intact, and an extensive neurological examination failed to reveal the slightest irregularity.

Capgras and Reboul-Lachaux noticed that M only saw *doppelgängers* of people she knew: strangers were never *doppelgängers*. And the problem was not that she didn't recognize faces: she always knew whose *doppelgänger* the imposter was. She saw the resemblance. The disorder lay not in recognition but in identification. According to Capgras and Reboul-Lachaux, the disorder appeared to be an 'identification agnosia'.[4] But what was the origin of this disorder? Recognition, they maintained, consisted in achieving agreement between an observation and the memories that go with the person observed. The memories lend the observation a sense of familiarity. The psychosis which M was suffering from brings with it an intense sense of alienation. As a result, loved ones no longer call up a feeling of familiarity. In the view of Capgras and Reboul-Lachaux, the *doppelgänger* is a creation of the 'logique des émotions': if a loved one no longer calls up the affection and the memories of the past, then it cannot be that loved one, and must therefore be someone else, someone who looks exactly like that person.[5] Paranoid suspicion does the rest: enemies are conspiring to eliminate one's loved ones and replace them with *doppelgängers*.

During a meeting of the Société Clinique de Médecine Mentale, Capgras organized a patient demonstration featuring Madame M. As soon as she entered the room, she began to recount her story: she was born as a Rio-Branco, her grandmother had 8,000 million

[4] *Ibid.* 127. [5] *Ibid.* 128.

Figure 11.1: Jean Marie Joseph Capgras (1873–1950)

francs, and someone had kidnapped her children, replacing them with *doppelgängers*. Clérambault, a colleague of Capgras, asked him whether 'auditory psychosensory phenomena' might play a role here, suggesting in discreet scientific wording that perhaps the patient was hearing voices or suffering from hallucinations. Before Capgras could reply, Mathilde de Rio-Branco spoke up: 'The noises are not "auditory phenomena", they come from bandits hiding in the cellars!'.[6]

Jean Marie Joseph Capgras was born in 1873 in Verdun-sur-Garonne, a village in the southwest of France.[7] He graduated from secondary school in Montauban with such brilliant marks that his teachers advised him to apply for the comparative examination of the École Normale Supérieure, an elite university in Paris. But Capgras opted for medicine instead. He had completed his stint as assistant houseman in Toulouse when a cousin who worked in an institution for the mentally disturbed persuaded him to switch to psychiatry. He was to continue in this specialization for the rest of his life, in institutions in the provinces and in Paris. For many years, he was associated with Maison-Blanche, where Madame M was a patient, and later with Sainte-Anne.

[6] *Ibid.* 130.
[7] J.-P. Luauté, 'Joseph Capgras and his syndrome', *Bibliotheca Psychiatrica*, 164 (1986), 9–21.

Capgras was a psychiatrist of the eager, inquisitive type. He began his rounds early in the morning, in order to have more time for his patients. By the time the study focusing on Madame M appeared, Capgras already had an established reputation in the field of delusions. In 1909, he and his colleague Paul Sérieux had written a classic work on this very subject: *Les folies raisonnantes. Le délire d'interprétation.*[8] They identified a 'chronic interpretative delusion', which was marked by complex but coherent delusions, the absence of hallucinations, intact intellect and a gradual extension. Unfortunately for the patient suffering from this condition, there was no hope of a cure. It is the type of delusion in which the patient's reasoning is based on facts which, in themselves, have been correctly perceived, but which lead to a totally false interpretation. This is known as a 'folie raisonnante': the conclusions are logical but ridiculous.

The delusions of Madame M bore some resemblance to a 'folie raisonnante', but the motives were different from those which Capgras had encountered up to then. The explanation which Capgras and Reboul-Lachaux themselves put forward for the *doppelgänger* delusion resembled a hypothesis which would not be formulated until sixty years later, when during the 1980s the neurological theories pertaining to facial recognition were drawn up. It is ironic that Capgras himself was responsible for the temporary disappearance of the explanation he had proposed. A year after the first publication, he and his co-authors wrote two more articles on the 'illusion des sosies'.[9] And this time, he explained the delusions in terms derived from psychoanalysis, which was then taking French

[8] J. Capgras and P. Sérieux, *Les folies raisonnantes. Le délire d'interprétation* (Paris, 1909).

[9] J. Capgras and P. Carrette, 'Illusion des sosies et complexe d'Œdipe', *Annales Médico-Psychologiques*, 82 (1924), 48–68; J. Capgras, P. Lucchini and P. Schiff, 'Du sentiment d'étrangeté à l'illusion des sosies', *Bulletin de la Société de Médecine Mentale*, 12 (1924), 210–17.

psychiatry by storm. By the time the psychiatrist, Levy-Valensi, proposed that the 'illusion des sosies' henceforth be known as the Capgras syndrome (in 1929), the *doppelgänger* delusion was already being interpreted entirely along Freudian lines.[10] It was a situation that would continue for another half-century.

A mind that found itself

Following Madame M's demonstration, one of the psychiatrists present remarked that he, too, had had such a patient: she was convinced that her husband, and also the doctor and the nurses, had been replaced by *doppelgängers*. The syndrome of Capgras was apparently not as rare as originally assumed, nor was Capgras' case study the first to make mention of the condition. In 1866, the German psychiatrist, Karl Kahlbaum, described a patient who took the people who visited him at the institution for imposters, marvelling at the fact that for purposes of this sham it had been possible to find 'extras' who bore such a striking resemblance to his friends and relatives.[11] He also regarded his wife as an imposter, even after, at the director's urging, he had submitted her to a rigorous examination.

The first description of the syndrome 'from the inside' appeared in 1910, long before Capgras' study. In his autobiography *A Mind that Found Itself*, the American Clifford Beers wrote about the protracted psychosis he had suffered from since the turn of the century.[12] He believed that first his brother and later his parents were *doppelgängers*. He felt as if he had been deserted by everyone, and that it would have been a betrayal for him to respond to the woman sitting next to his bed, who claimed she was his mother. For two years, Beers

[10] J. Levy-Valensi, 'L'illusion des sosies', *Gazette des Hôpitaux*, 55 (1929), 1001–3.

[11] K.L. Kahlbaum, 'Die Sinnesdelirien', *Allgemeine Zeitschrift für Psychiatrie und psychisch-gerichtliche Medizin*, 23 (1866), 56–78.

[12] C. Beers, *A Mind that Found Itself: an Autobiography* (New York, 1910).

categorically refused to speak to his family. When he spent a day at home, under supervision, he expressed his admiration for the way the *doppelgänger* was able to capture the voice and intonation of his father. This delusion did not disappear until he asked a patient due for release to find out if his family was still living at the same address. That was indeed the case. Clifford wrote a letter to his brother George in which he explained that the previous Wednesday he had had a visit from someone pretending to be him. The letter was intended as a kind of passport: if George had the letter with him on his following visit, then Clifford would know he was indeed his brother. If the visitor had no letter, then he would tell him in no uncertain terms what he thought of such a subterfuge. Several days later, Clifford saw his brother's *doppelgänger* come through the gate. He walked towards him, wondering what kind of lies the despicable swindler was going to dish out this time. But he took out a leather notebook, and handed him the letter.

> 'Here's my passport' he said.
> 'It's a good thing you brought it', I replied, as I glanced at it and again shook his hand, this time the hand of my own brother.
> 'Don't you want to read it?' he asked.
> 'There is no need of that. I am convinced.'[13]

From that moment on, Beers wrote, it was 'as if the molecules of my mental magnet were finally all pointing in the right direction. In a word: my mind had found itself.'[14] He always regarded 30 August 1902 as his 'second birthday'.

One of the most puzzling aspects of the early literature on the syndrome of Capgras is the fact that it was long regarded as a disorder that only affected women. The present figures do show that women are overrepresented by a ratio of about two to one, but it is curious that, after Capgras, ten years passed during which not a single male patient was described. It may have been sheer coincidence that all

---

[13] Beers, *Mind*, p. 25.   [14] *Ibid.*

the patients studied by Capgras and his colleagues happened to be women, so that females are wrongly associated with the characteristics of the syndrome. Perhaps the switch to a psychoanalytic explanation had something to do with it, or the prevailing insight that certain psychiatric conditions, such as hysteria, were 'women's complaints'. In 1936, the psychiatrist, J. R. Murray, presented 'a case of Capgras syndrome in the male', the first in the literature. He considered it worth a mention, although he did hint at a latent homosexuality.[15] From the 1940s on, more men were being diagnosed with the syndrome of Capgras.[16]

In 1927, at a session of that same Société where in 1923 Capgras had presented Madame M, the psychiatrists Courbon and Fail drew attention to a patient with delusions similar to those of the Capgras syndrome.[17] A 27-year-old woman, who had a passion for the theatre, was convinced she was being followed by the actresses Sarah Bernhardt and Robine. The two women either made use of an endless series of disguises, or took on the outward appearance of her acquaintances. Robine, for example, regularly posed as one of her neighbours. After the patient attacked a woman on the street whom she took for Robine, she was admitted. On the ward she was convinced that Robine and Bernhardt, dressed as nurses, forced her to masturbate. Courbon and Fail proposed that the syndrome be named after Léopoldo Frégoli, an Italian actor who was famous for

---

[15] J. R. Murray, 'A case of Capgras syndrome in the male', *Journal of Mental Science*, 82 (1936), 63–6.

[16] In an analysis of ninety-five Capgras patients, collected from the literature from Capgras and Reboul-Lachaux on, 72 per cent of the cases involved women, cf. F. de Jonghe and O. Markx, 'Het verschijnsel van Capgras. Over l'illusion des sosies', *Tijdschrift voor Psychiatrie*, 21 (1979), 600–14. In an analysis of 129 cases, drawn from the English-language literature and with the accent on those dating from the 1970s, the overrepresentation was only 57 per cent, cf. R. J. Berson, 'Capgras' syndrome', *American Journal of Psychiatry*, 140 (1983), 969–79.

[17] P. Courbon and G. Fail, 'L'illusion de Frégoli', *Bulletin de la Société de Médecine Mentale*, 15 (1927), 121–4.

his impersonations. Patients with the Frégoli syndrome suffer from the delusion that their pursuers impersonate the people around them, including family members, neighbours and friends. Among these patients, it is the men who are overrepresented. In 1932, at a session of the Société, Courbon and Tusques described a third type of delusion, that of the 'intermetamorphosis', where the patient is convinced that well-known individuals in his surroundings are capable of exchanging identities at will.[18]

Thus, in less than ten years (from 1923 to 1932) three case studies appearing in French psychiatric circles identified the main subtypes of what is now known as the 'misidentification syndrome'.[19] Of these three, the syndrome of Capgras occurs most often; the other two are rare.

An extra cup of tea

The literature on the Capgras syndrome is still decidedly casuistic in nature; the cases described now number in the hundreds.[20] But each individual case, like a dot in a pointillist painting, contributes to the general profile of the syndrome. In most Capgras delusions, the patient thinks that the *doppelgänger* is a human being of flesh and blood, although there is the occasional variant where the patient believes that his loved ones have been replaced by a robot or, in a modern version, by aliens. Sometimes the patient is himself part of the delusion: he thinks there are *doppelgängers* of him walking around, or that he himself is such an imposter. Capgras' Madame M was convinced that her own *doppelgänger* was living in her apartment. The reactions of Capgras patients to the appearance of *doppelgängers* are varied. An older woman sat quietly crying at the loss of her

[18] P. Courbon and J. Tusques, 'Illusion d'intermétamorphose et de charme', *Annales Médico-Psychologiques*, 90 (1932), 401–5.

[19] The original articles on Frégoli and intermetamorphosis also appeared in an English translation in Ellis, Whitley and Luauté, 'Delusional misidentification'.

[20] Berson, 'Capgras' syndrome'.

husband. Another woman resigned herself to the fact that she would have to face life with a *doppelgänger* at her side. From then on, she always poured three cups of tea: for herself, the *doppelgänger*, and her husband, in case he should reappear. When the couple went out for a walk, she slipped back to leave a note for her husband. Another patient knew for certain that her daughter had been exchanged for a *doppelgänger*, but because they got along so well, she never confronted her with the deception. In most cases, however, there is sorrow and concern about the fate of the loved ones who have disappeared. Were they driven away, poisoned, murdered? Are they being held captive somewhere? Will they ever return? Some patients report the disappearance to the police. One woman took to wearing mourning and in the anamnesis she referred to herself as a widow. Understandably, many patients tend to think that the *doppelgänger* must know something about the disappearance, and even accuse him or her of murder. Some, in their paranoia, fear that they will be the next victim. Should they not take action before it is too late? The status of *doppelgänger* is not without risk. One Capgras patient in Missouri believed that his stepfather had been replaced by an alien, and beheaded him in search of the batteries and microfilm.[21] There are quite a number of documented cases in which Capgras patients have committed homicide.[22] Here, the delusion usually has a long history, and the murders are carefully prepared and executed, according to a plan which indicates that the perpetrators' intellectual powers are still intact.

The psychoanalytic explanations, introduced in 1924 by Capgras himself, varied within the boundaries drawn by Freud. The Capgras syndrome was said to be a defence mechanism designed to camouflage the incestuous feelings of the patient for her father. It is unthinkable that such desires could be directed toward the father, which must

---

[21] G. Blount, 'Dangerousness of patients with Capgras syndrome', *Nebraska Medical Journal*, 71 (1986), 207.

[22] K. W. de Pauw and T. K. Szulecka, 'Dangerous delusions and the misidentification syndromes', *British Journal of Psychiatry*, 152 (1988), 91–6.

mean that he is not the patient's real father. It was also suggested that the ambivalent feelings which the patient supposedly had for her nearest and dearest, not only love but also hate, would lead to an unbearable sense of guilt. The only solution was to create a split in the object of those feelings and then to project all the feelings of hate onto the *doppelgänger*. This explains the idealization of the lost loved one and the aggression directed towards the *doppelgänger*. Occasionally, the patient's compulsory admission provided ultimate proof of the delusion: her own husband and children would never have had her locked up. That projection of pure hate means that the *doppelgänger* is in real danger. For many years, defence, projection and substitution were the main mechanisms seen to be active in the minds of Capgras patients. This was particularly evident in the case of French patients, for psychoanalysis had by then taken possession of psychiatry in France. Well into the 1970s, explanations couched in any but psychoanalytic terms were rare.[23]

Cross-over

In the past twenty years, the Capgras syndrome has crossed over from psychiatry to neurology. Until the late 1970s, the symptoms were still being studied against the background of psychiatric diagnostics, notably paranoid schizophrenia. Little mention was made of organic disturbances, and where this did occur it was seen as a coincidental convergence of schizophrenia and a neurological abnormality.[24] There was also good reason to regard organic explanations as suspect: the delusion of the Capgras patient tends to focus on individuals with whom he or she has an affective bond. Neurological damage could not possibly display such selectivity.

---

[23] K. W. de Pauw, 'Psychodynamic approaches to the Capgras delusion: a critical historical review', *Psychopathology*, 27 (1994), 154–60.

[24] See, e.g., R. Kiriakos and J. Ananth, 'Review of 13 cases of Capgras syndrome', *American Journal of Psychiatry*, 137 (1980), 1605–7.

How could a cerebral infarction or a stroke impair one's ability to recognize the faces of people in one's direct surroundings, but not those of other people? It was more logical to search in the direction of a disturbance in the patient's emotional housekeeping. During the 1980s, a shift occurred in this pattern. The fact that the onset of Capgras syndrome may be quite acute (as a result of brain damage following an accident, a stroke, or a pinched blood vessel) is difficult to reconcile with an explanation in affective terms. There was a rapid increase in the number of Capgras cases accompanied by demonstrable organic disturbances. To an extent, this was due to new diagnostic instruments, such as imaging techniques, but a more important factor was the emergence of the organic perspective in psychiatry. This was an invitation to actively search for physiological or neurological disorders. The fact that the Capgras syndrome was increasingly being seen as a condition with an organic background was not the result of a succession of newly discovered organic factors. Indeed, almost the reverse was true: thanks to the growing interest in the organic perspective, more and more of those factors were coming to light.

This development is reflected in a reversal of foreground and background. In the past, this psychiatric disorder was regarded as primary and any organic disorder as secondary. Today, in many cases an organic abnormality is specified, and otherwise there is the suspicion of an organic disorder which cannot be detected with present-day instruments. The default for the syndrome of Capgras is now an organic cause; and the list of abnormalities and injuries associated with Capgras is long and varied: epilepsy, brain tumours, MS, Parkinson's, alcoholism, an extra Y chromosome in men, migraines, electroshocks and drug abuse.[25] Capgras-like symptoms

---

[25] D. Bourget and L. Whitehurst, 'Capgras syndrome: a review of the neurophysiological correlates and presenting clinical features in cases involving physical violence', *Canadian Journal of Psychiatry*, 49 (2004), 719–25.

appear in around 10 per cent of patients with Alzheimer's, so that, to their sorrow, loved ones are treated like imposters.[26]

At present, the major theories point towards the neurology of facial recognition. In 1986, the American neurologist, Anthony Joseph, put forward an ingenious explanation which was in line with a finding from the research into split brains.[27] In cases of epilepsy which are unresponsive to treatment, an incision is sometimes made in the corpus callosum, the band of nerve tissue which connects the two brain halves, ensuring that no communication is possible between the left and right halves of the brain. This procedure, which makes it possible to examine patterns of specialization in the brain, has revealed that the right half plays a greater role in facial recognition. According to Joseph's hypothesis, each hemisphere develops its own representation of the face which is seen, and in a healthy brain, with an intact line of communication between left and right, the two fuse into a single image. But where organic damage has interfered with the communication between the two brain halves, the patient is presented with two separate representations which he cannot align with one another. The patient has a feeling that he recognizes the face and at the same time does not recognize it. His brain solves this problem for him: he is left with the impression that he is looking at a *doppelgänger*. Because the final product of face recognition is withheld, and he must (almost literally) make do with a neuronal semi-finished article, the Capgras patient is granted a glimpse of the separate activities of the two brain hemispheres.

An opportunity to test this hypothesis presented itself during research into another rare neurological abnormality, prosopagnosia, or the inability to recognize faces. In *The Man who Mistook his Wife*

[26] D.G. Harwood, W.W. Barker, R.L. Ownby and R. Duara, 'Prevalence and correlates of Capgras syndrome in Alzheimer's disease', *International Journal of Geriatric Psychiatry*, 14 (1999), 415–20.

[27] A.B. Joseph, 'Focal central nervous system abnormalities in patients with misidentification syndromes', *Bibliotheca Psychiatrica*, 164 (1986), 68–79.

for a Hat, Oliver Sacks described a prosopagnostic patient who put out his hand to a grandfather clock, gave parking metres an affectionate pat on the head, and at the end of one session took hold of his wife's head and tried to put it on his own head.[28] For a long time it was thought that the Capgras syndrome could not possibly be connected to prosopagnosia, since Capgras patients usually have no trouble identifying faces, and even see the likeness of the person who has disappeared in someone whom they regard as a *doppelgänger*. Conversely, the selectivity of the Capgras syndrome is lacking in prosopagnosia, where it is not only the faces of people close to the patient which are not recognized. Moreover, the average prosopagnosia patient differs from the Capgras patient in other respects as well. They are usually men, middle-aged or older, who have had a stroke or, as in the case of *The Man who Mistook his Wife for a Hat*, are suffering from a brain tumour. Capgras patients tend to be women, the syndrome can present in all age groups (patients as young as eight have been described), and brain damage has not been established in all cases. And yet Capgras patients consistently score lower on facial recognition tests than other categories of psychiatric patients. For example, in the facial recognition test named after Benton, which involves a series of photos of unknown individuals, they have more trouble identifying different photos of the same person. In 1984, research on prosopagnosia produced a suggestive link to the Capgras syndrome.

The British neurologist, R. M. Bauer, discovered that prosopagnosia patients do continue to register autonomous reactions to familiar faces.[29] During the presentation of photos, it appeared that the skin resistance of the patient (the same measure used in lie detectors) reacted to familiar faces but not to unfamiliar ones. These results on

---

[28] O. Sacks, *The Man who Mistook his Wife for a Hat* (London, 1985).

[29] R. M. Bauer, 'Autonomic recognition of names and faces: a neuropsychological application of the guilty knowledge test', *Neuropsychologica*, 22 (1984), 457–69.

the 'guilty knowledge test' seemed to indicate that there is another recognition system active. Bauer suggested that facial recognition takes place along two independent routes in the brain. The first trajectory is responsible for identifying the face and leads to conscious recognition, while the second trajectory, on the unconscious level, brings about the link with the emotional significance of the face. In the case of prosopagnosia patients, the first route is damaged, and only the autonomous reactions betray that somewhere else in the brain, beyond the reach of their consciousness, the face has been recognized.

In 1990, two British neuropsychologists, Hadyn Ellis and Andrew Young, formulated the elegant hypothesis that the Capgras syndrome may well be the *mirror image* of prosopagnosia.[30] If the first route is still intact, so that the patient consciously recognizes faces, but the second route has broken down due to a neurological impairment, then the patient will be unable to connect the face he recognizes with the emotional significance which that face once had for him. Because it is among the people closest to us that the discrepancy between cool recognition and lack of familiarity is greatest, husbands and wives, parents and children are those most often seen as *doppelgängers*.

On the basis of this theory, a testable prediction can be made. If that second route is damaged, then the Capgras patient will *not* display the autonomous reactions which are spared in prosopagnosia patients. Experiments based on the guilty knowledge test have shown that this is indeed the case. The patient recognizes the face, but apparently it no longer calls up the same emotional significance as in the past. In another experiment, Ellis tested the hypothesis put forward by Joseph that the Capgras syndrome is rooted in an

---

[30] H. D. Ellis and A. Young, 'Accounting for delusional misidentifications', *British Journal of Psychiatry*, 157 (1990), 239–48. For a detailed and illustrated presentation of this theory, see H. D. Ellis and M. B. Lewis, 'Capgras delusion: a window on face recognition', *Trends in Cognitive Sciences*, 5 (2001) 4, 149–56.

inability to integrate the two representations of the right and left brain halves. He had an experimental group of three Capgras patients watch a screen onto which two faces were projected for 200 milliseconds. They were asked to indicate whether the two faces were the same or different. The control group consisted of three paranoid patients who in all relevant characteristics corresponded to the Capgras patients. The latter were able to carry out this assignment even faster than the control group. Joseph's hypothesis had predicted a longer reaction time.

In one crucial aspect, the line of reasoning suggested by Ellis and Young runs parallel to that of Capgras and Reboul-Lachaux in 1923. In both theories, the patient is no longer capable of linking the face that he recognizes with the familiarity of the past. The ensuing conflict calls up the paranoid suspicion of a *doppelgänger*, a true product of the 'logique des émotions'. What Ellis and Young add to this argument is a specification of the neurological processes responsible for the emergence of this conflict. It is the right hemisphere which is under suspicion, a fact which fits their theory: the right hemisphere plays a greater role in facial recognition than the left.[31] While elegant, this theory has not proved decisive. It had already been established that in certain psychiatric disorders, the skin resistance no longer responds to familiar faces, although these patients show no signs whatsoever of the Capgras syndrome. In some cases, the trigger for Capgras-like symptoms is an acute psychological crisis, such as a divorce or a death in the family. And most important of all: after the article by Ellis and Young, a number of pesky incidental findings emerged which were disturbingly incompatible with their theory. In 2002, the Brazilian physician Dalgalarrondo and his colleagues reported the case of a 26-year-old

---

[31] H. D. Ellis, 'The role of the right hemisphere in the Capgras delusion', *Psychopathology*, 27 (1994), 177–85. See also N. M. Edelstyn and F. Oyebode, 'A review of the phenomenology and cognitive neuropsychological origins of the Capgras syndrome', *International Journal of Geriatric Psychiatry*, 14 (1999), 48–59.

Figure 11.2: Capgras as medical director of the Asile Sainte-Anne

blind Capgras patient.[32] Her husband had been replaced by a *doppelgänger*. They didn't fool her, she said: her real husband was a little heavier and he also smelled different. A year later, the German neurologist Dietl and his colleagues described the case of a Capgras patient who believed that her daughter, who had emigrated to the United States, had been replaced by a *doppelgänger*.[33] She had reached this conclusion on the basis of telephone calls, as there had been no visual contact for many years. Apparently there is something more – or something different – going on than a disturbance in visual recognition.

The man who gave his name to this syndrome, which is just as mysterious today as it was eighty years ago, took leave of Sainte-Anne in the early years of the Second World War. But he would soon return, this time as a patient. Towards the end of his life, Joseph Capgras lost his mental faculties. He died in 1950 in the institution over which he had presided for so long.

[32] P. Dalgalarrondo, G. Fujisawa and C. E. M. Banzato, 'Capgras syndrome and blindness: against the prosopagnosia hypothesis', *Canadian Journal of Psychiatry*, 47 (2002) 4, 387–8

[33] T. Dietl, A. Herr, H. Brunner and E. Friess, 'Capgras syndrome: out of sight, out of mind?', *Acta Psychiatrica Scandinavia*, 108 (2003), 460–3.

TWELVE

Little professors: Asperger syndrome

CB is a 15-year-old boy with a long history of behavioural problems. Although he is of normal intelligence, and in some categories, such as mathematical insight and spatial puzzles, well above normal, he attends a school for children with learning disabilities. His main handicap appears to be a lack of insight into the emotions and intentions of others. On a test that measures the interpretation of emotions on the basis of facial expression, he scored very low. He recognized the expressions denoting happiness and sadness, but not those for puzzlement or surprise. His inability to 'read' emotions regularly leads to conflicts with other children. In the playground, he tends to stay close to the adults.

His knowledge of social conventions is extremely limited and appears to have been consciously learned, rather than acquired naturally. His interests are monomaniacal. He knows all the prime numbers up to 7,057, and can recite the name and capital city of every country in the world. His use of language is highly concrete and literal. He does not understand metaphors. The same is true of humour.

CB's behaviour is highly ritualized. He will only eat when the various foods on his plate do not touch each other. Colours have a strong emotional value: red is good, yellow and brown are bad.

He doesn't eat brown food. He wants his surroundings to remain constant: when the furniture is moved around, he puts things back where they were. He does not like to be touched. When his parents want to hug him, they spread one hand so that their fingertips touch his.

It is striking that CB invariably describes his own mental processes in mechanical terms. He compares his memory to a video recorder, and the reproduction of facts to the processes 'rewind', 'play' and 'fast forward'. In unfamiliar surroundings, where there is too much new information to cope with, he feels like a crashing computer. Then he shuts out the world around him by putting his hands over his ears and moaning softly. CB compares this to shutting down the computer by means of 'control-alt-delete'.

There are no details available on the delivery. His parents are of normal intelligence and display no neurological or psychiatric disorders. CB is their only child. Raising him has placed a considerable strain on their marriage. At the moment they are living apart.

Case studies such as this are to be found in the *DSM-IV Casebook*.[1] Given the abnormalities which CB displays, the autism spectrum immediately springs to mind: the lack of insight into the emotions of others, the monomaniacal interests, the low tolerance for change, the aversion to being touched, and the inability to think in abstract terms. The fact that he is of normal intelligence and has no fundamental language disorder points to a form of autism known as Asperger syndrome.

Except that CB is not based on the *Casebook*. He is a character in *The Curious Incident of the Dog in the Night-time* by Mark Haddon. Readers will have recognized the details.[2] The initials stand for Christopher Boone, who at the beginning of the book is 'fifteen years, three months and two days old'. Christopher imparts this

---

[1] R. L. Spitzer *et al.* (eds.), *DSM-IV Casebook* (Washington, 1994).
[2] M. Haddon, *The Curious Incident of the Dog in the Night-time* (New York, 2003).

information to a policeman who has been summoned in the middle of the night, and is now squatting next to Christopher, staring at the neighbour's poodle, cruelly impaled on a pitchfork. The novel centres on efforts to solve this cowardly murder, as lived and told by Christopher.

Reading Haddon's novel, you experience something which is not evoked by studying the Asperger casus in the *Casebook* or the *Casebook*-like description above. After ten or twelve pages, you find yourself being drawn into Christopher's mind. Another ten pages, and you are in an inner world which is at once bizarre and ordered, exotic and logical, eccentric and straightforward. As the story unfolds, you begin to see the world through his eyes and process information through his brain. One of the paradoxes of this unusual book is that you begin to experience the inner life of someone who has no notion of the inner life of others. As a reader, you find yourself slipping into the first-person perspective of someone who sees the world exclusively from a third-person perspective. At the end of the book, it is difficult to dispel the feeling that you have just experienced something which is actually impossible, as if you've caught a glimpse of the dark side of the moon.

Asperger syndrome is named after the Viennese paediatrician Hans Asperger (1906–1980). What Haddon has so brilliantly achieved in his portrayal of Christopher – constructing an autistic character on the basis of how he reacts to what happens to him – is quite similar to what Asperger was striving for in the case studies in 1943.

'Difficult children'

The history of autism begins with a series of coincidences. It was in 1943 that a physician named Leo Kanner described a new psychiatric syndrome. As head of the clinic for child psychiatry at Johns Hopkins University in Baltimore, he had noticed that a number of his children suffered from a disorder to which he gave the name 'early infantile autism'.[3] At the heart of the syndrome lay a severe contact disorder. In that same year, Hans Asperger presented the results of his own research into the syndrome which today bears his name, and which likewise focuses on 'autism'. Kanner and Asperger wrote independently of one another, and the two never met. Nonetheless, they chose the same name to characterize the disorder, and both borrowed the term from the Swiss psychiatrist, Eugen Bleuler. The children they describe in their case studies bear such a close resemblance to each other that to this day there are those who question whether they are actually two different syndromes.[4]

In the light of this parallel, what happened after that is even stranger. Following the publication of Kanner's description, psychiatric institutions and paediatric clinics began to identify children who met the description of autism: a syndrome that no one had ever noticed before proved to be anything but rare. This established Kanner's reputation as the discoverer of a new psychiatric syndrome. What happened after the publication of Asperger's article is quickly told: nothing. Until the early 1980s, references to his work could be counted on the fingers of one hand. It was not until 1981 that the English autism specialist, Lorna Wing, proposed that the disorder described by Asperger be incorporated into the autism spectrum under the name 'Asperger's syndrome'.[5] In the past fifteen or twenty years, we have seen a repetition of what happened in the case of Kanner's autism: once the syndrome had been described and given a name, its incidence rapidly increased. To illustrate the extent of the explosion: anyone searching for 'Asperger's syndrome' at the time of writing (August 2008) will get over two and a half million hits. In August 2004, that number was 183,000.

[3] L. Kanner, 'Autistic disturbances of affective contact', *Nervous Child*, 2 (1943), 217–50.
[4] For a detailed comparison, see L. Wing, 'The relationship between Asperger's syndrome and Kanner's autism' in U. Frith (ed.), *Autism and Asperger Syndrome* (Cambridge, 1991), pp. 93–121.
[5] L. Wing, 'Asperger's syndrome: a clinical account', *Psychological Medicine*, 11 (1981), 115–29.

Figure 12.1: Asperger (left) and his team test children at the University Paediatric Clinic in Vienna

Hans Asperger was born in 1906.[6] He grew up in Vienna, where he also completed his medical studies. His specialization was paediatrics, which took him to the University Paediatric Clinic, founded in 1918. This clinic specialized in *Heilpädagogik*, whereby children were treated using a combination of medical, pedagogical and psychotherapeutic interventions. In 1932, only a year after obtaining his doctorate, Asperger was appointed assistant physician at the clinic. Even then, it was clear to him that he would find his life's fulfilment in the study and treatment of 'difficult children', as he referred to them. With a few brief interruptions, he remained on the staff of the clinic in Vienna. After the war he was appointed professor of paediatrics, a chair which he would hold for twenty years.

Asperger's habilitation thesis was devoted to the syndrome that now bears his name. It appeared in 1944.[7] In the ten years which he devoted to this research, Asperger observed some 200 children.

---

[6] For a brief biographical sketch, see J. Lutz, 'Hans Asperger und Leo Kanner zum Gedenken', *Acta paedopsychiatrica*, 47 (1981), 179–83. A more extensive account is U. Frith, 'Asperger and his Syndrome' in Frith, *Autism*, pp. 1–36.

[7] H. Asperger, 'Die autistischen Psychopathen im Kindesalter', *Archiv für Psychiatrie und Nervenkrankheiten*, 117 (1944), 76–136. An abridged form of this article appeared in Frith, *Autism*, pp. 37–92.

He first encountered the disorder as a child at summer camp: there were always a couple of boys who couldn't seem to mix with the group and panicked when they were forced to take part in activities.

The opening of the text reads like a methodological confession of faith. Asperger felt the attraction of *Gestalt* psychology: a human being is not the sum of his parts, but rather an organism whose characteristics are interwoven. It is no accident, he wrote, that the word individual means 'indivisible'. The physician's main instrument is neither measurement nor experiment, but observation. A physician must trust his intuition and his impressions, and open himself up to the *Gestalt* of the individual: build, posture, gaze, facial expression, movements, intonation – in short, everything. The true art consists in listening to a person's *Zusammenklang* or harmony. Asperger did not believe in psychological tests, artificial diagnostic situations, or a strict, mechanical application of typologies. Even in the case of a characteristic such as intelligence, which appears to lend itself to precise measurement, the important thing is not the score on the intelligence test, but rather what the test says about the child's manner of working, interests and originality. Intelligence is only one of the threads from which an individual is woven, and it is coloured by all the others.

Sometimes, however, the pattern of the fabric displays an irregularity. This is seen in a type of child whom Asperger referred to as an 'autistic psychopath' (a term which can no longer be used, since 'psychopath' now refers to a different psychiatric disorder). What Asperger was trying to describe was more akin to a derangement of mind. The core of the disorder is 'autism' (from *autos*, or self): the state of being locked up in a private world, together with a lack of contact with one's social surroundings. Children with this disorder encounter problems – with their parents, with their teachers, and with themselves. They are so different from the average child that they require special pedagogical treatment if they are to find their place in society.

Fritz V

The core of Asperger's account consists of four case studies. The first is also the most detailed: Fritz V, born in 1933, admitted for observation at the age of 6. Fritz was the eldest of the children. His motor development proceeded more slowly than normal, but his speech was advanced for his age; indeed, he spoke 'like an adult'.[8] Fritz was totally unfit for school: he never completed an assignment, and was constantly grabbing things and smashing them to bits, or using them to hit other children, without ever stopping to think about whether he was hurting them. Equally noteworthy is the fact that he never entered into an affective relationship with anyone at the clinic. He could not abide the other children. It didn't bother him when someone got angry with him; in fact, he seemed to enjoy provoking people. In addressing adults, he never used the formal '*Sie*'. For him, everyone was '*Du*'.

Fritz's mother came from a family which also produced one of Austria's greatest poets, alongside a number of eccentrics. They were almost all intellectuals, whom she referred to as '*genial verrückt*' (in the 'mad-genius' mode).[9] As a young man the grandfather had had similar problems, and he was even expelled from school. Fritz resembled his mother. Once, Asperger saw them together, not far from the clinic: 'the mother slouched along, hands held behind her back, apparently oblivious to the world. Beside her the boy was rushing to and fro, doing mischief. They gave the impression of having absolutely nothing to do with each other.'[10] The mother always looked somewhat unkempt. When things got on top of her at home, she simply dropped everything and went off into the mountains for a week or so. Fritz's father was a well-placed civil servant,

---

[8] Quoted from the translation by Uta Frith: H. Asperger, 'Autistic psychopathy in childhood' in U. Frith (ed.), *Autism and Asperger Syndrome* (Cambridge, 1991), pp. 37–92, 39.

[9] Asperger, 'Autistic psychopathy', p. 40. [10] *Ibid.* p. 41.

painfully correct, pedantic and aloof: Asperger could not summon up any more sympathy for him than for his wife.

Fritz himself is tall for his age, he tends to slouch and his movements are clumsy. But he has a delicate face, and Asperger makes mention of his 'aristocratic features'.[11] His gaze is vacant, passing swiftly and absently over people and objects. He has a thin, high-pitched voice, with a strange lilting intonation. He speaks slowly, dragging out his words. When he replies, it is seldom in answer to the question. Sometimes he repeats the entire question, or only a word. Fritz has a peculiar relationship with noise: he throws toys, apparently because he likes the sound they make, and sometimes he drums rhythmically on his thigh or the table or a wall – or even another child – as if they are all the same to him. The paradox is that these impulsive actions are invariably so unpleasant, painful or downright dangerous that he must realize how disagreeable his behaviour is. But he seems to take no notice of his immediate surroundings. He will sit there with a sleepy, absent look on his face, and then suddenly jump up and sweep all the teacups from the table or give another child a box on the ears.

This peculiar behaviour also manifests itself during testing. One of the assignments involves copying a geometric pattern of sticks laid on the table. Fritz barely glances at the example, but lays the sticks down in the correct pattern, and does so more accurately than the other children in his age group. But with the exception of this example, he is impossible to test. He deliberately falls off his chair, slaps the teacher on the hand, and gives nonsense answers. When asked what the difference is between glass and wood, he says 'Because the glass is more glassy and the wood is more woody.'[12] It is only in the area of figures and arithmetic that he is able to hold his own. He can remember a sequence of six numbers and repeat them, which according to Binet's intelligence test, corresponds to the level of a child

---

[11] *Ibid.* p. 42.   [12] *Ibid.* p. 45.

of 10. Like almost all children of this type, according to Asperger, Fritz has one specific *Sonderinteresse*, or talent, and that is arithmetic.[13] He taught himself to count to a hundred and within that range his arithmetic is good, not only numbers over 10 but also fractions. Fritz can ask himself which is larger, one-sixteenth or one-eighteenth, and come up with the right answer. As a joke, someone once asked him what two-thirds of 120 was, and the answer came back in a flash: 80. Small wonder that the assessments of such children range from genius to mentally retarded.

Asperger explains that while this isolated intellectual skill is intact, Fritz's emotional life is severely disturbed. Even before a 'normal' child (the quotation marks are Asperger's) has any knowledge of words, he or she learns to obey the look, the gestures and the tone which accompany what the father or mother is saying. He or she learns how to interpret facial expressions, body language and voice, via a process which is totally unconscious. In Fritz's case, it is as if the ability to make contact with others by means of such non-verbal communication is lacking. One indication of this is the fact that his own means of expression deviate from the normal. The way he looks at people is odd, his voice is strange, and his motor system and speech are different. It is not surprising that he fails to understand the expressions of others.

Conversely, no one can empathize with Fritz. No one knows why he's laughing or hopping around on one foot, why he suddenly turns angry, or starts pummelling another child. His feelings are totally unrelated to the situation, and his mood swings so abrupt that it is almost impossible to make contact with him. Any show of affection appears to irritate him.

This means that the usual instruments of instruction and education are all but useless. Where there is no contact with the child's emotional life, nothing has any effect on his behaviour, neither a friendly

[13] *Ibid.*

request nor an angry threat. Asperger's advice is to issue all assignments 'with the affect turned off'.[14] The teacher must never become angry, nor should he strive to be liked. Good results were obtained with assignments issued in a mechanical, stereotypical manner. Fritz proved susceptible to this approach: it was as if he was unable to resist an order given in the tone of an automaton.

No matter how disturbed his concentration seemed, Fritz managed to pick up enough from the individual, custom-tailored schooling which he was offered to ensure that he did not lag too far behind his peers. This was an aspect which fascinated Asperger: how someone with such a severe handicap was capable of keeping tabs on his surroundings out of the corner of his eye, as it were. Often by accident, those who deal with such boys discover that 'their thoughts can be unusually rich. They are good at logical thinking, and the ability to abstract is particularly good. Indeed, it appeared that even in perfectly normal people an increased distance to the outside world is a prerequisite for excellence in abstract thinking.'[15]

Fritz is followed by Harro L, 8 years old, just as aggressive as Fritz, and just as clumsy. He displays the same vacant expression, the sudden laugh that no one understands, the unexpected replies: 'Glass is transparent. Wood – if you wanted to look through it, you would have to make a hole in it. If one wants to beat on a piece of wood then one has to beat a long time until it breaks, unless it's a dry twig. Then that would break easily. With the glass you need to hit only twice and then it's broken.'[16] His 'special interest' is also doing sums, and he has developed his own systems, which are totally different from the conventional methods, so original and yet often so complicated that he ends up making mistakes. Harro is incapable of learning via the normal, much simpler, methods. In his case, it is the father who is 'strange': the man has no contact with anyone and he has exchanged his dream of becoming a painter for the trade of

[14] Ibid. p. 47.   [15] Ibid. p. 49.   [16] Ibid. p. 54.

brush-maker. On the ward, Harro avoids all contact with the other children in his group. He reads a great deal and when he is absorbed in a book, he is oblivious to everything around him. His verbal powers of expression are downright precocious, comparable to those of an adult: he takes pleasure in recounting fantastic stories which go on interminably and gradually become incoherent.

After Fritz and Harro, the case of 7-year-old Ernst K conforms to a pattern which is beginning to take shape: he cannot abide other children, makes a scene if things are not in precisely the place he wants them or is used to, and he is so clumsy that he has to be helped with the simplest procedures, such as eating and dressing himself. Ernst also does sums according to his own methods. He looks straight past objects and people: the eye does not seem to grasp anything. His voice is high and nasal and, according to Asperger, he sounds like 'a caricature of a degenerate aristocrat'. He, too, has an eccentric father, and like Fritz, he is lanky and has delicate features.

Asperger presents a fourth case, that of 11-year-old Hellmuth L, which illustrates that brain damage can also lead to behavioural abnormalities resembling those of the boys described above. In Hellmuth's case, that brain damage was caused by a lack of oxygen during the delivery. He displays the same pattern: the absent expression, the precocious use of language, and an inability to interact with other children. Unlike Fritz, Harro and Ernst, he does not excel at arithmetic, but he does have a preference for poetic language which is lacking in the other three.

'Intelligent automata'

According to Asperger, the differences between Fritz, Harro and Ernst were variations within a common profile. It was a profile which over the previous ten years he had diagnosed in some 200 boys. For example, their voices were often high or shrill or, by contrast, very soft or monotonous; in either case they were unusual enough to invite derisive imitations. Although their special skills and interests were wide-ranging, they were all eccentric. One of the children could recite by heart the entire timetable of the Vienna tram lines, while another was a 'calendar savant', able to calculate instantly the weekday for any calendar date in any century. The profile begins to take shape quite early in life, from the age of about 2. As the child grows up, there may be many changes in the expression of the disorder, but it will never go away. To those familiar with the profile, it is instantly recognizable, as soon as the child enters a room or opens his mouth to speak.

Often the faces of these children are 'old', as if they belong to a 'degenerate aristocracy'.[17] When they look at something, their gaze seems to glance off the object, as if it is only visible on the periphery of their field of vision. 'One can never be sure whether their glance goes into the far distance or is turned inwards, just as one never knows what the children are preoccupied with at a particular moment or what is going on in their minds.'[18] Their intellectual skills are also different. In 'normal' children, intelligence takes shape between two poles: at one end, the spontaneous original expressions, at the other end, the copying activities, the learning from others. The latter without the former is empty and mechanical. But the former without the latter is a true handicap: children with this disorder are incapable of being anything but original, spontaneous and impulsive. They dream up new words that no one understands, and design worlds known only to them. The transfer of knowledge via normal learning channels is impossible. The combination of originality and an inability to learn often leads to conflict between parents and teachers. The parents see only the surprising, original side of the child's behaviour, while the teachers know only that the child is impossible to teach. Asperger appeals to his readers to see the positive side of the handicap. At the core of the disorder is the lack of contact with the environment. But it is precisely this which creates the distance which is

[17] Ibid. p. 68.   [18] Ibid. pp. 68–9.

indispensable for abstraction. In the most favourable case, this can lead to great scientific accomplishments.

Asperger believed that the profile was rooted in disturbances in the deepest layers of the personality. While their intellect may be above average, the drives and instincts of these children are often severely disturbed.[19] They are totally egocentric, and have no respect whatsoever for others: this is not the reflection of a conscious insolence, but rather a defect in their understanding of other people. They have no sense of social distance, and they touch people as they might a piece of furniture. Young or old, acquaintance or stranger: such considerations play no role in the way they respond to others. Lessons in social mores must be explicitly taught. Only via the intellectual route are these 'intelligent automata' able to learn behaviour patterns.[20]

Their approach to objects is also different. Ordinary children are capable of bringing objects to life during their play – dolls become playmates. Children with autism are barely aware of such objects or, conversely, they turn them into a kind of fetish, like the wooden spool that one boy always carried around with him. They can be equally obsessive about living creatures: one of the boys had two white mice which he cared for with touching dedication. At the same time, he drove his parents to distraction with his constant badgering.

Asperger was reluctant to make sweeping statements concerning the possible hereditary nature of the condition. Any conclusion would have to be based on extensive genealogical studies. But in *every* case where he had become acquainted with the parents or relatives, he had discovered psychopathological features. Often the children came from prominent families of artists or scholars, but instead of inheriting the original talent present in the genes, they seemed to display only the accompanying whims and eccentricities.

[19] *Ibid.* p. 79.　　[20] *Ibid.* p. 58.

In the majority of cases, the father had an intellectual profession, and the one or two manual workers among the parents, such as the brush-maker, seemed to feel that they had missed their calling. There were more than the usual number of only children, in Asperger's view the result of the parents' autistic leanings and the coldness and aloofness of their marital life.

The disorder affected only boys. From time to time, Asperger saw one or two of the symptoms in girls, but never the complete syndrome. The disease was 'an extreme variant of male intelligence, the male character'.[21] Boys and girls have their own characteristic pattern of intelligence: that of girls is directed toward the concrete, the practical and the sensible, while that of boys focuses on logical thinking, abstraction and independent investigation. In autistic boys, abstraction takes on such proportions that instinctive contact with people and objects is lost. Asperger admitted that he, too, found it puzzling that so many of his autistic boys had a mother with distinct autistic characteristics.

And then there were the incongruities *within* the syndrome. The children developed no affective bond with the people around them. Why, then, did they display such obsessive affection for, say, a pet rat? Why did precisely these children show signs of extreme homesick-ness? Most of the children who were brought in for observation were accustomed to the ward after a day or so, while the autistic children remained inconsolable for days, and were eloquent in describing how much they missed their beloved parents. Asperger had noticed that autistic children had a preference for rhythmical swaying movements. But why did they have no sense of rhythm in music, and why were their motions so wooden during rhythmic gymnastics? Children with this disorder give the impression that they are totally oblivious to their surroundings. And why was there sometimes that one detail which suddenly seemed to attract their attention? One of the boys

---

[21] *Ibid.* p. 84.

could not be persuaded to eat his soup because he was so fascinated by the fat globules floating on the surface, and kept blowing them back and forth. And finally, why was it so difficult to get these children to carry out assigned tasks, while orders which were not formulated as a personal assignment, but rather as something which was objectively necessary, were duly carried out when they were recorded in a detailed roster?

Finally, Asperger discusses what is likely to happen to these children. A great deal depends on their level of intelligence. Children who are also mentally subnormal have the poorest prospects. Many end up doing odd jobs or, in the least favourable cases, roaming the streets as 'originals, grotesque and dilapidated, talking loudly to themselves or unconcernedly to passers-by'.[22] Children with a normal or above-normal intellect clearly have better prospects. Once they have chosen a profession, some of them achieve a remarkably good social integration. Asperger followed the career of an autistic man over an extended period of time. At a young age he was found to have exceptional mathematical abilities. 'When he was three, his mother had to draw for him, in the sand, a triangle [*Drei-eck* or three-corner], a square [four-corner] and a pentangle [five-corner]. He then took a stick himself, drew a line and said "And this is a two-corner [*Zwei-eck*], isn't it?", then made a dot and said "And this one is a one-corner [*Ein-eck*]."'[23] After an extremely difficult time at secondary school, where he had trouble with all his subjects except maths, he took up theoretical astronomy. He later discovered a calculation error in the work of Newton and made it the subject of his dissertation.

Nor was he an exception. In the experience of Asperger, almost all autistic children of normal intelligence ultimately find a suitable job, often thanks to their exceptional skills in subjects like maths, technology or chemistry. There was also one boy who became an authority on the subject of heraldry. The one-sidedness, the clearly defined

---

[22] *Ibid.* p. 87.   [23] *Ibid.* p. 88.

areas of interest, and the 'blinkers' made him eminently suited to such a profession.

The closing passage is worth quoting in full:

> We are convinced, then, that autistic people have their place in the organism of the social community. They fulfil their role well, perhaps better than anyone else could, and we are talking of people who as children had the greatest difficulties and caused untold worries to their care-givers. The example of autism shows particularly well how even abnormal personalities can be capable of development and adjustment. Possibilities of social integration which one would never have dreamt of may arise in the course of development. This knowledge determines our attitude towards complicated individuals of this and other types. It also gives us the right and the duty to speak out for these children with the whole force of our personality. We believe that only the absolutely dedicated and loving educator can achieve success with difficult individuals.[24]

Let us remind ourselves of the courage it took to publish these words in Vienna in 1944.[25]

Asperger and Kanner

Asperger's account is an elegant demonstration of his methodological convictions. In all his observations, he strove to absorb into his consciousness the *Gestalt* of an individual. Fritz, Harro, Ernst and Hellmuth are not paper cases, precisely because the minutiae of their comings and goings feature in the description of their disorder. They begin to move, come to life, and imprint themselves upon the reader's memory as the difficult children they were: insolent, wayward, aggressive and a danger to other children. That characterization also reflects the pedagogical climate in an Austrian clinic during the

[24] *Ibid.* pp. 89–90.
[25] In the Vienna hospital 'Am Spiegelgrund', some 800 mentally and physically handicapped children died as a result of Nazi experiments.

1930s: Asperger once gave as an example of a cheeky reply in response to an assignment: 'Well, I'm not going to do it!' And yet at the same time, the man must have had a super-human ability to see through the exasperating behaviour of these children, and to identify it as a manifestation of their disorder. This is in the nature of a *Gestaltswitch*, to keep to Asperger's psychological sphere: for him, unmanageability, impulsiveness and inaccessibility were no longer the characteristics of a bothersome child, but rather the signs of a serious disorder.

Asperger did not address the question of how the condition arises. He was convinced that there was a hereditary factor involved, but what actually caused the disorder and how it was passed on was also a mystery to him. There are a few allusions to theories related to degeneration and the link between genius and madness. On several occasions, Asperger describes the voice and outward appearance as reminiscent of 'degenerate nobility', and in the psychiatry of the day it was assumed that in the course of generations families sometimes came close to foundering in sickness, alcoholism and psychiatric disorders. The theory that exceptional artistic or scientific accomplishments often go hand in hand with characteristics which are dangerously close to psychopathology also resonates in Asperger's text: Fritz's mother described certain relatives of theirs as *genial verrückt* (in the 'mad genius' mode), and the view that her son's disorder combined elements of both was apparently shared by Asperger.

Equally striking here is an element which is *lacking*: namely all trace of the influence of a man who, until his forced departure in 1939 by order of the Gestapo, was a prominent fellow townsman of Asperger. The text contains only one acerbic passage devoted to the *Individualpsychologie* of Adler, a pupil of Freud, who was still blaming the problems of autistic children on the fact that they were often only children and therefore did not have sufficient contact with youngsters of their own age. The slightly old-fashioned vocabulary was also understandable, since they associated almost exclusively with adults. But Asperger would have none of it: 'As so often, this particular psychological approach confuses cause and effect.' The child was not autistic because he remained an only child. He remained an only child because the parents were latently autistic, and other children did not fit into their life. (In actual fact, a child with the syndrome of Asperger is not more likely to be an only child.) Psychoanalysis played no role in Asperger's views on autism, and he would not have regarded Freud as a colleague. Asperger was a paediatrician, not a psychiatrist.

By the time Asperger's own article appeared, Kanner's had already been published in the United States. Leo Kanner, twelve years older than Asperger, was born in 1894 in Klekotow, in the Austro-Hungarian empire.[26] Although he originally had writing ambitions, he ultimately opted for a career in medicine, obtaining his doctorate in 1920 in Berlin with a dissertation on electrocardiography. To an extent, Kanner was schooled in the same German academic atmosphere as Asperger. After emigrating to the United States, he made a name for himself with *Child Psychiatry*, a handbook that launched the field of study devoted to the psychiatry of the child.[27] Kanner was also the founder and director of the Johns Hopkins Children's Psychiatric Clinic.

In Baltimore, Kanner observed children who bore a strong resemblance to the boys described by Asperger. On the basis of eleven case studies, eight boys and three girls aged between 2 and 8, he described the clinical picture of what would become known as 'the classic autist': a child who appears incapable of social contact or communication, displays stereotypical behaviour, is averse to change, and has one or two obsessive interests. Kanner also noted several specific

---

[26] V. D. Sanua, 'Leo Kanner (1894–1981): the man and the scientist', *Child Psychiatry and Human Development*, 21 (1990) 1, 3–23. See also K.-J. Neumärker, 'Leo Kanner: his years in Berlin, 1906–1924: the roots of autistic disorder', *History of Psychiatry*, 14 (2003) 2, 205–18.

[27] L. Kanner, *Child Psychiatry* (London, 1935).

abnormalities which do not appear in Asperger's account: parroting (echolalia), and the tendency to use 'you' or 'he' instead of 'I'. In the same way, Asperger noted abnormalities which Kanner did not mention: the peculiar gaze, the strange voice and intonation, the pedantic language, and the lack of a sense of humour.

Reading Kanner's case studies, one also comes across striking similarities to those of Asperger: Donald, who could count to 100 by the age of 5, was good at memorizing things, and threw his toys around because he was fascinated by the sound they made when they hit the floor; Virginia, who avoided all eye contact; George, who forlornly followed his mother around, even though she was caught up in her own world and never once looked back at her son. After the war, scientific communication was resumed, together with the usual correspondence and congresses, and many child psychiatrists, paediatricians and remedial educationalists (including Asperger himself), were inclined to see the disorders identified in Baltimore and Vienna as one and the same condition. Asperger later distanced himself from that view. The children whom Kanner observed barely spoke, and when they did, they used language in a stereotyped manner, rather than as an instrument of communication. Another difference was that the type of child described by Asperger was of normal or higher intelligence. Kanner's children, to the extent that they could be tested, were retarded.

For many years, comparisons such as these were an exclusively European affair. Asperger's text was not translated into English until 1991, and even in that part of the academic world which had access to the German sources, there was limited interest in his work. Kanner's first article was followed by a long series of follow-up studies which appeared in prominent psychiatric publications and journals of remedial education. His writings appear to have eclipsed those of Asperger, just as the fluttering, parroting autists described by Kanner eclipsed Asperger's pupils, with their antiquated manner of speaking.

Figure 12.2: Hans Asperger (1906–1980)

But Asperger was not entirely ignored, and if there was one country where his work received an early and favourable reception, then it was most surely in the Netherlands. In 1949, Asperger was in Amsterdam as an invited guest at the second international congress devoted to remedial education.[28] He delivered a lecture on his 'autistischen Psychopathen' which convinced the leading lights of the first generation of Dutch child psychologists and child psychiatrists that this was a syndrome which did indeed differ from that described by Kanner. During the 1960s, the Leiden child psychiatrist Van Krevelen (credit where credit is due) went to considerable lengths to focus attention on the work of Asperger. In an English-language article published in 1971, he even included a reference to 'Asperger's syndrome', but did not succeed in getting the eponym accepted.[29]

Hans Asperger died in 1980 at the age of 74, followed six months later by Leo Kanner. Asperger's career was one of lectures, consultations, observations, ward rounds, reports and surgery hours. Following

[28] H. Asperger, 'Bild und soziale Wertigkeit der autistischen Psychopathen' in *Proceedings of the Second International Congress on Orthopedagogics 18–22 July 1949* (Amsterdam, 1950), pp. 257–69.

[29] A. A. van Krevelen, 'Early infantile autism and autistic psychopathy', *Journal of Autism and Childhood Schizophrenia*, 1 (1971), 82–6.

his retirement in 1977, he remained active as an author, and in 1979 he spoke at a Swiss congress devoted to the condition which he had described back in 1944. At that time, there was no such thing as 'Asperger syndrome'. The article by Lorna Wing which launched his name (and that is no exaggeration) appeared exactly one year after his death.

Refrigerator mothers

Researchers who claim that Kanner and Asperger identified two different syndromes often point to characteristics described by Van Krevelen back in 1971, albeit without mentioning his name. In the Kanner-type autist, the disorder comes to light soon after birth. As a rule, speech fails to develop. In the case of the Asperger autist, the disorder generally does not become apparent until 2 or 3 years of age, so that the child can walk before he can talk. While the language of these children is aimed at communication, it is still 'one-way communication', and there is often something pedantic about their 'antiquated' word choice. Indeed, Asperger children are sometimes referred to as 'little professors', a term which is never used to describe Kanner's patients. In the matter of eye contact, the Kanner child acts as if other people do not exist, while the Asperger child avoids contact with others. Asperger children have a better social prognosis. In a succinct characterization, Van Krevelen once observed that Kanner's autists live in a world of their own, while Asperger's autists live in our world, but in their own way.

Today, both syndromes are regarded as disorders of neurobiological origin, although there is no sign of agreement on the nature, location and cause of the defect. In his description of Hellmuth L, Asperger pointed to similarities between the behavioural consequences of brain damage sustained during delivery and certain symptoms of autism, but he also noted that in the case of the first three boys, there was absolutely no indication of a cerebral disorder. The brain research carried out over the last fifty years presents a highly diffuse picture.[30] On average, autistic children are thought to have a slightly larger brain volume. There may also be abnormalities in the production and breakdown of the neurotransmitter serotonin. The neurons in the hippocampus appear to be less numerous and less branched. Subtle abnormalities in the cerebellum are thought to be responsible for the motor clumsiness. The execution of certain tasks, such as recognizing faces, appears to evoke a different pattern of activation in the various brain areas than in the case of non-autistic children. Few researchers doubt that autism will ultimately be attributed to a congenital developmental disorder of the brain, but up to now no more precise identification of the disorder has been forthcoming.

During the 1950s, this gap in theory formation left room for suspicions which have had a particularly disastrous effect on the mothers of autistic children. Both Asperger and Kanner had noted that the parents of autistic children were often intellectually minded. Asperger did not clarify the nature of this connection. It appeared to be related to a genetic factor, but he could not say how the transmission took place, and whether it followed the male or female line, or perhaps a combination of the two. There was simply not enough information available. Kanner did not have the necessary data at his disposal either, but he was convinced that the child's autism was a natural reaction to the lack of a warm, intuitive contact with the mother. This marked the birth of the 'refrigerator mother', a cool, rational creature who was too detached to develop a strong bond with her child. This hypothesis became intertwined with the psychoanalytic theory that experiences in the early years are decisive for a child's development,

---

[30] J. A. Meyer and N. J. Minshew, 'An update on neurocognitive profiles in Asperger Syndrome and High-Functioning Autism', *Focus on Autism and Other Developmental Disabilities*, 17 (2002) 3, 152–61. See also B. S. Myles and R. L. Simpson, 'Asperger syndrome: an overview of characteristics', *Focus on Autism and Other Developmental Disabilities*, 17 (2002) 3, 132–8.

as well as with the attachment theory of John Bowlby, who foresaw catastrophe for mothers who, due to their lack of sensitivity, were unable to develop a proper bond with their newborn child. The psychoanalyst, Bruno Bettelheim, wrote in *The Empty Fortress* that there was one fundamental, fatal factor in the development of autism: 'the parent's wish that his child should not exist'.[31] He was referring in particular to the mother: as a result of her defensive, negative or ambivalent responses to the child's overtures, the disappointed child retreated into an extreme isolation. Bettelheim (who before the war had been imprisoned in Buchenwald and Dachau) likened autistic children to prisoners in a concentration camp. He had seen Muselman prisoners who had given up all hope. They retreated into themselves and wandered through the camp like living dead.[32] Autistic children displayed that same psychological absence; and the strange expression which had so fascinated Asperger resembled that of the prisoners. On the one hand, you had to keep a sharp eye out for danger but, on the other hand, it was important to avoid eye contact with the guards. This resulted in the averted, seemingly empty gaze of the children. Citing a colleague, Bettelheim wrote: 'the child can see and hear, but he does not look or listen'. It was a perspective calculated to rob the mother of an autistic child of all hope. In 1960, *Time Magazine* quoted Kanner as saying that mothers of autistic children only warm up long enough to bear a child. The therapy was focused on liberating these children from the isolation in which they found themselves: the fault of a cold-hearted, often university-educated mother.

Historians of psychiatry have put forward evidence that this form of 'mother-blaming', which is also seen in theories on the origin of depression and schizophrenia, cannot be dissociated from the increasing liberation of women, their access to higher education, and their

---

[31] B. Bettelheim, *The Empty Fortress: Infantile Autism and the Birth of the Self* (New York, 1967), p. 125.

[32] *Ibid.* p. 67.

steady rise in traditionally male professions.[33] In 1977, studies involv-ing autistic twins concluded that autism has a genetic foundation, and thus originates before birth. The fact that, at the crossroads of the 1950s, psychology went down Kanner's road and not Asperger's has been the cause of much unhappiness, guilt and self-recrimination.

The exact nature of the link between autism and the intellectual level of the parents is still controversial. There are those who see this as a false connection: it is simply easier for parents with a higher education to find the way to professional help, which means that they are overrepresented in the statistics. Others maintain that autistic traits predestine individuals for intellectual professions. The theory has recently been put forward that the overrepresentation of children with Asperger's among parents in Silicon Valley may have to do with the profile of the 'nerd' and his autistic leanings: it is no coincidence that the nerd, usually a man, immerses himself in the abstractions of virtual worlds.[34] The condition is known locally as the 'Geek syndrome'.

Theory of mind

In the 1980s, the notion that autism is caused by a severe contact disorder gained support from a theory inspired by a combination of developmental psychology and philosophy. It suggested that the core of the defect was the inability to see the world from someone else's perspective. As the British psychologist, Simon Baron-Cohen, put it in 1985, an autist has no *theory of mind*, no realization of the inner life of others, perhaps because he has no access to his own inner life.[35] Baron-Cohen asked himself whether autists are not in fact

---

[33] E. Dolnick, *Madness on the Couch: Blaming the Victim in the Heyday of Psychoanalysis* (New York, 1999).

[34] M. J. Nash, 'The Geek Syndrome', *Time*, 5 June 2002, 50–1.

[35] S. Baron-Cohen, A. M. Leslie and U. Frith, 'Does the autistic child have a "theory of mind"', *Cognition*, 21 (1985), 37–46.

behaviourists who do not speculate on the feelings and intentions of others, but simply establish which behaviour follows which behaviour.[36]

In a series of relatively simple tests, he demonstrated that autistic children find it difficult to work with mental representations of objects. Ordinary children learn at a young age to distinguish between the qualities of a real cookie and a remembered, imagined or promised cookie. Autistic children apparently find it difficult to imagine that an object which is not present in a concrete form, but exists in someone's memory, can still influence behaviour. Baron-Cohen found a similar difference when he asked the question 'What does your brain do?'. Children around 5 years of age and children with Down's syndrome gave answers which had to do with mental activities: you use your brain to think, remember, learn, keep secrets. The autistic children (whose average age was 14) came up with mainly motor and physical functions: your brain helps you to move, run, sleep, etc. They saw the brain as just another mechanical organ.

Due to the absence of a theory of mind, autists live in a social world inhabited by individuals with an inaccessible inner life: in other words, they live among people who will never become another 'I', but will always remain an external 'he' or 'she'. This hypothesis likewise presupposes that autistic children exist in a kind of social isolation, but the therapeutic recommendations which follow from this conclusion are quite different. Baron-Cohen designed a programme of 'mind reading', whereby children are explicitly taught associations which an ordinary child learns quite naturally, such as those between facial expression and emotion, intonation and mood, body language and intentions. Today, the perspective of the theory of mind is found in many diagnostic tests and behavioural observations,

[36] S. Baron-Cohen, 'Are autistic children "behaviorists"? An examination of their mental-physical and appearance-reality distinctions', *Journal of Autism and Developmental Disorders*, 19 (1989) 4, 579–600.

although it is more of an extended characterization of the defect rather than a clarification of the underlying causes of autism.

Poor Kate

Kanner-type autism has been part of the *DSM-III* since 1980. Asperger syndrome made its first appearance in the *DSM-IV* in 1994. The inclusion of both syndromes has not ended the discussion on the relation between them, but rather intensified it. The criteria for the diagnosis 'autistic disorder' overlap those of Asperger syndrome. When a child meets six or more of the criteria for autism, the diagnosis is 'autistic disorder'. In order to avoid double diagnoses, *DSM* users are instructed to consider the diagnosis Asperger syndrome only in those cases where the child meets fewer than six of the autism criteria and, moreover, has no language deficiency. This diagnostic procedure has led to a paradoxical situation: according to a recent analysis, Fritz, Harro, Ernst and Hellmuth met so many criteria for autism that a diagnosis of Asperger syndrome was out of the question.[37] The logical conclusion was that the children described by Asperger himself did not have Asperger. Some researchers maintain that this result is proof that there is no essential difference between the two syndromes, while others conclude that the *DSM* is apparently incapable of describing Asperger syndrome in the manner intended by Asperger.

No such confusion presents itself when the *Casebook* accompanying the *DSM-IV* is used, since it contains a case of Asperger that displays all the features described by Asperger himself. This case study is called 'Cartographer', and it is borrowed from the same article in which Lorna Wing proposed the name 'Asperger syndrome'. The main character is CB, a boy of 13. He is in special education, is good

---

[37] J.N. Miller and S. Ozonoff, 'Did Asperger's cases have Asperger disorder? A research note', *Journal of Child Psychology and Psychiatry*, 38 (1997) 2, 247–51.

at learning things by heart, has several monomaniacal hobbies, including high-tension masts, traffic signs, and, above all, maps. CB is clumsy when it comes to social behaviour, he cannot get a handle on abstractions, and jokes are largely lost on him.

Over the last few years, the diagnosis of Asperger has become more and more frequent, in some cases posthumously: Einstein, Bartok and Wittgenstein are often mentioned in this respect.[38] Making use of quotations from a biography dating from 1851, Oliver Sacks has made it plausible that the English physicist, Henry Cavendish, suffered from Asperger syndrome: 'His brain seems to have been but a calculating engine; his eyes inlets of vision, not fountains of tears; his hands instruments of manipulation which never trembled with emotion.'[39] The syndrome is slowly becoming part of the body of medico-psychiatric knowledge. Those two and a half million hits for 'Asperger syndrome' include autobiographies of people with Asperger, books written by and for partners of people with Asperger, alongside self-tests, support groups, therapies, manuals for remedial teachers, discussion groups and pedagogical advice.

The degree to which specialized knowledge of the background and diagnostics of autism is now finding its way to a broader audience will be clear from a passage in the above mentioned *The Curious Incident of the Dog in the Night-time*. It's about a test that Christopher had to take at his special-ed school. His teacher Miss Julie comes in and sits down next to him. She puts a tube of Smarties on the desk and asks him what he thinks is inside. 'Smarties', Christopher says. She picks up the tube, opens it and pulls out a small red pencil. Then she puts it back in, closes the tube, and asks Christopher: 'If your mummy came in now and we asked her what was inside the Smarties tube, what do you

---

[38] See for analyses in this genre M. Fitzgerald, *Autism and Creativity: is there a Link between Autism in Men and Exceptional Ability?* (Hove/New York, 2004).

[39] O. Sacks, 'Henry Cavendish: an early case of Asperger's syndrome?', *Neurology*, 57 (2001), 1347.

think she would say?' 'A pencil', Christopher says.[40] This exercise is a standard situation taken from theory-of-mind tests, and it has been copied almost literally from a guide for people who work with autistic children.[41]

There is a detail in the theory-of-mind tests devised by Baron-Cohen which eminently reflects the tragedy of the syndrome of Asperger. The experimenter explains that there are two dolls, Sam and Kate, both of whom would like a cookie. Unfortunately, Sam is the only one who gets a cookie from his mother, since Kate's mother isn't home. All this is 'make-believe', of course: Sam doesn't really get a cookie. But children aged around 5 and children with Down's syndrome feel sorry for Kate because Sam got a cookie and she didn't. The autistic children show no sign of sympathy. Why should they? In the literal world which they inhabit, there are simply two dolls and neither one of them has a cookie. If you feel for these children, then there is something intact in you which is lacking in them.

---

[40] Haddon, *Curious Incident*, p. 116.
[41] P. Howlin, S. Baron-Cohen and J. Hadwin, *Teaching Children with Autism to Mind-read: a Practical Guide* (Chichester, 1999), pp. 253–4.

THIRTEEN

The Cardan suspension of science

In 1875, Jean-Martin Charcot celebrated his fiftieth birthday. He had spent the previous ten years at La Salpêtrière, where he focused his attention on diseases of the elderly and disorders of the nervous system. Charcot's reputation was already established. He was the first to distinguish between multiple sclerosis (his coinage) and Parkinson's disease; he identified amyotrophic lateral sclerosis (ALS, characterized by a rapid atrophy of muscle tissue, also known as Charcot's disease); and described Charcot's foot, a sudden softening of the bones of the foot as a result of nerve damage.[1] Of the dozens of eponyms which include Charcot's name, the majority refer to his work in neurology. He had been a member of the Académie de Médecine since 1872, but the prestigious membership of the Académie des Sciences lay years into the future. Much of what would determine how Charcot is remembered (his research into hysteria, the semi-public *Leçons du Mardi*, the theatrical hypnosis demonstrations) dates from the second half of the 1880s. In 1875, Charcot was first and foremost a neuroanatomist.

Like many physicians of his generation, Charcot was an excellent draughtsman, and many of his sketches have been preserved.

---

[1] C.G. Goetz, M. Bonduelle and T. Gelfand, *Charcot: Constructing Neurology* (New York, 1995).

Figure 13.1: Charcot during an anatomy lecture in the amphitheatre of La Salpêtrière (1875). In 1895, the maker of the drawing, Brissaud, would be the first to formulate the hypothesis that Parkinson's disease is caused by damage to the substantia nigra

He always encouraged his students to develop their drawing skills.[2] He believed that drawing had a formative influence: it taught you to observe and to be attentive to details. A number of his doctoral students illustrated their own dissertations. And Charcot himself was often portrayed. In 1875, Brissaud, then still a student, secretly sketched the professor during an anatomy lecture. One of the senior physicians caught him at it, confiscated the drawing, and showed it to Charcot. Brissaud must have held his breath. The portrayal is of an overwhelming simplicity. Charcot is holding a brain in his hands and pointing out to his students something which is apparently on the underside. If he had not been wearing a high hat, he could

[2] H. Meige, 'Charcot artiste', *Nouvelle iconographie de la Salpêtrière*, 11 (1898), 489–516. In 1902, Henry Meige published, with Feindel, a monograph on what is now known as the syndrome of Gilles de la Tourette.

Figure 13.2: Formal portrait of Charcot

easily have been mistaken for a butcher showing a customer his wares, before wiping his hands on his apron. Charcot had the drawing framed. Perhaps the one draughtsman had seen what the other was trying to express: concentration, hard work, an organ that only gives up its secrets to someone who is not afraid to dirty his hands.

In later life, Charcot also had his iconography. Photos and paintings dating from the last ten years of his life are dominated by grandeur and glory. In 1882, Premier Gambetta had personally instituted a Chair of Neurology for him, the first in the world.[3] By then his reputation reached far beyond the borders of both France and medical science. In an official portrait (now in the possession of the Académie de Médecine) he is portrayed as a scholar, attired as for an academic ceremony. This is Charcot as he must have appeared at the degree-giving ceremony of a student, or during the acceptance of yet another honorary degree. He was a member, honorary member or president of various distinguished scientific societies, and the most famous psychiatrist of his day, called in for consultation by the Emperor of Brazil and the Queen of Spain. Together with Pasteur, he was the face of French medical science.

---

[3] Gambetta died later that year. He had donated his brain to the recently formed Société d'Autopsie Mutuelle.

Charcot distributed eponyms on a scale that was unequalled, both before and after him. This was the achievement of *both* Charcots, the man in the apron and the man wearing academic robes.

When Charcot proposed attaching someone's name to a syndrome, disease, test or symptom, that proposal was in the nature of a royal decree. Regardless of whether it happened quasi-casually, as in the case of Jackson's epilepsy, or after the presentation of medical arguments, as in the case of Parkinson's disease, Charcot was assured of the endorsement of the scientific community. The bestowal of an eponym was an expression of his power, and the same held true for Kraepelin when he named 'Alzheimer's disease'. But that power was rooted in the authority which Charcot had gained as a neurologist, and it was not sacrosanct. Power can be undermined, sometimes by the manner in which it is exercised. If Charcot had consistently given precedence to French researchers, his authority would soon have stopped at the French border. Chauvinism can erode even a reputation hewn from marble. But that was not a mistake which Charcot was likely to make. While discussing with students and colleagues the attribution of the eponym to Jackson, he mused aloud about whether it might be better to include Bravais in the eponym. Charcot was making it clear that for him science was above simple patriotism. Passing Bravais over in 1887 helped to do away with any lingering suspicion of favouritism following the bestowal of the 'syndrome of Gilles de la Tourette' in 1885.

The fact that prestige plays a role in the granting of eponyms is likewise reflected in those bestowed by other scientists. In almost every case, the eponym is recorded together with the name of the person who proposed it: proof enough that in the scientific world the words 'I baptize you' is itself a source of prestige.[4] Almost every article

---

[4] The eponym 'syndrome of Clérambault' was awarded by a committee, while the adoption of 'Brodmann's areas' in neurology was too scattered to justify the designation of a single person as name-giver.

devoted to the Bonnet syndrome contains a reference to De Morsier (1936), while the syndrome of Asperger is wedded to the name of Wing (1981). Broca has his Ferrier (1876), Korsakoff his Jolly (1897) and Capgras his Levy-Valensi (1929). But, as in the case of Charcot (although on a less monumental scale), scientific prestige is both condition and consequence. If Ferrier, Jolly and Wing had not themselves been researchers with a solid reputation, it is unlikely their proposals would have been honoured, if indeed they had been in a position to put them forward. Without exception, the eponyms were proposed in what were then prominent organs of scientific communication, such as a published clinical lesson (Charcot), a monograph (Ferrier, Damasio), a handbook (Kraepelin) or a professional journal (De Morsier, Jolly, Levy-Valensi, Wing). A certain measure of prestige is required for admission to such a podium. Moreover, the launch of the proposal is not the end of the affair. On several occasions, De Morsier had to remind the scientific community that it was he who introduced the Bonnet syndrome and endowed it with a clearly defined meaning, and that one could not alter the diagnostic criteria with impunity. His concern is clear: with other criteria, it would no longer be 'his' syndrome. Wing was faced with the same problem. According to the criteria employed by *DSM-IV*, Asperger syndrome tends to dissolve into the diagnosis 'autistic disorder'. Indeed, in the view of some researchers, one is justified in questioning whether the boys described by Asperger actually had 'Asperger'. Looking back on the consequences of her article on Asperger syndrome, Wing writes that, of all the criteria proposed, those of *DSM-IV* bear the *least* resemblance to those of Asperger himself.[5] Not only the borders of the syndrome are at issue here, but also the position of the person who proposed the eponym, and this requires alert surveillance.

[5] L. Wing, 'Reflections on opening Pandora's Box', *Journal of Autism and Developmental Disorders*, 35 (2005) 2, 197–203.

Modern historians do not think in terms of causes. Causes are made of steel, and to work with them you need an oven and an anvil to hammer your explanations into shape. Fortunately there is a more manageable option: factors. And they are available in abundance: latent and manifest factors, dominant and subordinate factors, vital and contributing factors. Factors can trigger, facilitate, interfere with, mediate and even – where they provide that last push – precipitate. You can weave with factors. Anyone who attempts to describe the processes which play a role in eponyms, not only the discovery, the attribution and the acceptance, but also the postponement of acceptance (Asperger), the temporary disappearance (Gilles de la Tourette), and the reintroduction (Alzheimer), will encounter explanations woven out of factors. One factor that we would intuitively regard as indispensable proves, on closer examination, to be highly attendant: priority.

Stigler's law

The Russian neurologist, Dr Ewa Ssucharewa, was a scientific assistant at the Sanatorium School affiliated with the Psycho-Neurological Children's Clinic in Moscow. Of the children admitted for observation (often for a period of years) there were six who differed from the others and who had so much in common that they appeared to represent a specific disorder. She christened the disorder 'schizoid personality'. Her analysis of the six cases, all boys, appeared in a prominent German neuropsychiatric journal.[6]

All six were 'of an autistic nature': they never played with other children, preferring to live in their own fantasy world. Three of the

---

[6] G. E. Ssucharewa, 'Die schizoiden Psychopathien im Kindesalter', *Monatsschrift für Psychiatrie und Neurologie*, 60 (1926), 235–61.

boys came in for a lot of pestering, due to their odd behaviour. Their language was precocious and a trifle pedantic. They enjoyed playing with the sound of words, especially by means of repetition or rhyme. All of them were highly impulsive. There was one who would go over to another boy and, without the slightest provocation, begin to hit him, while another once pushed a boy into the water for no apparent reason. Their interests were bizarre and monomaniacal: one told interminable stories about the French campaign against Russia in 1812. Although all six were of above-average intelligence, they all had trouble keeping up. Sometimes they got bogged down in the details. In motor skills, they were downright clumsy, and eating and getting dressed invariably presented problems. Their voices were odd: one talked through his nose, while the other had a high, whiny voice, but spoke 'like an adult'. Several of the boys had a real aptitude for maths or music. They tended toward rigidity (a certain 'stiffness of the soul') and automatism: they had trouble breaking off an activity they were engaged in.[7] They all found it difficult to adjust to new things.

Ewa Ssucharewa's six Moscow boys were the spitting image of the boys whom Hans Asperger described in Vienna in 1944, and who would together form the prototype of the Asperger syndrome. The article by Ssucharewa contains no reference to Asperger. Indeed, that would have been impossible, since her piece appeared in 1926. Chronologically, the disorder which Asperger 'discovered' in 1944 was actually a rediscovery.

In fact, I discovered that *most* of the discoveries of eponymists are rediscoveries – and that that, too, had already been discovered and even immortalized in an eponym: Stigler's law.[8] The official wording of the law, named after the statistician who rediscovered the

---

[7] Ssucharewa, 'Schizoiden Psychopathien', 256.

[8] S. M. Stigler, 'Stigler's law of eponymy' in T. F. Gieryn (ed.), *Science and Social Structure: a Festschrift for Robert K. Merton* (New York, 1980), pp. 147–57.

phenomenon in 1980, is even more radical: 'No scientific discovery is named after its original discoverer.'[9] Stigler did not go so far as to claim that eponyms were simply handed out willy-nilly. He acknowledged that 'it is rare that an eponym is awarded to an individual who has not done some work at least tangentially connected with the discovery', but when it comes to identifying the original discoverer, eponyms are liable to lead you up the garden path.

Stigler's law is principally irrefutable. No matter which eponym you choose as proof to the contrary, it is always possible that some earlier discoverer will be discovered. Ewa Ssucharewa, for example, was not discovered (or rediscovered) by the Scottish psychiatrist, Sula Wolff, until 1995.[10] But there is abundant corroboration for Stigler's law, also with regard to the eponyms presented in this book. On occasion the eponymists themselves have noted the existence of a predecessor. At the presentation of Tan's brain, Broca explained that the damage to the frontal lobe appeared to confirm the theory of Bouillaud. Alzheimer wrote in 1911 that his colleague Redlich had discovered plaques in the brain of senile patients as far back as 1898. Korsakoff called attention to the Swedish physician Magnus Huss, who half a century earlier had written about memory disorders attributable to alcoholism. Jackson referred to the epilepsy that now bears his name as 'Bravais epilepsy', after the Frenchman who had described this variant in 1827. And in 1885, Gilles de la Tourette incorporated into his own article the complete case history of the Marquise of Dampierre, which Jean Marc Itard had published in 1825. As a rule, however, the earlier discoverers do not turn up until after (and as a result of) the work of the eponymists. Although, in

---

[9] Stigler, 'Stigler's law', p. 147.

[10] S. Wolff, *Loners: the Life Path of Unusual Children* (London, 1995). In 1996, Wolff published a translation of Ssucharewa's article: S. Wolff, 'The first account of the syndrome Asperger described?', *European Child and Adolescent Psychiatry*, 5 (1996), 119–32. The question mark betrays a sense of history.

many cases, the eponymists were not the 'original discoverers', as Stigler refers to them, in a historical sense it was their contribution which opened up a new field of research. It is in this area that others (primarily colleagues and historians of science) can discover something on their own, namely: 'predecessors'.

Predecessors, precursors and earlier discoverers swim against the tide of chronology: they all come after the eponymist. Without the eponymist, no one would ever have heard of them, their work would still be languishing in the paper graveyard of back volumes and archives. Who would ever have heard of Dax Sr and Dax Jr if Broca had not mentioned them in his 1865 article? There is no doubt that the memory disorder described by Robert Lawson, physician at the Lunatic Hospital in Exeter in 1878, corresponds to what we now know as the Korsakoff syndrome. But without Korsakoff, Lawson would have been forgotten. It was Lawson who needed Korsakoff, and not the other way around. After Joseph Capgras identified his *doppelgänger* syndrome in 1923, it appeared that Clifford Beers had written about this delusion in his 1908 autobiography, while later historians of psychiatry discovered an even more senior predecessor in the person of the German psychiatrist Kahlbaum (1866). In fact, the discovery of predecessors is a special case of a general law. Once someone points out something exceptional, something you have never noticed before, it is suddenly not that difficult to find other examples. Thus, in the case of Lawson and Kahlbaum, it was not so much a question of 'discovering' as 'recognizing'.

Not only the predecessors of eponymists swim against the tide. The same can be said of the eponymists themselves. What counts as the 'discovery' of Broca, Alzheimer or Korsakoff is determined by what happens *after* that discovery. This is clear from the case studies published by the eponymists themselves. In 1760, Bonnet described the images which his grandfather saw. In 1944, Asperger wrote about his 'difficult children'. In the nearly two centuries which lie between these two dates, the sciences of brain and mind altered unrecognizably. What has not changed, however, is the fact that Bonnet, Asperger and all the eponymists in between made use of case histories. Sometimes there was only that one case. For Bonnet, it was no more than an observation in passing. Other eponymists initially published on a single case, but implied that later on similar cases would be examined. Broca's 'Monsieur Tan' (1861) was followed that same year by Lelong, and within two years by six nameless cases. Alzheimer presented the case of Auguste D in 1906, but he himself went in search of new cases, and in due time found Johann Feigl. Both Clérambault (Léa-Anna B) and Capgras ('Mathilde de Rio-Branco') highlighted individual patients, but in the years that followed they also published the details of new cases. From the start, Parkinson, Hughlings Jackson, Korsakoff, Gilles de la Tourette and Asperger described several cases, although they often chose to examine one or two patients in more detail, so that the others simply provided more examples of the same prototype. Thus the description of only one patient is an exception, and when the eponym was *attributed*, there were always multiple cases. In 1936, De Morsier added his own patients to Bonnet's grandfather. Charcot had assembled a room full of trembling women for the lecture in which he renamed the 'paralysie agitante' Parkinson's disease. Damasio saw in his own practice new examples of the Gage matrix. And Jolly had admitted to the Berlin Charité Hospital the same type of patients as those described by Korsakoff. The syndromes of Capgras and Clérambault were only named after a number of cases had been described. Wing collected a series of cases involving children who displayed the same symptoms described by Asperger, and added her case history of the 'Cartographer'. In short, 'the first' is a designation only awarded by virtue of the cases which followed. Thus it was Johann Feigl who made Auguste 'the first Alzheimer patient'.

The statistical universe

The physician of today lives in what Meulenberg and Oderwald call a 'statistical universe'.[11] The same may be said of the researchers who over the last fifty years have devoted themselves to the eponymic disorders. Bonnet described one case, while Teunisse's dissertation focused on sixty visually impaired individuals who saw Bonnet images. While Parkinson mentioned six cases, one of them a man he had seen shuffling by with his manservant on the other side of the street, modern research into Parkinson's disease combines the data on thousands of patients. Between 1861 and 1865, Broca reported on individual cases of aphasia and left-sided brain damage (fortunately, the cases of right-sided injury and aphasia did not appear until after that regularity had become a 'law', making the injuries on the right 'exceptions'). Conrad's research into the 'mirror-image theory', which stated that the language centre is located opposite the preferred hand, was carried out among 800 soldiers with brain damage. Hughlings Jackson described in detail the behaviour and experiences of 'Dr Z' during his 'dreamy state'; the present research into this symptom makes use of large groups of epileptic patients in an effort to establish the relationship between age, medication, type of epilepsy, brain areas involved, and dozens of other factors. Other diseases were also included in this statistical universe: Parkinson's disease and Alzheimer's and the syndromes of Gilles de la Tourette, Capgras, Clérambault and Asperger. What we now know about the risk factors, gender distribution, links to other diseases, hereditary factors, course and prognosis has been collected by means of statistical research.

In the statistical universe, case histories now only play a role in meta-analyses, where an entire series of cases are examined. Today,

---

[11] F. Meulenberg and A. Oderwald, 'Wat wil het geval...? Gevalsbeschrijvingen in medische wetenschap en journalistiek' in F. J. Meijman and F. Meulenberg (eds.), *Medische publiekscommunicatie. Een panorama* (Houten, 2002), pp. 288–316, 290.

observations such as those of Bonnet, Parkinson or Clérambault would be dismissed as 'casuistic' or (even worse) as 'anecdotal evidence'. Anyone who recalls the clinical course of Korsakoff's patient who could not rid himself of the thought that somewhere in Moscow lay the unburied body of a friend, Jackson's description of 'Dr Z' and his dreamy state, or 'the confessions of a tiqueur' by Meige and Feidel will realize just what has disappeared from medical science, namely the experience of the patient. Parkinson, Broca, Jackson, Korsakoff, Gilles de la Tourette, Alzheimer, Clérambault, Capgras and Asperger were practising physicians, and their accounts reflect something of what it meant to suffer from the disease they described. Disease histories which do justice to the 'inside' of the condition, the subjective experience, are now a 'lost art', as the Russian neuropsychologist Luria once wrote to Oliver Sacks.[12] Nowadays, they are associated mainly with 'romantic science', a genre whose greatest appeal lies *outside of* medical science. And, in the view of Meulenberg and Oderwald, where individual patients do figure in medical articles, the accounts are often so objectified that the reader may wonder whether there is really any point in including them: 'It becomes a kind of standardized account of a certain Mrs A which appears to be scientific, but which also raises the question of why it is presented so specifically as the story of Mrs A.'[13]

While case histories focusing on the experience of suffering from the disease have been relegated to the margins of medical literature, this does not mean they have disappeared. They have simply acquired other authors. In *Out of Mind* (1989), J. Bernlef attempts to enter the mind of a patient with early Alzheimer's. The first-person narrator in *Scar Tissue* (1993) by Michael Ignatieff has a mother who displays the early signs of dementia and is aware of this fact. The main character in

---

[12] See Sacks' foreword in A. R. Luria, *The Man with a Shattered World* (Cambridge, 1987).

[13] Meulenberg and Oderwald, 'Wat wil het geval …?', p. 291.

The Suspect (2003), a thriller by Michael Robotham, suffers from Parkinson's and through him the reader gradually realizes what it must be like to inhabit an increasingly wooden and unresponsive body, and to see in the mirror the reflection of his frozen features. Mark Haddon's *The Curious Incident of the Dog in the Night-time* (2003) explores the mental world of a boy with Asperger syndrome, the same condition which affects the main character in Stefan Brijs' *The Angel Maker* (2008). The narrator in *Motherless Brooklyn* (1999) by Jonathan Lethem is called Lionel Essrog, but his nickname is 'freak show'. He is a private detective who suffers from Tourette syndrome, which does not make it easy to shadow people unnoticed. The introspection of Lionel gives the reader a better insight into the thoughts, actions and experiences of a Tourette patient than can be found in any medical study. Writers have long been fascinated by mental disturbances – Guy de Maupassant was only one of the authors who regularly attended Charcot's *Leçons du Mardi* – and in their work they have given expression to that fascination. But today it is almost as if each disorder has its own literary spokesmen.

These 'literary case histories' evoke insights which over the years have been culled from the fields of neurology and psychiatry, providing an often startling reflection of the accepted view during a particular period. In 1938, Georges Simenon wrote a Maigret story called 'Monsieur Lundi'. The intrigue turned on an older, unmarried woman who suffered from the syndrome of Clérambault: she believed that her doctor was in love with her. In *Enduring Love* by Ian McEwan, one of the characters is a Clérambault patient: the unemployed, mildly religious fanatic, Jed Parry. He believes that the science writer, Joe Rose, is in love with him and starts stalking him. These two patients typify two different chapters in our theorizing about the Clérambault syndrome. In the psychiatric world of 1938, the typical Clérambault patient was still an old maid who had her eye on a man of high social standing (indeed, the syndrome was also known as 'old maid's syndrome'). In the psychiatric world of

1998, a Clérambault patient may well be a man. The fact that the sufferer is trying to initiate a homosexual relationship and, out of sheer frustration, begins to stalk the man makes for a psychiatric profile that did not exist half a century ago.

But now that the medical men have relinquished their monopoly, the most obvious authors of disease histories are the patients themselves. Bonnet, Parkinson, Jackson, Korsakoff, Gilles de la Tourette, Alzheimer and Asperger have become the name-givers of foundations and patient associations. Their sites refer visitors to patient autobiographies and other ego-documents. Someone who has just been diagnosed with Parkinson's disease and wants to know what kind of life he can expect does not visit his doctor, but rather reads what his fellow patients have to say on the subject. These disease histories are not divorced from medical science. The 'proto-professionalization' which features in the chapter on Gilles de la Tourette often appears in a very pure form, for example, when an Asperger patient writes that his problem is that he has no 'theory of mind'. Ego-documents written by patients have their limitations. The story of one's recovery from aphasia can only be described in retrospect, that of an Alzheimer's patient only in the initial stages.

According to expectations

In an article on Charcot as draughtsman and art lover, his pupil Henry Meige recounts that when 'le Maître' was diagnosing a patient, his artistic temperament also came into play.[14] It is important to see the pattern of the symptoms, to separate the essential from the coincidental, to note a detail in which the disorder is expressed. And above all, like a novice draughtsman, he will have to learn to *look*, to free himself from what he expects to see or thinks he sees.

---

[14] Meige, 'Charcot artiste', 491.

Referring to the role of expectations in medicine, Charcot warned that we all have a tendency to see only what we have learned to see, and to overlook what does not fit in with our prejudices. A recurring theme in all his lectures and patient demonstrations was the importance of learning to observe without preconceptions: 'You know that, as a matter of principle, I pay scant attention to preconceived notions. To see something clearly, you must take things exactly the way they are.' As a diagnostician, he described himself in visual metaphors which underline the passivity of his judgements: 'I only observe, nothing more' and 'All I am is a photographer'.[15] Freud, who was himself a listener, referred to Charcot as a *visual*.

Charcot's vision of diagnosis and observation, and of himself, is eminently nineteenth-century. The advice that follows from it – present yourself as a *tabula rasa* – is impossible to follow. The fact that Charcot the neurologist was an excellent diagnostician was due not to passive registration, but rather to his ability to apply to his observations inventive and wide-ranging conjectures. In the accounts of his diagnostic sessions we see someone carrying on a seemingly casual conversation with his patient, asking questions, giving instructions – and all the while, testing one hypothesis after the other. Towards the end of the visit, there was a diagnosis: the one hypothesis which had survived a systematic, and perhaps to some extent unconscious, process of elimination. The averred 'I only observe' was above all a question of serious reflection.

Even in today's literature on 'discoverers' we find the familiar rhetorical argument that their successes can be traced to an ability to break free of what one has been taught to see, to notice something that up to then had remained invisible to others, burdened as they were with their private prejudices. Today, this is an outdated notion. The work of eponymists contains observations and perceptions prompted by a background teeming with existing expectations and

[15] Goetz, Bonduelle and Gelfand, *Charcot*, p. 90.

interpretations. Many of the facts (or what pass for facts) collected by the eponymists have quietly disappeared, because the background in which those facts were significant no longer exists. The 'ape sulcus' which Brodmann found in the brains of three Javanese was only of significance in a conceptual world which placed those 'primitive races' somewhere half-way between Man and monkey. Broca's claim that the brain of a dog is more asymmetric than that of a fox acquired credibility from the now abandoned theory that training leads to asymmetry and that that asymmetry is hereditary.

Some theories have taken such a broad and lasting grip on science and society that they are in the nature of an ideology supported by findings which largely *flow from* them. Morel's theory of degeneration and the progressive corrosion of the genetic material produced a whole series of 'facts' which have since disappeared, together with the degeneration theory itself. According to Gilles de la Tourette, children with tics came from families which displayed the neuropathological symptoms of degeneration: a brother who stutters, a bizarre aunt, a grandmother with asthma. In the view of Meige and Feindel, tiqueurs are weak-willed individuals: degeneration has affected their ability to control their impulses. Alzheimer believed that some people are eager to have themselves declared unfit to work, and that 'degenerates, psychopaths or mentally disordered individuals' (i.e., 'the children of epileptics, criminals or alcoholics') were especially susceptible to this 'benefit neurosis'. It went without saying that the silk thieves whom Clérambault interviewed were all degenerate women. That was clear from their behaviour, and otherwise from their background: a grandmother who went to her grave insane, or a cousin who masturbated. As late as 1944, Asperger was still employing the guarded terms appropriate to a theory whose extreme, even criminal, consequences had become so highly visible that his 'difficult children' were reminiscent of degenerate nobility, often the last scion of a family where genius and madness held each other in a precarious equilibrium.

Psychoanalysis and the theories on hysteria which it propounded have long manufactured their own facts. The notion that Bonnet images are seen by people who, as a result of regression, long for the small, safe world they knew as children fit into the theory which claimed that the ego is seeking compensation for loss in old age. The fact that Capgras' *doppelgänger* syndrome was long viewed as a female complaint followed from the prevailing interpretation of hysteria as a condition peculiar to women. The emergence of the male Capgras patient reflected not only the waning vitality of the psychoanalytical perspective, but also the simultaneous change of course in the direction of a neurological explanation which could no longer apply exclusively to women. The 'refrigerator mothers' of autistic children who featured in so many studies during the 1950s and 1960s have faded into the background, along with opposition to the independence of women. All these facts, findings and conclusions, whether gathered by observation or measurement, did not disappear as a result of new research, but due to the disintegration of the theories which had given rise to them.

Docility of facts

For anyone who believes that historic awareness, methodology, common sense, peer review, or any other corrective factor has led to a beneficial tempering of the ideological dependence of facts, there is no case so instructive as the research, past and present, into the relationship between the two hemispheres of the brain.

The fact that different functions can be represented in the right and left half of the brain was first suggested in the 1820s and confirmed by Broca in the 1860s by means of autopsies. According to Broca, the asymmetry between the two brain halves developed through education and training; in other words, thanks to what culture has contributed (per individual and per generation) to the natural situation. Thus, asymmetry had become a measure of civilization. Neurologists now had an instrument at their disposal by which an entire series of objective, scientifically sound hierarchies could be constructed: that asymmetry was more common among whites than among blacks, among men than among women, among the rich than among the poor, among city-dwellers than among villagers. Asymmetry was not neutral: the left was superior. The functional qualities of the left hemisphere (logical thought, control, will power) made it the 'masculine' hemisphere, while the 'feminine' right hemisphere became the seat of intuition and passion, but also of impulsiveness and instability. With this distribution of properties, it was inevitable that the left hemisphere would take the lead, reflecting the natural situation in a marriage between husband and wife. Towards the end of the nineteenth century, 'asymmetry' and 'left' had executed a kind of pincer movement, whereby the thinking, white, cultured male automatically dominated everything associated with 'right' or 'symmetrical'. Among the many Broca epigones who have attempted to underpin these neuropolitical relationships by means of the most wide-ranging forms of 'proof' was a certain Delaunay. 'With perfect ease of conscience, he offered up his work to the altar of disinterested science – and it was accepted, because the *weltanschauung* it sanctified was so deeply-rooted in late-nineteenth-century consciousness that its ideological nature had become essentially invisible.'[16]

If there is an apology inherent in the understanding of the historian, his scathing analysis of Broca's 'great circle route' (see Chapter 4) showed that Gould has little patience with it. In his eyes, Broca is the *bête noire* of French neurology, notably because of the unacceptable contrast between his reputation as an objective, impartial and, in a political sense, reformist researcher, and the real Broca: a sexist, racist, French chauvinist pseudo-scientist who fiddled the facts. Exact measurements, which Broca saw as the best safeguard against prejudice,

---

[16] A. Harrington, *Medicine, Mind, and the Double Brain: a Study in Nineteenth-Century Thought* (Princeton NJ, 1987), p. 92.

especially when the measurement can be left to the instrument, are for Gould part and parcel of his perfidious rhetoric: all those figures and instruments lent a semblance of objectivity to what were in fact the prejudices of Broca himself and the well-to-do bourgeois class to which he belonged.[17] He did not test them, he reproduced them.

What can we learn from this? The gist of Harrington's analysis (see Chapter 4) is that convictions shared in wide circles have a tendency to absorb the science of the day, complete with findings, methods, interpretations, etc. According to that view, there is a pre-existing bedding into which results automatically flow. New findings do not shift the bedding, but rather deepen it. In Gould's view, science is diametrically opposed to ideological interpretations. Science is there to correct, refute and eradicate prejudices. To that end, it must be practised as honestly and as precisely as possible. Moreover, if Broca had taken a few elementary methodological precautions, he would not have ended up with such absurd results. He should have measured brains and skulls without any prior knowledge of their origin. He should have used statistical tests to correct for chance and set up control groups. And he should have predicted his results, so that they did not fall into line with his hypothesis thanks to 'corrections' after the fact.

In 1961, precisely 100 years after Broca held aloft the brain of 'Monsieur Tan' at a gathering of the Société d'Anthropologie, the neuropsychologist Roger Sperry published an article in *Science* on the surgical separation of brain-halves.[18] The technique involved the bisection of the corpus callosum, the thick bundle of nerve fibres joining the two hemispheres. The first experiments with 'split brains' which Sperry carried out made use of animals, but in later years his pupils Gazzaniga and Bogen performed the same operation on patients with severe, untreatable epilepsy, thereby making available a powerful new method for the study of functional differences

---

[17] S. J. Gould, *The Mismeasure of Man* (New York, 1981), p. 85.

[18] R. W. Sperry, 'Cerebral organization and behavior', *Science*, 133 (1961), 1747–57.

between the hemispheres. This work would earn Sperry the Nobel Prize in 1981.

Most of the experiments involving split-brain patients are performed in a laboratory setting. The examination of separated brain-halves requires highly artificial conditions. Visual stimuli which are meant for only one half of the brain (the right, say) must be presented only to the left field of vision of both eyes, and dichotic listening tasks are essential in order to measure differences in the reaction to sound stimuli. The outcomes of split-brain experiments have resulted in a spectacular rehabilitation of the right brain-half.[19]

When Sperry, Gazzaniga and Bogen began their research, there was no one who still associated the right brain half with animality, instinct, criminal tendencies, female impulsivity, mental disease and all the other characteristics which neurology had attributed to it around 1900. The right hemisphere was no longer identified with *any* specific qualities. It had become the 'inferior', 'minor' hemisphere. Thought took place in the left brain. According to Henschen's summary of the general consensus in 1926, the right half of the brain was perhaps no more than a spare organ.[20] But split-brain research suggested that the right hemisphere was even better at some tasks than the left hemisphere. Most of those tasks had to do with the processing of spatial patterns, such as the recognition of faces or the mental rotation of forms. The interpretation of emotions on the basis of facial expressions and the recognition of melodies likewise proved more right-sided. The left hemisphere supports tasks which require a strict linear structuring in time, such as the language function or rhythm in music. However, with the exception of the processing of language, the differences between the capacities of the left and the right hemisphere are minimal. There are absolutely no

---

[19] An excellent overview of methods and findings related to lateralization is that of S. P. Springer and G. Deutsch, *Left Brain, Right Brain* (New York, 1993).

[20] S. E. Henschen, 'On the function of the right hemisphere of the brain in relation to the left in speech, music and calculation', *Brain*, 49 (1926), 110–23.

grounds for such claims as 'emotions are located on the right' or 'logic is on the left'. It is always a question of one half playing a slightly larger role in a certain process. According to the most conservative researchers in the area of hemispheric specialization, it is even misleading to refer to 'specialization': the right hemisphere is only better at certain tasks because the left hemisphere, already responsible for language, has relinquished some of its competence.[21] Unlike the left hemisphere, the right hemisphere has no special talents.

In 1969, Joseph Bogen authored a series of three articles under the collective title 'The other side of the brain'.[22] The first dealt with the 'ordinary' neurological subjects, such as the consequences of the transsection of the corpus callosum for writing or the copying of figures, but the following two articles were set out along broader lines. Bogen characterized the left hemisphere as 'propositional', a term used by Hughlings Jackson to indicate that the left half thinks in language and provides for its verbal expression. In Bogen's view, the right hemisphere was 'appositional', implying a form of thinking which is spatial and intuitive. The differences were not absolute but gradual, and together they formed a relationship: the A/P ratio. Depending on the personal A/P ratio, a person would tend to think in a 'left-brained' or 'right-brained' manner, even without a severed corpus callosum. According to Bogen, dichotomies related to 'propositional' and 'appositional' included atomistic vs. global, abstract vs. concrete, successive vs. simultaneous, digital vs. analog, analytic vs. synthetic. In 1972, three sociologists collaborated on a later

---

[21] M. C. Corballis, 'Are we in our right minds?' in S. Della Sala (ed.), *Mind Myths: Exploring Popular Assumptions about the Mind and Brain* (Chichester, 1999), pp. 25–41.

[22] J. Bogen, 'The other side of the brain I: dysgraphia and dyscopia following cerebral commissurotomy', *Bulletin of the Los Angeles Neurological Societies*, 34 (1969) 2, 73–105. The following two articles were published in parts 3 and 4.

article, the fourth part of 'The other side of the brain'. They helped to lend the A/P ratio a broader social significance.[23]

The authors suggest that the tendency to think more with one hemisphere could be the result of early cultural influences. In societies where children follow intensive instruction in reading, writing and grammar, a left-brain, propositional thought style will be dominant, while in unlettered societies, with other forms of education (focusing on spatial skills, for example), an appositional thought style will develop. This meant that it was possible to establish the A/P ratio not only of individuals, but also of entire societies or cultural groups. In the United States, this could mean that 'for example, Blacks or Hopi Indians would differ from middle-class Whites in having less success in problems making greater demands upon the left hemisphere than the right'.[24]

This supposition was subjected to further testing. In recent demographic studies, differences were observed between the performance of various ethnic groups on psychological tests. Bogen and his co-authors focused on two of these. In the Similarities test, one component of a widely used intelligence test, the subject has to give a verbal answer to a verbal question pertaining to similarities between, say, a statue and a poem. The Similarities test is designed primarily to appeal to the propositional style of thought. In the second test, the Street test, the subject is shown a silhouette-like figure, portions of which have been removed, and asked to identify it. This test requires an appositional thought style. The combined scores on the two tests form a new ratio, the Street/Similarities ratio, which lends quantitative expression to the A/P ratio. When combined with the performances of various ethnic groups, this

---

[23] J. E. Bogen, R. De Zure, W. D. Tenhouten and J. F. Marsh, 'The other side of the brain IV: the A/P ratio', *Bulletin of the Los Angeles Neurological Societies*, 37 (1972) 2, 49–61.

[24] Bogen *et al.*, 'Other side IV', 50.

produces the following ranking (the higher the position, the more left-brained):

white city dwellers;
white country dwellers;
black male city dwellers;
black female city dwellers;
Hopi Indians.

Let us now take several bewildered steps backwards. This is the same – the *exact same* – order established for asymmetry by Broca and his followers a hundred years ago: a hierarchy in which white men were at the top, primitive peoples at the bottom, and women half-way down. But the *interpretation* of the ranking which Bogen presented was quite different from that of Broca. In the 1970s, the values which in Broca's day had been linked to the left brain (reason, control and culture) began to be associated with a style of thinking and acting which had created serious social problems. Thanks to science and technology, there was now the spectre of depleted natural resources, environmental pollution, and a nuclear arms race that was running out of control. The development of intellectual, analytical skills in education came at the expense of creativity and intuition. The linear, masculine thinking of the left hemisphere was at odds with the more feminine, wordless knowledge of the right hemisphere. Soon the left hemisphere came to stand for the industrialized and urbanized world, the right hemisphere for an intuitive, meditative approach to knowledge, one which had been so much better preserved in the Orient than in the Western world. Just as in Broca's day, the results of neurological research had an unmistakable ideological charge. But because the moral plus and minus poles had by then exchanged places, the hierarchy was turned upside down. Now it was the Hopi Indians, still living close to nature, who had upheld the morally superior right-brain thinking. And black women, even when they lived in the city, thought more with their right brain than black men did. And at the very bottom of the new hierarchy were the white city dwellers, with an A/P ratio that pointed to a questionable dominance of the left hemisphere.

Bogen's results did not go unchallenged. Fellow neurologists pointed out that the differences in A/P ratio were simply the result of differences in performance on the Similarities test, since everyone scored about the same on the Street test. This meant that conclusions pertaining to the share of the right hemisphere were somewhat premature.[25] But approval predominated, and soon there were additional results which followed the same lines. Among the children of Navajo Indians, there were findings indicating that the left ear performed better in listening tests than the right ear, while the reverse was true among white children: clear proof that the Navajo Indians were right-brained (stimuli presented to the left ear go to the right brain and vice versa). EEG studies showed that the brains of Hopi children display more activity on the right when listening to a story in Hopi than when listening to the same story in English.[26] According to other researchers, the brains of Indians are more symmetrical than those of whites. Results such as these appeared in authoritative journals, and within ten years after Bogen's article appeared, the idea had taken root that neurologists and neuropsychologists had presented scientific proof that the American Indian is right-brained.

The reactions in Indian circles were reserved. Two psychologists, Peters and Chrisjohn (the latter an Oneida Indian from a Canadian reservation), wrote with a fine sense of history that it was time to start worrying when someone claims to have come up with 'anatomical

---

[25] J. A. Zook and J. H. Dwyer, 'Cultural differences in hemisphericity: a critique', *Bulletin of the Los Angeles Neurological Societies*, 41 (1976) 3, 87–90.

[26] L. Rogers, W. Ten Houten, C. D. Kaplan and M. Gardiner, 'Hemispheric specialization of language: an EEG study of bilingual Hopi Indian children', *International Journal of Neuroscience*, 8 (1977), 1–6.

proof' of differences between the brains of whites and non-whites, and that the myth of the right-brained Indian could have disastrous consequences for the schooling of Indian children.[27] The next step might be a decision to remove left-brain components from the curriculum, since apparently the brains of Indian children were not equipped for that type of learning. The upshot of the affair would be that due to their neurological limitations, there were certain things that Indians simply could not learn. It is quite possible that Bogen and his colleagues had no more of a political agenda than Broca did. But their findings clearly had political implications, and in the same area: differences between men and women, between various ethnic groups, between lettered and unlettered cultures.

Apparently, the fact that the 1870s and the 1970s are separated by a hundred years of progress in methodology has not resulted in the change that Gould had hoped for. There was some methodological criticism levelled at Bogen's research, but on the whole the methodology he employed, with validated and reliable tests, refined statistical checks and references to factor analysis, actually reinforced the impression that these were objective, scientifically reliable results. Bogen's findings did not clash with the then current views on the brain and the differences between individuals. In fact, they lent them an exact expression, formulated in figures.

What has been demonstrated here in such great detail, on the basis of the neurological hierarchies of Broca and Bogen, also emerges as a pattern in other fields of research. That second proud dogma proclaimed by Broca, about the large white brain and the smaller black brain, had a long history lasting well into the twentieth century: until after the Second World War, volume measurements were still being carried out, using new techniques.[28] A few years ago, an

[27] R. E. Chrisjohn and M. Peters, 'The right-brained Indian: fact or fiction?', *Journal of American Indian Education*, 13 (1986), 62–71.

[28] Much of that research was gathered by the psychologist, J. Philippe Rushton, who, despite a questionable reputation as regards his thinking on 'races', had

anthropologist demonstrated that the outcomes of those measurements varied according to a society's views on differences between ethnic groups.[29] A fellow anthropologist summarized the docility of facts as follows: 'First we must admire the apparent cranial expansion of Asians over the last half-century, when earlier researchers consistently reported their having *smaller* brains than whites. Obviously this implies the possibility of a comparable expansion in blacks. But more likely it implies the possibility of scientists finding just what they expect when the social and political stakes are high.'[30]

Distance in time makes it easier to identify the shared convictions and prejudices of past generations. This holds true for historians of brain science and for brain scientists themselves. Even the (for the historian) relatively brief distance of thirty years helps present-day neurologists to place the findings of Bogen: the 1970s, California, the bulletin of the Los Angeles Neurological Societies. With the passage of time, the perspectives of historians and scientists begin to converge. The *absence* of a temporal distance creates a deceptive transparency. The view held by prominent scientists in the 1960s that the 'refrigerator mother' was responsible for her child's autism is today recognized as contestable, but how will later generations see the now widely held view that autistic children have no 'theory of mind'? Will this explanation one day be rejected as denigratory and simplistic, because it typifies a specific philosophical trend rather than the reality of autistic functioning?

The sixteenth-century Italian Girolamo Cardan was a physicist, astrologer and mathematician. As an inventor, his name has been perpetuated in the eponym of Cardan's rings: one ring, which rotates

access to the most prominent professional journals. Representative of this type of theory formation is J. P. Rushton and C. Davison Ankney, 'Brain size and cognitive ability: correlations with age, sex, social class, and race', *Psychonomic Bulletin and Review*, 3 (1996), 21–36.

[29] L. Lieberman, 'How "caucasoids" got such big crania and why they shrank', *Current Anthropology*, 42 (2001), 69–96.

[30] J. Marks, *Human Biodiversity* (New York, 1995), p. 271.

freely on its axis, hangs in a second ring, which can turn freely in the plane which is perpendicular to it. As a result, what is hanging in the inner ring can move freely in all directions. Each researcher hangs suspended in time, like a ship's compass in Cardan's rings. He makes use of the methods deemed most appropriate, chooses the instruments available to him at the time, appeals to arguments accepted as valid, and is dependent on the dozens of conventions which he shares with his contemporaries and which are therefore barely noticed. Even when he adopts a position which runs counter to the prevailing views and strives to remain independent of the movements around him, he will unconsciously be carried along, compass and all, by the insights of his day.

Index